HADRIAN'S WALL

From construction to World Heritage Site

NOTES, ABBREVIATIONS AND ACRONYMS

Dates

All BC dates are identified BC; to avoid misinterpretation, up to 100, all AD dates are identified AD.

First published in June 2018

A catalogue record for this book is available from the British Library.

ISBN 978 1 78521 189 8

Library of Congress control no. 2017949648

Published by Haynes Publishing,
Sparkford, Yeovil, Somerset
BA22 7JJ, UK.
Tel: 01963 440635
Int. tel: +44 1963 440635
Website: www.haynes.com

Haynes North America Inc.,
859 Lawrence Drive, Newbury Park,
California 91320, USA.

Printed in Malaysia.

MILECASTLES

Type I Short-axis: so, broader than deep (where deep is between gateways). These milecastles were usually built by *legio II Augusta*.

Type II Long-axis: so, the distance between the gateways was more than the width. These milecastles were built by *legio XX Valeria Victrix* and are only found on the Narrow Wall (the western end of Hadrian's Wall).

Type III Long-axis milecastles built by *legio VI Victrix*.

Type IV Long-axis milecastles built by *legio XX Valeria Victrix* on the Broad Wall (central and eastern section of Hadrian's Wall).

ROMAN MEASUREMENTS

The basic Roman *pes* or foot could be divided into three 4in-long *palmi* (handbreadths), 12 *unciae* (inches) or 16 *digiti* (fingerbreadths). There are many interpretations of exactly how long a Roman pes was, but today most commentators have settled on 11.65in (296mm). The Roman mile was 1,000 paces (the Latin for 1,000 – *mille* – gives us our word mile) or 5,000 Roman feet. This gives 1,481m (4,860ft).

HADRIAN'S WALL

From construction to World Heritage Site

Operations Manual

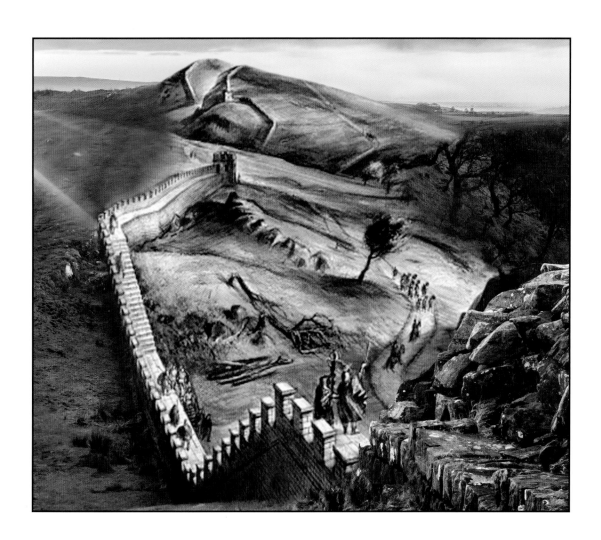

A JOURNEY ALONG THE WALL, AND BACK IN TIME

Simon Forty

CONTENTS

INTRODUCTION

A UNESCO World Heritage Site since 1987, the wall has seen a substantial increase in visitors since a national trail footpath opened in 2003. It's hardly surprising when the path affords views such as this. Shutterstock

'And so, having reformed the army … he set out for Britain, and there he corrected many abuses and was the first to construct a wall, 80 miles long, to separate the barbarians and the Romans.'

Most studies of Hadrian's Wall include that quote from Aelius Spartianus' *The Augustan History*, written at the end of the 3rd century AD. There's not much choice because that's the only significant mention of the wall in what remains of Roman literature. In a world where TV history programmes spin the smallest parcels of fact into huge hypotheses, it shouldn't come as a surprise to learn how little we know about the much-covered subject of Britain in the 2nd century AD, and how little we know about Hadrian's likely visit to the country, why he ordered the wall and how it was built. The building blocks of our knowledge include the epigraphic evidence – inscriptions on stones and quarries along the wall, often built into farm buildings; the archaeological evidence,

including the wonderful Vindolanda letters; and not much else except extensive theories and extrapolation from other sources such as Trajan's column in Rome.

Then there's the wall itself: robbed for building stone from the start, plundered for General Wade's Military Road, more of the wall is visible in the castles and buildings along its length than there exists *in situ*. English Heritage estimates that only 10 percent is visible today, and what exists has been extensively rebuilt by Victorian 'archaeologists', the Department of Works and, latterly and more sympathetically, by English Heritage and the National Trust. On top of this, today it is inundated with tourists from all over the world: so many of them that the path along the wall is in danger of collapsing under the strain and requires remedial work to ensure the safety of the monument and its visitors.

It's hard to blame them. I've been to Rome and seen the Forum. I've wondered at the beautiful Pont du Gard and the engineering that allowed the 45km (30 mile) aqueduct to take water to Nîmes. I've been amazed by the streets of Pompeii and

▼ *The Roman Empire in the Hadrianic period with wall in place. On the eastern edge, Hadrian would withdraw from Assyria, Mesopotamia and Armenia.* Andrei nacu/WikiCommons

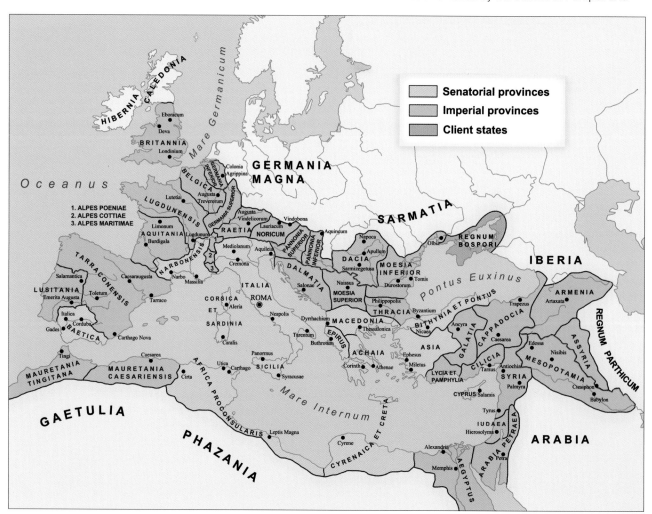

Herculaneum, fascinated by Baalbeck and wept as the desert ruins of Palmyra were ravaged by Isis – but nothing beats standing by a watchtower above the Whin Sill crags on a grey, wet day as the clouds scud overhead. Quite simply, Hadrian's Wall is one of the most important surviving Roman artefacts that, seemingly daily, extends our knowledge of the Roman world through the brilliant work of such organisations as the Vindolanda Trust. We might not know exactly where it ran through today's urban sprawl of Carlisle and Newcastle, whether it had a rampart walkway running its entire length, if it was painted white to dazzle the natives and what the Vallum is – but there is every likelihood that one day, some day, we will. It's only comparatively recently that archaeology has started to get to grips with the *vici* – the towns and settlements that built up around the forts – and it's safe to say that there's much more evidence still under the ground.

THE SOURCES

The main Roman legions and auxiliaries who built and manned the wall are known by the archaeological evidence they left behind and by references to the province of Britain that occur in such Roman literary records that have survived. Regarding the written information, all three writers who mention Britain never actually visited the island itself. Tacitus (around AD56–120) is the most contemporary primary source for the province in the 1st century AD. His *Annals* cover the period AD14–68 and his *Histories* AD68–96. Elevated by Vespasian to senatorial rank, he wrote about events that occurred during his or the previous generation's lifetime through interviews with those directly involved and also through access to the

Senate's reports and records. In a biography of his father-in-law, Gnaeus Julius Agricola, Governor of Britain AD78–84 , he describes Agricola's northern campaigns and some of the tribes he fought.

Cassius Dio (around AD155–235) was a senator, provincial governor and consul who wrote an 80-volume history of the Roman Empire from its earliest times to 229, not all of which survives. The parts that concern Britain – cover the period of Caesar's first expedition (55BC), the Claudian conquest (AD43) and the Neronian revolt (AD61).

Ammianus Marcellinus, c. 325–330 to c. 391–400 was a retired soldier who wrote a history of Rome (the *Res Gestae*) from the accession of the Emperor Nerva in AD96 to the death of Valens at the Battle of Adrianople in 378, of which only the sections covering the period 353–378 survive. These include details about Britain as a chief source of grain for Gaul during the reign of Julian, the multiple attacks of the 'barbarian conspiracy' that it suffered in 367 and a reference to the existence of a brief fifth British province known as Valentia.

Gildas was a monk who lived in Britain and Brittany in the 6th century. His *De Excidio et Conquestu Britanniae* ('On the Ruin and Conquest of Britain') looks at British history from the conquest and is an important source.

Other written documents are important. We don't know who wrote the *Ravenna Cosmography* in the 8th century – and the mistakes and corruptions in it mean it is less well regarded than Ptolemy's *Geographia* written in the 2nd century, the *Itinerarium Antonini Augusti* (probably of the 3rd century) or the *Tabula Peutingeriana*, 4th–5th century (from a 13th-century copy) – but it does

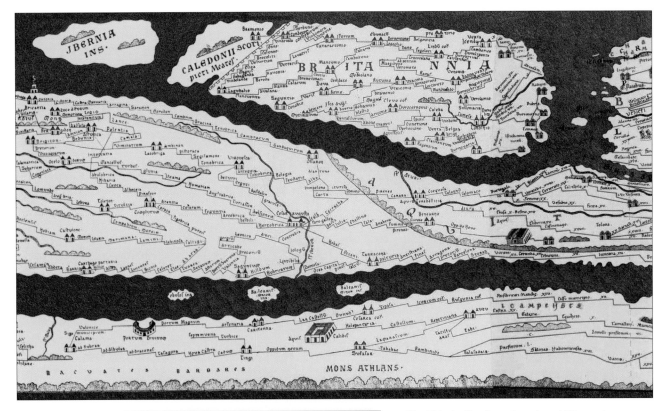

▲ *The* Tabula Peutingeriana *is a 13th-century copy of an earlier – possibly Roman – map showing the ancient world's road system. This 19th-century facsimile shows Hadrian's Wall, but the white, western section was added by Konrad Miller in his 1887 edition.* WikiCommons

► *Epigraphy – the study of inscriptions – provides much information about the wall, particularly the many votive altars dedicated by military units involved in its construction. This one, from the Tullie House Museum, is dedicated by legio II Augusta to Cocidus, the Celtic god of war and hunting. It was found near Milecastle 65.*

supply more British place names than the others.

The archaeological evidence is mainly epigraphic in the form of sometimes intact but for the most part partial remains of stone inscriptions on buildings, milestones, votive altars, gravestones, etc giving details of units and individuals along with the emperors they served and gods they worshipped. Coin deposits are an important way of dating occupation levels, and other more fragile artefacts have occasionally been preserved by unique soil conditions – such as the personal letters, possessions, shoes and fabrics at Vindolanda, which give tanatalising glimpses into the more personal everyday human lives of those involved in such a huge enterprise. Aerial photography and the increasing sophistication of geo-physical ground-penetrating radars and other high-tech sensory equipment enable a much more sensitive and astute archeology than before – but there are still major gaps in our knowledge that stone-robbers, coastal erosion (particularly for the Cumbrian coast) and time itself have caused. Only some of these will ever be filled in.

Some evidence can also be gleaned from

THE NAMES OF THE FORTS

Frustratingly, history is an imprecise science. Sources contradict each other and we don't always know which is correct. The names of the major forts along the wall are a good example. Some – such as Vindolanda – are fixed; others – like Banna and Magnis – are open to interpretation, where 'open to interpretation' means argument between experts. Of specific interest for Hadrian's Wall, therefore, are three pieces of material culture: cups and pans that not only show sequences of locations but also are evidence of the power of merchandising famous engineering feats a staggering near 2,000 years ago.

- The Rudge cup, found in 1725 in Wiltshire and probably dating to the 130s, lists five forts in order:
  MAIS ABALLAVA VXELODUM CAMBOGLAN SBANNA
  (Mais = Bowness; Aballava = Burgh; Uxelodunum = Stanwix; Camboglanna = Castlesteads;
  Banna = Birdoswald … probably).

- The Amiens *patera* (libation bowl) found in France in 1949, lists:
  MAIS ABALLAVA VXELODVNVM CAMBOG...S BANNA ESICA
  (as above with the addition of Aesica = Great Chesters).

- The Staffordshire pan, created in the 2nd century lists:
  MAIS COGGABA TUXELODUNUM CAMMOGLANNA RIGOREVALIAELI DRACONIS
  (Mais, Coggabata = Drumburgh, Uxelodunum; Cammoglanna = Castlesteads. There are a number of interpretations of the final RIGOREVALIAELIDRACONIS. It's possible that Rigorevali = on the line of the wall and Aelidraconis could give the maker's name (Aeli Draco). However, another interpretation is that Rigorevaliaeli = the name of the wall, which is Vallum Aelium, the latter after Hadrian's family name Aelius; Draconis = the maker's name is Draco.)

elsewhere in the Empire, again through inscriptions or references, especially to higher-ranking legionary officers who moved on or to units who were transferred from Britain to the continent. Military diplomas issued on each non-citizen soldier's retirement are another valuable source of information about the troops of the Auxilia and their movements. Inscribed in bronze, they certified that the holder had been honourably discharged on completion of service and had thus received Roman citizenship.

However, despite a wealth of material there are still many gaps in our knowledge and more sites that have yet to be excavated. Literary records have to be interpreted with the understanding that the writer concerned usually followed his own particular political or personal agenda. Some things have to be surmised, taking into account the degree of uniformity reached by the Roman military, although Rome and its legions, as in all human societies, were in a constant state of change. Tactics, equipment, uniforms and even beards underwent considerable evolution to meet new challenges, cope with the inevitable reductions in resources available at any given time or just reflect contemporary fashion.

▶ *While often a hobby practised by amateurs, re-enactment can supplement academic studies with experimental archaeology and provides a human dimension to what can otherwise be a dry subject.* Graham Sumner

CLAUDIAN CONQUEST

After Caesar's initial reconnaissance in 55BC and show of force in 54BC, Emperor Claudius – driven by the same imperative for justification and glory that firmly linked the political and military spheres in the upper echelons of Roman society – invaded Britain in AD43. Under the pretext of restoring King Verica of the friendly Atrebates to his throne and to chastise the aggressive Catuvellauni who had displaced him, Claudius initiated the conquest that would eventually see most of the island incorporated into the Roman Empire for some 400 years.

Britain in the 1st century AD was not unknown to the Roman world. Pytheas of Massalia had described his circumnavigation of the island around 330BC; there had been trading links – mainly valuable tin – between Cornwall and the Mediterranean for many years; many British tribes were related to or had close links with those in Gaul and some supplied British warriors to aid the Gaulish tribes in the struggle against Rome.

Britain was rich in metal resources – gold, silver, iron, lead and tin – and had a well-established agricultural economy, exporting corn, wool, cattle, hides and hunting dogs. It wasn't a single united entity, but rather a collection of rival tribal kingdoms, some with continental ties and trade and therefore familiar with Roman ways. Others were wild and free, rejecting any trappings of Mediterranean civilisation: fierce warriors of the prehistoric era rather than well-trained, armour-

clad soldiers. Such disunity was always exploited by Rome, who was happy to make alliances with friendly tribes but whose disciplined troops invariably won any pitched battles and who also, as experts in siege warfare, found the hillforts of the natives easy enough nuts to crack.

So it proved. The Claudian conquest saw the southern areas of Britian taken and Romanised. The years that followed brought further expansion with the absorption of Wales and parts of Northern Britain. This island caught the Roman imagination for military action in wild places: a mission of forced civilisation similar, perhaps, to that of the European expansion following the Industrial Revolution in more recent times. It was a frontier where a man could cut his teeth and prove himself worthy of higher rank and more reward, for some even the purple (a colour associated with emperors).

The backbone and major source of power in Rome were its legions. Emperors both feared and courted them. Although they were the source of the emperor's power, they were kept discreetly away from the Italian mainland, guarding the edges of the Roman world and keeping the foreign provinces under control. At first, as one such frontier province, Britain merited four legions, but then later – around AD86, following serious trouble on the continent – three. This was still a large number of troops for a relatively small geographical area and one that would cause problems later, for these troops made the governor of Britannia a powerful political player even if he was far from the centre of power. Various governors went on to become emperors or began rebellions and seceded from Rome's control. To curtail the power of the governor and resolve the problem, Britain was first split into two – *Britannia Superior* and *Britannia Inferior* – around 197; later, c. 296, into four: *Britannia Prima* (the south of England), *Britannia Secunda* (Wales), *Flavia Caesariensis* (the Midlands and East Anglia) and *Maxima Caesariensis* (northern England up to Hadrian's Wall). Neither change stopped the problem of power-seeking governors.

▶ *Emperor Claudius reigned from AD41–54. Born in Gaul, he was expansionist and initiated the invasion of Britain and start of the conquest. This head is from the Ny Carlsberg Glyptotek Museum in Copenhagen.*
Cnyborg/
WikiCommons

THE IMPOSITION OF ROMAN RULE

Twenty years after the initial Claudian invasion, the subjugation of Britain had progressed roughly to a line between the Humber and the Mersey: the territory of the Brigantes and Parisi. Most of the southern tribes seemed to have accepted Roman control. More importantly, the Romans had removed the main focus of resistance to their rule when the Brigantine queen Cartimandua handed Caratacus over to Rome following his defeat at Caer Caradoc in AD50. The campaigns of Publius Ostorius Scapula (AD47–52), Aulus Didius Gallus (AD52–57), Quintus Veranius (AD57) and Gaius Suetonius Paulinus (AD58–60) had pushed Roman power into Wales. In AD60, as Tactitus – the Roman historian and son-in-law of Agricola who was probably on the campaign – so vividly describes, Suetonius Paulinus attacked the isle of Mona (Anglesey), the centre of the Druids, who seem to have been the Celts' religious and legal class. However, Suetonius Paulinus was forced to break off the conquest of the island when the eastern tribes rose up under Queen Boudicca of the Iceni.

The reasons for the rebellion are detailed in two Roman sources, Tacitus and Cassius Dio, and boil down to inept, heavy-handed and rapacious Roman administration. The summary handling of the Iceni tribe following the death of King Prasutagus was the obvious primary factor in the Boudiccan rebellion, but it's too easy to focus on this and not look at the wider issues. The causes of the revolt and its ramifications echoed over the next century and provide good reasons for Romans to fear unrest in Britain as a whole and not just in those places that had not been subjugated or settled.

First, there are the problems engendered by settling army veterans or others on confiscated land. These are exacerbated by local politics and finance, especially when religious differences are included. In Camulodunum (Colchester), the provincial capital and before that the centre of the Trinovantes, the veterans had forced the locals to pay for a temple to the Emperor Claudius. Perhaps more importantly, it can hardly be unimportant that Suetonius Paulinus was in the process of attacking Anglesey, and destroying the Druidic centre – possibly the religious heart of Celtic Britain.

Another important lesson from the revolt would be its ferocity. The Britons aimed first of all for Camulodunum, burning down Claudius' temple, and systematically destroying the city, which had been inadequately protected. The Romans sent *legio IX Hispana*, then commanded by Quintus Petillius Cerialis, whose name will reappear in British history as governor in AD71–74: it was destroyed by the rebels, and the commander was lucky to escape with his life and his cavalry. After Camulodunum, Verulamium (St Albans) and Londinium (London) were both destroyed and many citizens were horribly slaughtered and soldiers killed – modern estimates are half Dio's 80,000 dead, but still sizeable – before Suetonius Paulinus brought the British to battle and defeated them.

In the aftermath of the revolt, Emperor Nero strengthened the Roman forces in Britain – Tacitus records that he sent from Germany 2,000 legionaries, eight cohorts of auxiliaries and a thousand cavalry – and Suetonius Paulinus embarked on severe reprisals on the Iceni and other rebel tribes to destroy their fighting capacity. A new procurator, Julius Classicanus, replaced the rapacious Catus Decianus and, later, after an assessment by Nero's envoy Polyclitus, Suetonius Paulinus was also replaced. The new governor was Publius Petronius Turpilianus, who had an altogether less warlike outlook than Suetonius Paulinus – so much so that he was criticised by Tacitus for being lazy.

The rebellion also engendered a more defensive mindset in the Romans who had, perhaps, been lulled into a false sense of security following Caratacus's capture. In reality, the conquest of Celtic Britain would prove rather more difficult than Rome had anticipated, and continued rebellions would require a larger military presence than elsewhere in the empire. Although disparaging about the British, the Romans had good cause to treat their warriors with caution.

▲ *The classic view of Boudicca as seen next to the Houses of Parliament. Sculpted by Thomas Thornycroft and erected in 1902 some years after his death, the bronze typifies the fanciful Victorian view of the British heroine with her daughters beside her and wonderful stallions pulling her Roman chariot.* Rafesmar/ WikiCommons (CC BY-SA 3.0)

THE TRIBES OF BRITAIN

There were many more tribes than the ones identified by Tacitus or Ptolemy, but information about them is patchy.

1 Cantiaci, 2 Trinovantes and 3 Catuvellauni

These three tribes were united under Cunobelinus – Shakespeare's Cymbeline – and it was the attack on the neighbouring Atrebates (4) by Cunobelinus's son Caratacus that provided Claudius with the pretext for the invasion in 43BC, when the Atrebates' king – Verica – fled to Rome. The Trinovantes had been the most powerful tribe in Britain when Julius Caesar invaded in 54BC.

4 Atrebates

Linked closely to the Belgica of northern France, they sided with Vercingetorix. After the defeat at Alesia in 52BC by Julius Caesar, the ruling group – headed by King Commius, who had been a client of Caesar's – left for Britain. During the reign of Augustus, the tribe must have rejoined the ranks of client states, because Commius' sons Tincomarus and Eppillus approached Augustus as mediator. When another brother Verica appealed to Rome for help against the Catuvellauni, Claudius used the opportunity to invade Britain.

▶ *Although the main tribes of Britain in the Roman period are almost impossible to map completely accurately, this gives a rough idea of their areas. The Brigantes seem to have had the largest territory of the British tribes – particularly if it includes the Carvetii as a sub-tribe, although this is disputed.*

5 Durotriges

One of two major West Country tribes, the Durotriges proved strong opponents of Roman rule, with many hillforts (including Cadbury Castle in Somerset and Maiden Castle near Dorchester). They were taken over in the 4th century by their neighbours, the Dumnonii.

6 Dumnonii

Linked for posterity to the Roman city of Isca Dumnoniorum – Exeter – this tribe, or more likely collection of tribes (including one of the Cornovii – see 13), had cultural connections with the peoples of Brittany (Armorica as it was then). Tin and lead mining had led to Mediterranean connections as early as the Phoenicians.

7 Iceni

A thorn in the Roman side in the early years after the invasion, the Iceni had initially sided with Claudius before rebelling in AD47 when Ostorius wanted to disarm them. Their rebellion under Queen Boudicca in AD60 is an iconic moment in British history. However, it ended in defeat and there are few mentions of the tribe subsequently.

8 Dobunni

Based around the Avon gorge, the Dobunni are not known for being warlike. They paid tribute to the Catuvellauni and effectively surrendered to the Romans without a fight – although elements of the tribe are thought to have sheltered Caratacus before his final campaign.

9 Silures

Centred in south Wales, the Silures proved staunch opponents of the Roman invaders who were forced to site there a legionary fortress – Isca, later Caerleon – which housed *legio II Augusta*. The Romans were probably still there as late as 380.

10 Demetae

The southwest peninsula of Wales was their home – an area known for gold mining. They don't seem to have caused the Romans many problems. Indeed, the presence of a fort – Leucarum (today's Loughor) – suggests that the Romans had to defend the area from the neighbouring Silures.

11 Ordovices

Caratacus moved here from the Dobunni, leading a rebellion in AD50. Agricola put down another rebellion in AD79 with extreme prejudice and no further mention is seen of the tribe.

12 Deceangli
After defeating the Ordovices, Agricola moved on to the northwest tip of Wales where the Deceangli and Gangani tribes lived. The isle of Anglesey, known for Druids and copper-mining, was pacified in AD78

13 Cornovii
Other tribes in Britain have the same name – one in northern Scotland and the other in Cornwall. There are many theories why this should be, but whatever the reason they lived in a strategically important area through which Watling Street led to the fourth largest town in Britain: Viroconium (Wroxeter). The tribe is linked to Hadrian's Wall because the *cohors Primae Cornoviorum* – the only native unit that served in Britannia – garrisoned Pons Aelius in the 4th century.

14 Corieltauvi
On the border between the southern lands taken by Rome after the invasion, this unwarlike tribe, centred on today's Leicester (Ratae Corieltauvorum), was – it seems – happy to have a Roman presence, as it kept down the raids of the more warlike Brigantes.

15 Parisi
Possibly linked to the Parisi in Gaul (who give their name to today's French capital), this tribe gets larger in the 1st century AD, perhaps a result of an influx of their continental bretheren.

16 Brigantes and 17 Carvetii
The Brigantes seem to have been a large and powerful collection of tribes – including the Carvetii – who were originally happy to accept client status with the Romans. This changed in AD69, when Rome had to intervene against King Venutius, hitherto a client. Around 100–105 the northern Brigantes rebelled, and again in 138, when Quintus Lollius Urbicus moved from Hadrian's Wall into Brigantine territory. The rebellions were easily put down, but in 154, after another, the Brigantes territories were broken up and the Romans took direct control.

18 Votadini
With their lands northeast of the wall, centred on the hillfort at Dunpelder, the precursor to Edinburgh, the Votadini were under direct rule when the Antonine Wall was in use (138–162).

19 Selgovae and 20 Novantae
Northwest of the wall in today's Dumfries and Galloway were two tribes: the Selgovae and, farther west, the Novantae.

21 Damnonii
A troublesome tribe that never accepted the Roman yoke. Some of their territory may have been held by the Romans when the Antonine Wall was in place.

23 Venicones
Unusual in that they may have had a navy – the Venicones lived northeast of the wall. They were subjugated by Agricola in AD81 and a defensive line along the Gask Ridge was established in their area to help keep the highland tribes at bay.

22 Epidii, 24 Taexali and 25 Caledonii
The northern tribes were never conquered by Rome, although Agricola's campaigns saw them beaten at Mons Graupius in AD83 or 84.

▲ *Cadbury Castle, one of the hillforts that stood against Roman occupation, probably under the Durotriges. There's debate about whether the fighting took place at the time of the original invasion around AD43–44 or later.*
Shutterstock

▼ *Antonine Wall ditch on Bar Hill above Twechar, East Dunbartonshire, Scotland.*
Shutterstock

THE ADVANCE INTO SCOTLAND

Probably in AD83, somewhere still not precisely known in the far north of the island, Gnaeus Julius Agricola defeated the Caledonian tribes at Mons Graupius. It was the culmination of more than 10 years of fighting, which started when Vespasian's brother-in-law, Quintus Petillius Cerialis, became governor of Britain in AD71, and was continued under Agricola from AD77.

The year of the four emperors – AD69 – saw civil war across the empire and movement of legions to and from Britain. The tribes in the south remained peaceful, but there was fighting in Brigantes' territory involving the governor, Marcus Vettius Bolanus, but he had insufficient forces to take this further, so simply contained the problem. Vespasian's enthronement as emperor ushered in

the dynamic Flavian dynasty, which saw the legions return to Britain and Roman power extend into the north of Scotland. The new governor was Quintus Petillius Cerialis, who saw the Boudiccan revolt at first hand as commander of *legio IX Hispana*. Subsequently he suppressed the Batavian revolt of Julius Civilis on the Rhine using *legio XIV Gemina* from Britain. Quintus Petillius Cerialis then went to Britain with *legio II Adiutrix,* and so had four legions (*II Adiutrix*, *II Augusta*, *IX Hispana* and *XX Valeria Victrix*) to hand for his campaigning.

We know a lot about this period – albeit from

a partial source: it is covered in the histories of Agricola's son-in-law, Tacitus. First as commander of *legio XX Valeria Victrix* and then as governor himself, Agricola was instrumental in the expansion of Roman rule. He was alongside Petillius Cerialis as the governor attacked the Brigantes, defeating their king Venutius at Stanwick in AD70, advancing north as far as Carlisle on the west coast and even possibly towards Newcastle in the east. This was the first time that Roman power extended as far as what would become the line of the wall.

Agricola had left Britain in AD73 to govern Gallia Aquitania when Petillius Cerialis was succeeded by Sextus Julius Frontinus. Governor from AD73, Frontinus defeated the Silures in south Wales and started building the great legionary fortress of Chester. Wales had not been completely subdued when Agricola returned as governor around AD77: his first action was against the Ordovices as he finished off the conquest of north Wales and Anglesey that Suetonius Paulinus was undertaking when Boudicca's revolt intervened.

Next, Agricola advanced into Scotland, his progress held up more by lack of imperial permission to advance than difficulties subduing the tribes whom he finally drew into a major battle, eventually defeating the northern elements at Mons Graupius. At this point Agricola was recalled, and there was no immediate resumption of military action. The new emperor, with troubles on other frontiers, reduced the Roman forces available for action in Britain. Domitian's campaign (AD84) against the Chatti of the mid-Rhine region of Taunus used vexillations (temporary task force detachments) from all four British legions, and in AD86, *legio II Adiutrix* was transferred from Britain

▲ *Agricola built the stronghold of Segontium in North Wales to ensure the Ordovices were contained.*
Nilfanion/ WikiCommons (CC BY-SA 4.0)

◄ *As the Romans advanced northwards they built forts from turf and wood, which were sometimes later consolidated into permanent stone structures. Mediobogdum – now known as Hardknott – was probably built in Hadrian's reign and although abandoned in the Antonine period, was revivified in the 3rd century, and surrounded by a bustling vicus. Note the baths on the left outside the walls.*

► *The major locations in Roman Britain and the Roman roads that joined them. Note the three legionary fortresses of the three permanent legions in Britain.*

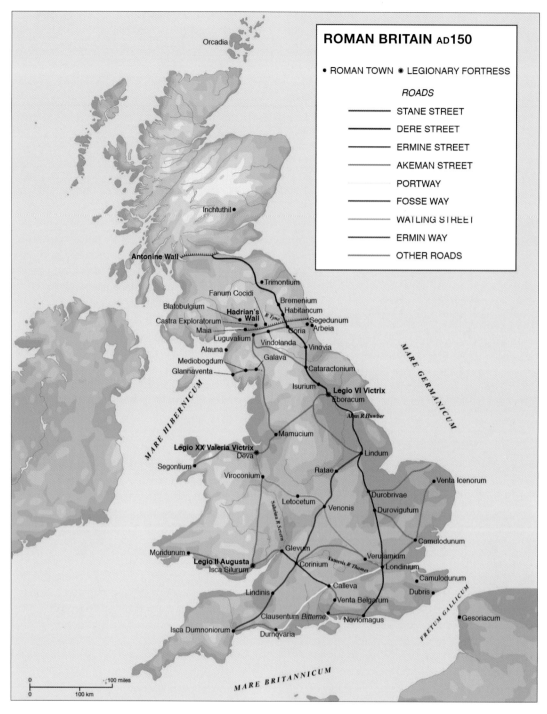

ROMAN BRITAIN AD150

● ROMAN TOWN ● LEGIONARY FORTRESS

ROADS

— STANE STREET
— DERE STREET
— ERMINE STREET
— AKEMAN STREET
— PORTWAY
— FOSSE WAY
— WATLING STREET
— ERMIN WAY
— OTHER ROADS

for the European campaign and never returned. The loss of a legion precluded the subjugation of the Caledonian tribes, but while the victories of Agricola in Scotland were soon negated, he left his mark on Britain in the form of two lines of forts – the Gask Ridge line and the Stanegate.

THE STANEGATE FORTS

The early Stanegate forts were the longer-lasting of the two and were sited not far behind where Hadrian's Wall would be built. The name 'Stanegate' was not contemporary; it has an old

Norse origin and was not used by the Romans. The line began as a link between two major forts that guarded important river crossings heading north on either side of the country: it soon became an artery linking the east and the west. On the eastern side, guarding the Tyne and on the major route north (Dere Street), was Coria (Corbridge). Originally, Agricola built a supply camp nearby, and the first fort dates to around AD84 (it was rebuilt in stone in the middle of the next century). In the west, overlooking the River Eden, was Luguvalium (Carlisle), started around AD72.

The Stanegate forts evolved to follow the river valleys of the Tyne and the Eden's main tributary, the River Irthing. Another eight major and minor forts have been found between them: at Newbrough, Vindolanda, Haltwhistle Burn, Carvoran, Throp, Nether Denton, Castle Hill Boothby and Brampton Old Church. Of these, pottery evidence makes it likely that Vindolanda and Nether Denton – like Carlisle and Corbridge – were the earliest; there is less dating information for the others. Although later superseded by the extension of the frontier farther north, the Stanegate line never fully lost its importance and was a prime reason why Hadrian chose to site his wall where he did, since the two could be combined to make more of a defence in depth, with the Stanegate fort garrisons able to reach the wall quickly when needed.

THE GASK RIDGE FORTS

Agricola didn't build a defence line here: there was no reason for him to do so as he expected the border to be much farther north. Agricola's role was to set up the opportunity by building the road and certain key forts. He also built a line of forts along the Gask Ridge in Scotland, anchored on a legionary fortress at Inchtuthil. Part of a system built by Agricola as he moved ever northwards, again these forts could not be called a defence line or even a frontier. They were designed to bottle up the native Caledonians until such time as the Roman juggernaut swung into action once more and continued its conquests. Later in his life, Agricola would bemoan the fact that Ireland hadn't been tamed and that he could have done so with a legion and some cavalry.

The Gask Ridge forts or fortlets were sited much closer together from south to north at Camelon, Drumquhassie, Malling/Mentieth, Doune, Glenbank, Bochastle, Ardoch, Kaims Castle, Strafeath, Dalginoss, Bertha, Fendoch, Cargill, Cardean, Inverquharity and Strathcaro, backed up by the legionary fortress of *legio XX Valeria Victrix* at Inchtuthil. The southwestern ones (Drumquhassle, Menteith/Malling, Bochastle, Doune, Dalginross and Fendoch) are collectively known as 'Glenblockers', located to monitor traffic in and out of various glens and valleys.

As already discussed, this series of forts and watchtowers sited between the mountain highlands and the lowlands wasn't constructed as a defensive line, and there's no reason to suppose the troops who were left there when Agricola departed did not expect to proceed further. However, within six years – at the latest – of Mons Graupius, the forts were abandoned and the Roman forces withdrew back into the lowlands.

Recent research has shown that although these most northern Roman installations were not occupied continuously for very long, many saw service later when the Romans advanced northwards again under Quintus Lollius Urbicus (governor during the reign of Antoninus Pius) and Septimius Severus.

At some time in the next 20 or 30 years – between AD84 and around 110, and it is not clear when or which emperor ordered the withdrawal – Roman forces accepted that containment around the Solway Firth – Stanegate – Tyne line was the best course of action. To give the Stanegate a defensive function, a series of smaller forts was needed to fill in the gaps: Haltwhistle Burn and Throp might be such forts, but there is insufficient evidence to confirm this. The final retreat from Scotland probably took place in about 105, and so the strengthening of the Stanegate defences – if this happened – could date from about that time.

David Breeze argues persuasively that it was Trajan (r. AD98–117), the otherwise aggressive emperor, who decided that he wanted to use his forces elsewhere. The trouble was that for the tribes north of this line, in spite of Roman money and political savvy in the pursuit of divide and rule, this can only have served as a green light for reversing the events of the early AD80s. There is some record of Roman honours for fighting along this border and it's likely that the tribes expanded south, raiding into the Romanised areas and increasing the pressure on the Stanegate defences – so much so that reinforcements and replacements had to be sent from the continent. The stage was set for the arrival of the Emperor Hadrian.

▼ *Doune Castle in Perthshire, sits on a promontory above the confluence of the Ardoch Burn and River Teith. The Roman Gask Ridge fort could have been similarly sited but there are no obvious signs – such as can be found a few kilometres away at Ardoch.* Shutterstock

PUBLIUS AELIUS HADRIANUS

▶ *Hadrian was an autocrat who travelled extensively around his empire.*
Shutterstock

▼ *The remains of Roman Italica, the likely birthplace of Hadrian. A well-preserved site near Sevilla, Spain, with a huge amphitheatre (at the time, the third-largest of the Roman world) it benefitted from Hadrian's patronage during his lifetime.*
Shutterstock

Hadrian was the 14th Emperor of Rome and a popular ruler for 21 relatively peaceful years, from 10 August 117 to 10 July 138. In time he became known as the third of the 'Five Good Emperors' (namely: Nerva, Trajan, Hadrian, Antoninus Pius and Marcus Aurelius). There are more surviving portraits of Hadrian than any other emperor except Augustus. This is not only down to his long reign but also because he founded numerous cities: accordingly, statues of him were erected throughout the empire in appreciation and also in anticipation of his visits. He was much travelled, and his retrenchment of the empire led to the creation of a stable border – and of course his eponymous wall.

Education and training

Born 24 January AD76, probably in Italica, Hispania (modern Seville, Spain), Hadrian had an aristocratic education. At around the age of 14 he was summoned to Rome by his distant cousin, the Emperor Trajan, who had been his nominal protector since his parents died. Trajan was the first Roman ruler to come from a provincial background (also Spain) and Hadrian would follow in his footsteps.

Trajan gave Hadrian his first military position and he would serve in legions all over the empire, including as a tribune of *legio II Adiutrix* in Britain (around AD95). When Trajan died on campaign in Cilicia (southern Anatolia) in 117, Hadrian was with him in command of his rearguard and through the offices of Trajan's wife, Pompeia Plotina, was named as his successor.

Hadrian was a believer in the Augustan warning to his successors – that they should keep the empire within the natural boundaries of the Rhine, the Danube and the Euphrates. After years of almost reckless Roman expansion, throughout his reign Hadrian sought to define and retain what was worthwhile and give up or contain what was not. In this way – and uniquely for a Roman emperor – he began making lengthy tours of most of the empire, reviewing all infrastructure, especially military, in each province, from a practical, strategic and geopolitical perspective. He also inspected his legions and, to keep the troops fit, instil discipline and maintain morale, he introduced new intensive drill and manoeuvre routines. He liked to wear military attire and made a point of sleeping and eating among his soldiers (probably as much for security as morale) and in turn was respected and loved by his men.

Projects and legacy

Hadrian also loved building and everywhere he went he built: he left his legacy in a rake of cities across the Balkans, Greece, Asia Minor and Egypt. For the Romans he rebuilt the Pantheon (destroyed by fire) and revived Trajan's Forum, as well as building many other notable structures, including baths and villas.

To emphasise Roman power, Hadrian instigated a new policy of strengthened frontier defence, with the addition of visible physical fortified barriers to delineate the empire's frontiers wherever possible: Africa, Germany and, of course, Britain all saw work on linear barriers of varying degrees of strength.

Around 122 Hadrian almost certainly visited Britain and ordered the construction of what became known

as the *Vallum Hadriani*, the huge project that we now know as Hadrian's Wall. In the life of Hadrian that was written in the 4th century, it was stated that the wall was built to divide the Romans from the Britons. He had decided that because of the relatively small distance involved, northern Britain should have a unique solid curtain-walled barrier set within a defence zone to monitor civilian tribal traffic, intercept problems and act as a first line of defence against a determined attack. It was to be a visual manifestation of the power and capabilities of Rome – *qui barbaros Romanosque divideret*, i.e. dividing the barbarians from the Romans.

The wall was a prestige project. It showed Rome's – and by extension Hadrian's – power, financial muscle and technical abilities as well as the emperor's munificence and concern for the welfare of Britons and their province. To the Romans, who were used to extraordinary buildings – pyramids, amphitheatres, aqueducts of over 50km (30 miles) in length, huge temples and palaces – the wall may not have been one of the wonders of the world. To anyone living in Britain, however, it must have been spectacular.

Hadrian left his mark on Britain in another, subtler way that is less well known than his wall. Starting around 119, coins – bronze *asses* – were issued in Rome with a seated female on the reverse. Below was the legend *Britannia*, identifying the pacified nation. While it was not unusual for Romans to do such a thing, it was a first for Britain. Subsequently, in 134–138 more coins bearing a similar legend were minted and there are also examples – very rare today – of the legends: ADVENTUS AUG BRITANNIAE (arrival in Britain) and EXERCITUS BRITANNICUS (inspection of the army in Britain). The symbol was chosen for use on the penny in 1797 and was used subsequently on British coins until 2008, the modern version seeing her spear altered to a trident to emphasise how 18th-century Britannia ruled the waves.

Finally, after many years of travelling and in failing health following a punitive campaign in the near east around Jerusalem, Hadrian returned to Rome and a quiet life of administrative affairs and writing poetry. He named Antoninus Pius as his successor.

Hadrian died – probably as a result of a heart attack – on 10 July 138, aged 62. Temples were soon built in his honour as he was deified by his successor, but perhaps his greatest legacy is his great wall.

THE CONCEPT OF A BORDER

Up until the 2nd century Rome wasn't very good at borders: it was too busy expanding and conquering. To be seen to achieve something, to show capability, prowess and honour, a man – especially an emperor whose hold on power was tenuous – had to win victories, defeat enemies or acquire land for Rome.

The Roman Empire reached its greatest extent during the reign of the Emperor Trajan – some 5 million sq km (19.3 million square miles) and upward of 50 million souls. Its nominal border stretched over 5,000km (3,100 miles) from the Atlantic coast of northern Britain, through Europe to the Black Sea, and from there to the Red Sea and across North Africa to the Atlantic coast and then up to Britain again. It had enemies, it's true, but it did not fear those enemies and expected not only to vanquish them but also to continue its growth. There may not have been a cult of 'manifest destiny' but there seemed few limits to Roman power and so no need for hard borders. Where there were problems, money or duress could usually provide a client kingdom or buffer state.

In reality, however, the empire had reached a point where expansion was hard work: lines of control and communication had become too stretched for a world without the technology needed to govern at such distances. Additionally, the expense of far-off military operations – particularly in the deserts of Africa or forests of northern Europe – was considerable. On top of this, there were the problems of civil strife – often caused by strong, charismatic provincial leaders with the backing of their armies at times when there were imperial succession problems. All these factors contributed to the need for retrenchment. And then there were those outside the empire who looked in: greedy warriors who glimpsed the tantalising wealth of the empire, or those to whom the prospects of work, advancement and citizenship were important. The empire needed to control access to its markets and improve its finances: how better to do that than at a customs post?

The easiest way to control borders was first and foremost to ensure friendly, co-operative neighbours who were in Rome's pocket; one example is provided in Armenia. Hadrian gave up Trajan's conquests, instead exercising control through allies, and he 'showed many favours to many kings' and provided the empire with useful buffer states.

▶ *Hadrian's Wall is a permanent reminder of the Romans' campaigns in the north, restraining raids on farms and livestock.* Shutterstock

▼ *Borders were important to the Romans to delineate ownership and responsibilities. Near Trajan's Gates the emperor ordered a fort to be built to emphasise the border between Thrace and Macedonia.* Shutterstock

The other way to control passage of people and goods – then as now – was a policed linear barrier. In Africa the *Fossatum Africae* – African ditch – if it really did exist, is a good example. In length, it dwarfs Hadrian's Wall. Mentioned in the 312 *Codex Theodosianus*, in more recent times it was championed by French archaeologist Jean Lucien Baradez, who had been involved in military aviation in World War I as an observer. When he went to Algeria after World War II, he conducted aerial surveys that showed evidence of a frontier barrier made up of ditches, embankments and watchtowers. He identified four main segments – Hodna or Bou Taleb (100km/62 miles), Tobna (50km/30 miles), Gemellae (60km/37 miles) and Ad Majores (70km/43 miles) – and the obvious similarities between it and other Roman *limes* suggested an African barrier up to 750km (465 miles) in length. Conjecture it may be, but the idea of a customs barrier is certainly feasible: the *portorium* (duty on imports, mostly on luxuries such as spices, precious stones, silks and other fabrics, ivory, animals and slaves) was an important source of revenue in Roman times and those who collected it – the *portitores* – as reviled then as they are today.

Elsewhere, local circumstances – such as a major river or natural feature – helped. While it's dangerous to consider the length of the Rhine-Danube frontier as a single entity, nevertheless it was an easy choice to control egress to the empire along a large river obstacle and tax whatever crossed.

The Roman word *limes* is the root of our word 'limits' and the Romans used it to define a marked border. Today, the Roman *limes* is preserved through UNESCO's 1987 world heritage grouping of the Frontiers of the Roman Empire. Elements of the border system can be seen everywhere along its length – watchtowers, ditches, embankments, walls – but nowhere more obviously than Hadrian's Wall.

The Germanic and Rhaetian *limes* started at the North Sea and ran along the banks of the Rhine to the Danube: from Lugdunum Batavorum (Katwijk) to Castra Regina (Regensburg), a length of 550km (340 miles). But there's a 300km (185-mile) gap between the two rivers from Mogontiacum (Mainz) to Castra Regina and this had to be filled with a ditch, mound and palisade, watchtowers and fortresses (there's a reconstruction at Saalburg). These defences wouldn't stop a concerted effort by armed warriors, but they certainly acted as a barrier against raiders and helped channel legitimate travellers and merchants through an administrative system.

In Britain, one wonders whether a number of years in the highlands and glens had taught the practical Romans that Scotland wasn't worth the bother. It was just too meagre in resources, awful in climate and filled with intransigently hostile natives to justify maintaining the large military presence required. Whatever the reason, the wall created between the Tyne and The Solway Firth was more permanent both in fact and in legend than any other.

▼ *Hadrian's Wall should not be seen in isolation. It was part of an integrated system that includes the German limes and North Africa. Today part of the Frontiers of the Roman Empire World Heritage Site, the German section includes the reconstructed fort of Saalburg. It was rebuilt on its current footprint in Hadrian's reign, and reconstructed in the early 20th century.*
Shutterstock

TIMELINE

55–54 BC	Julius Caesar's expeditions to Britain.
AD 43	The Emperor Claudius organises the invasion of Britain by four legions commanded by Aulus Plautius.
43–47	Aulus Plautius advances to a line from Exeter to Lincoln, with Vespasian (then commander of *legio II Augusta*) attacking to the west.
50	Battle of Caer Caradoc sees Caratacus defeated.
58	Suetonius Paulinus becomes governor.
60–61	While Suetonius Paulinus is attacking the Druids on Anglesey, the Iceni revolt under Boudicca. Petillius Cerialis escapes when the infantry of his *legio IX Hispana* sustain heavy losses. The revolt is extinguished as Suetonius Paulinus rushes back.
69	The Year of the Four Emperors ends with Vespasian in power.
72–74	A new governor, Petillius Cerialis, arrives in Britain with *legio II Adiutrix*. Ably assisted by Agricola (commanding *legio XX Valeria Victrix*) Petillius Cerialis conquers the Brigantes, defeating Venutius and advancing as far north as Luguvalium (Carlisle), where a fort is constructed.
76	Emperor-to-be Hadrian is born on 24 January, probably at Italica, Hispania.
77–84	Agricola returns to Britain as governor and holds the position for an unusually long time, enabling him to advance deep into Scotland where he defeats the tribes at Mons Graupius. He sets up forts along the Gask Ridge anchored on Inchtuthil, a legionary fort on the Tay. Farther south he constructs the Stanegate and a supply fort at Red House Farm that will later move a quarter-mile south and become Coria (Corbridge).
85	Construction starts on the first fort at Vindolanda. It is made from wood and possibly overlays an earlier structure from the 70s. It is garrisoned by the *cohors I Tungrorum*. The Tungrians (from today's Belgium) are linked to a number of locations on the wall – such as Brocolitia and Vindolanda in 122–138 – until the end of the 4th century.
86	The Red House Farm supply fort is moved to Coria.
87	Inchtuthil (legionary fort on the Tay) is evacuated before completion; the legions have left all forts north of Newstead by 90. *Legio II Adiutrix* leaves Britain for Dacia.
90–103	The Vindolanda letters, the first known surviving examples of the use of ink letters in the Roman period, are written.
92–97	Vindolanda expanded as the Tungrian cohort gets bigger. It will be further enlarged 97–103 as *cohors VIIII Batavorum* replaces the Tungrians. The Batavi

	come from around the Rhine delta in present-day Netherlands.
94–95	Hadrian serves as a military tribune in *legio II Adiutrix*.
98	Trajan becomes emperor.
100	Claudia Severa's birthday party invitation to Sulpicia Lepidina, perhaps the most famous of the Vindolanda letters.
100–105	During this period, probably under imperial command, the army withdraws to the Stanegate line. The northern Brigantes chase them down, possibly under Arviragus, who seems to be responsible for the burning of the fort at Coria, as well as others including Trimontium (Newstead). *Cohors I Tungrorum* returns to Vindolanda and a new fort is built for them and a cavalry unit from Spain (the Varduli or Vardulli).
117	Hadrian becomes Rome's 14th emperor.
118	Pompeius Falco becomes governor.
119–122	Fighting in Britain; losses are heavy as exemplified by *cohors I Tungrorum* who lose their commander, Titus Annius, in battle around this period (as evidenced by a memorial found at Vindolanda). The *Expeditio Britannica* is sent from the continent with 3,000 legionaries. At some time in this period *legio IX Hispana* leaves Britain and *legio VI Victrix* arrives. The latter is certainly in Britain in 122, when it helps build Pons Aelius.
122	Hadrian visits Britain with his friend, the new governor Aulus Platorius Nepos. The wall is probably planned and started during this visit. Nepos oversees much of the construction work on the wall. Stone inscriptions citing him (and, in a number of cases, the emperor) have been found at a number of forts including this on a granary at Condercum: IMP CAES TRAIANO HADRIAN AVG A PLATORIO NEPOTE LEG AVG PR P VEXILLATO CLASSIS BRITAN 'Built for Emperor Caesar Trajanus Hadrianus Augustus by Aulus Platorius Nepos, the pro-praetorian legate [governor of the province] of the emperor, and a detachment of the British Fleet'.
125	There's a big change in the building plan as forts are added to the wall itself. This often leads to dismantling of milecastles and turrets that had already been built.
126	Most of Hadrian's Wall has been constructed. The Vallum was also added to the defences, after the forts were built. It runs from around Milecastle 5 to Bowness, with a short disruption in the marshy area from Milecastles 73 to 76.
128	Arbeia at South Shields – seaport and supply base for the wall – is built by *legio VI Victrix*.

132/133 Governor P. Mummius Sisenna probably oversees the final stages of construction. The largest fort on the wall, Uxelodunum (Stannix) may be the HQ for the wall's senior unit commander.

138 Hadrian dies on 10 July. He is succeeded by his choice of successor, his adopted son Antoninus Pius. Although he is regarded as a non-military man, his actions in Britannia are aggressive. His new governor, Quintus Lollius Urbicus, is instructed to advance into Scotland.

140–160 At Vindolanda, a smaller auxiliary fort replaces the one built to accommodate men building the wall. The garrison is not confirmable but may be Nervii, whose tribe originate from northern Gaul, particularly Belgium.

140–143 The Romans move north to the Forth–Clydeline, reoccupying Lowland Scotland on a permanent basis and beginning construction of the turf-and-timber Antonine Wall. Around this time, the defences of Hadrian's Wall are decommissioned and sometimes abandoned. Parts of the Vallum are filled in, and civilian settlements build up around the forts that are still in use. Many milecastles and turrets fall out of service, with their gates removed.

144 The Antonine Wall is complete: a 3m (9ft 10in) turf wall, a 5m (16ft 5in) ditch, 19 forts, 9 fortlets and upwards of 6,500 defenders.

148 A serious attack on the wall by a descendant of Caratacus, Corvus of the Damnonii, leads to heavy fighting – particularly at Trimontium (Newstead). This will be a continuing story for the next 20 years.

150s New governor Gnaeus Julius Verus arrives in Britain during this period – at least by 158 – possibly bringing reinforcements for the legions. It is debated whether there is a short retreat to the Hadrian's Wall defences in this period. Many historians have suggested that the Forth–Clyde line is abandoned around 158 and then reoccupied around 160. There is no doubt that Roman forts in the Pennines and on the Solway–Tyne line are reoccupied, and Hadrian's Wall sites recommissioned, but the Antonine Wall remains in use until the mid-160s, and it's certainly possible that there was just one slow withdrawal.

160s The first stone fort is built at Vindolanda. This is identified by the Vindolanda timeline as the seventh on the site.

160 Around this date Coria bridge is rebuilt in stone and there are detachments from *legio XX Valeria Victrix* from Deva (Chester) and *the legio VI Victrix* from Eboracum present there.

161 Emperor Antoninus Pius dies and is succeeded by Marcus Aurelius and Lucius Verus as joint emperors. Their first job is to defend a Parthian invasion. The war continues until 166.

163 Rebuilding at Coria.

163 In response to a growing need for troops elsewhere in the empire, the Romans seem to abandon the northern, Antonine Wall, although some outpost forts may remain in use until at least the 180s. A fort excavated at Camelon, just 2 kilometres or so east of Falkirk in the territory of the Damnonii, seems to confirm a withdrawal date of this time. Hadrian's Wall itself is certainly still garrisoned, as archaeology has proven, especially at Newsteads.

165 The Antonine Wall has been abandoned again following tribal unrest and the death of the Emperor Antoninus. The recent restoration of Hadrian's Wall appears wise.

165–180 The Antonine Plague – perhaps a smallpox or measles pandemic – decimates Rome and the Roman Army, reducing capabilities on the Rhine, and affecting Britain, too, as exemplified by a mass grave at Glevum (Gloucester), in the civitas of the Dobunni.

166 Hardly had the Parthian wars ended – and the Antonine plague reached the empire through the returning troops – than Rome was threatened by the Marcomannic wars: an invasion of Rhaetia and Germania Superior and, later, Dacia.

175 After crushing the Lazyges, the *expeditio sarmatica*, the peace treaty, saw 5,000 surrendered Sarmatian cavalry sent to Britain and assigned to *legio VI Victrix*.

177 Second Marcommanic War starts with rebellion by the Quadi and Marcommani. Commodus becomes joint emperor with his father, Marcus Aurelius.

180 Marcus Aurelius dies after his forces defeat the Marcommani. There's a third war that finishes in 182. The Germanic frontier will be a problem henceforth. Commodus continues as sole emperor. He sends Ulpius Marcellus (governor 176–80) back to Britain when northern tribes – the Caledonii – take advantage of the death of Marcus Aurelius and cross the wall, destroying Onnum, Vindobala and Coria.

184–185 Roman victories in Britain (Commodus takes the title *Britannicus*) and Ulpius Marcellus possibly advances to the Antonine Wall to chastise the enemy.

192–193 Commodus assassinated; his successor Publius Helvius Pertinax is murdered by the Praetorian Guard. The year of the five emperors ends with Clodius Albinus, Governor of Britain, siding with Septimius Severus, who wins the throne.

196 Clodius Albinus is proclaimed emperor at Eboracum and takes his army into Gaul to further his claim, buying off the alliance of northern tribes – the Maeatae.

197 Albinus loses the battle of Lugdunum, leaving Severus in command. In Britain, the Maeatae, Brigantes and Caledonii attack and cross Hadrian's Wall to cause major problems. They are too strong for the weakened Romans, and the new governor, Virius Lupus, has to buy peace.

205	Under governor Alfenus Senicio extensive rebuilding takes place, but further encroachment by northern tribes see him ask Severus for direct assistance.
208	After successful campaigns in Parthia and Africa, Severus brings 40,000 troops to Britain. The army marches north, re-establishes the Antonine Wall and defeats the tribes ranged against him, although his losses against the guerrilla tactics of the Caledonii are substantial. The new position doesn't hold for long after Severus's death in 211.
c. 208	Circular stone huts found at Vindolanda were probably built during Severus's reign. There were some 250 of them, and the Antonine fort was demolished to make room for them. No one is sure who was housed in them – theories range from local farmers under threat from raiders to prisoners of war or African troops.
c. 211	Britain is divided into two provinces: Britannia Inferior, run from Eboracum by a praetorian governor, and Britannia Superior, commanded by a consular governor in London. The victories of Severus keep the north fairly quiet for some years.
211	Death of Septimius Severus at Eboracum. He is succeeded by his sons Caracalla and Geta. Neither wants to fight in Britain and peace is made with the Caledonians – or so Dio suggests. As he wasn't a Caracalla supporter he may have suggested this to dishonour him. Either way, Hadrian's Wall becomes the boundary of empire once again.
213	Vindolanda sees a new stone fort as the circular huts are stripped away. The garrison is *cohors IV Gallorum*, who are there by 213.
220	The first Saxon raids start in southeast Britain.
240	Longovicium (Lanchester) on Dere Street is rebuilt and regarrisoned by Roman troops.
259–274	Crisis in the empire: the Rhine frontier is collapsing; Britain and Gaul revolt. Marcus Cassianus Latinius Postumus declares himself emperor (259). Britain, Germany and Gaul support him and create the Empire of the Gallic Provinces.
270	In spite of the febrile political atmosphere, a large *vicus* has developed at Vindolanda but…
c. 280–300	Vindolanda is abandoned. This may have something to do with changes within the army structure, or the turbulent infighting between emperors and usurpers, but no one yet knows why such a thriving site was suddenly vacated with no obvious sign of military action.
274	Postumus is defeated at Châlons by Emperor Aurelian, who also disposes of the Germanic tribes, bringing peace at last. He is honoured with the title *Restitutor Orbis* (Restorer of the World) but is murdered by the Praetorian Guard.
284	Diocletian wins the empire by defeating his nearest rival, the emperor Carinus, who had been fighting in Britain. Carinus beat another rival for the crown, Julianus, before losing to Diocletian, who soon co-opted a military strong man, Maximian, as co-emperor.
285	Diocletian assumes the title of *Britannicus Maximus* – probably following a victory in his name in Britain, possibly by Carausius.
286	Maximian gives Carausius – based with the fleet at Bononia (Boulogne, also called Gesoriacum) – the job of dealing with Frank and Saxon pirates in the Channel and North Sea.
287	Maximian suspects Carausius of withholding too much booty and orders his death. Carausius rebels and takes over Britain and northern Gaul as Emperor in the North, beating Maximian in 288–9.
293	Carausius's position weakens as Constantius subdues the Germanic tribes and nibbles away at northern Gaul. Carausius is murdered by Allectus, who takes over as emperor.
296	Constantius Chlorus is finally strong enough to recover the province of Britain from Allectus. The fact is recorded on a milestone of around 306 in Luguvalium, which reads: FL(avio) VAL(erio) CONSTANT [i-] NO NOB(ilissimo) CAES(ari) ['For Flavius Valerius Constantinus, most noble Caesar'] The battles for empire cause problems around the wall and as far south as Eboracum and Deva (Chester) as troops were taken south.
296	After Constantius takes Britain he imposes a new governmental system (the reforms are named after the senior emperor of the Tetrachy, Diocletian), dividing it first into four provinces and later possibly five. There is academic disagreement over both the names and location of these. Constantius also institutes a regime of repair and renovation along the wall.
297	First use of the word Pict to describe the northern tribes – assumed to be the Caledonii and others.
296–305	Aurelius Arpagius is identified as the provincial governor of the wall area in an inscription found at Banna (Birdoswald), which also mentions rebuilding as the cohort 'restored the commandant's house, which had been covered with earth and had fallen into ruin, and the Headquarters Building and the bath-house…'
c. 300	The troops – in the form of *cohors IV Gallorum* – move back into Vindolanda, building a new stone fort. However, it houses fewer men and, for the first time, it seems as if the accommodation includes their families, housed in chalets rather than long barrack blocks.

c. 303 One of the legends of St. George has it that Diocletian puts to death an officer of his army who has travelled from Britain to plead the Christian cause (they are being persecuted at this date).

305 Constantius and his son Constantine arrive in Britain to campaign in the north. That happens, it would appear successfully, but Constantius is unwell…

306 He dies at Eboracum and Constantine is proclaimed emperor. It takes 20 years but by 324 he is sole emperor of the Roman world and he rules until 337, the last seven years from his new capital of Constantinople.

314 Constantine's army is very different to the old imperial army, with a delineation of troops into garrison troops – *limitanei* – and the mobile field army, the *comitatenses*. The *Dux*, or commander, of the army in Britain, is based at Eboracum. The effectiveness of this change will be evaluated later in the century.

320 A unit of Tigris bargemen (from Iraq) are employed by the Romans at Arbeia Fort on the Tyne.

343 Constans, the current emperor, unusually for the time, braves the winter seas in a surprising visit to Britain. There is much conjecture as to why he came, but touble in the north is inferred from fire damage to at least three forts – Risingham, High Rochester and Bewcastle – and the widespread refortification of cities that follows the visit.

360–361 The Caesar is now Julian (the Apostate) and he's in Lutetia Parisiorum (Paris) when he hears that the northern tribes have attacked the lands near the border. He sends his *magister militum* (master of soldiers), Lupicinus, with troops to Britain, although it's unknown how the campaign is prosecuted, if at all, because Lupicinus is recalled when Julian is proclaimed emperor. Ammianus Marcellinus tells of an attack by Picts, Scotti, Saxons and Attacotti. How well this is countered is debatable, but the events are overshadowed by the Barbarian Conspiracy, which is identified as starting in 367.

367 A rebellion by the Romans on Hadrian's Wall allows the tribes to overrun the north (the Picti) in the biggest revolt against Roman rule since the Iceni. There are concerted attacks by sea on western (by the Irish Scotti and, probably, Attacotti) and eastern areas of Britain (by the Saxons). The country is plunged into chaos, with cities sacked and the Roman commanders of navy and land forces killed and captured respectively.

368 Flavius Theodosius clears Britain of the invaders and restores the wall. Some units – especially the scouts – are seen as traitors and disbanded; others are treated with more clemency in an amnesty that helped provide Theodosius with men. There's a new garrison – and a Christian church – at Vindolanda. The warning signs for the future are clear, however, and Theodosius's rewards would be fleeting; in 376 he was executed for reasons unknown.

369 Raiding continues but the wall has been restored to a semblance of order. Watchtowers are erected down the east coast to warn against Germanic invaders and along the northern coast to defend against them.

379 Theodosius's son becomes emperor. On his death in 395, the Roman Empire is split into east and west under his children and is never reunited.

381 Another Pictish invasion is quelled by Magnus Maximus a senior commander who had fought with his uncle, Theodosius's father.

383 Magnus Maximus is proclaimed emperor by his troops, and he takes them to Gaul to make a play for the throne. He defeats Gratian and negotiates with Theodosius I, who recognises him as Western Augustus. However, he continues to wage war against the eastern emperors.

384–390 With Maximus away, what Gildas calls the first Pictish War begins.

388 Magnus Maximus is defeated and killed. Theodosius II sends help to fight against the Picts.

395 The empire splits into east and west and a register of all the offices is compiled: the Notitia Dignitatum, an important sourcebook for the historian.

398 Gildas's account of the second Pictish wars ends in victory over the enemy by Sticho. In fact, there is little evidence for this, and the drain of forces eastwards continues.

402 The last date of Roman coinage found in Britain.

410 Nearly all Roman troops have left Britain to defend Rome against the Visigoths.

900 Vindolanda's final occupants desert the site, which becomes a desolate ruin. Hadrian's Wall becomes a quarry and 90 percent of it will be used before it is conserved.

1746 The Military Road is built by General Wade to ease mobility after the second of the Jacobite rebellions. Much of the stone needed to build the road is robbed from Hadrian's Wall.

1800s Some reduction in quarrying as people seek to protect the remains of the wall – the best-known being John Clayton (1792–1890) and John Collingwood Bruce (1805–1892), whose numbering system for the castles and turrets on the wall was the foundation for what is used today.

1964 Corbridge Hoard discovered.

1970 Digging begins at Vindolanda.

1973 The first Vindolanda letters are discovered.

1987 Hadrian's Wall becomes a World Heritage Site.

2005 Creation of the Frontiers of the Roman Empire WHS, German *limes* and Hadrian's Wall.

1

BUILDING
THE WALL

Castle Nick – Milecastle 39 – was consolidated by John Clayton, but is nevertheless a striking location only a short distance north of Vindolanda. The milecastle appears to have been occupied until the late 4th century. Shutterstock

ROMAN ENGINEERING

Hadrian's Wall, the forts and their associated bath houses, temples and buildings speak volumes for the Romans' technical and engineering capabilities. Making maximum use of the natural features of the landscape – such as the ridge of the Whin Sill – they sited the wall effectively and built it to last. In spite of the depredations of time, the Cumbrian and Northumberland weather and the stone-robbers it has endured for 1,900 years and is enjoying a revitalisation thanks both to its position as a UNESCO World Heritage Site and a continuing stream of architectural finds – particularly the fabulous Vindolanda letters.

The people who built this wall were highly skilled professionals who used what we would term crude surveying instruments and tools. As far as we know, they didn't use compasses, had no method of magnified viewing (telescopes came into use during the 17th century) and couldn't measure latitude or longitude and so couldn't produce effective maps. While there are a number of extant Roman writings about their techniques, as with so much of our knowledge of the Romans, much is left to interpretation and conjecture. Take the *groma*, the tool of the Roman surveyor. Most literature suggests it was their main tool – but there's a convincing argument to suggest it was too inaccurate to be able to perform over long distances and that a version of the later surveyor's square might have been used instead.

It is clear that, whichever instruments were in their hands, the Romans had a brilliant and sophisticated engineering and surveying system capable of building large cities, immense bridges and lengthy aqueducts. Measuring and marking out tracts of land was important socially for farmers and cities – in particular to settle land disputes – but it was also vital for soldiers.

The concept of linear barriers as frontiers wasn't new to Hadrian. Many ancient cities had walls (think of Jericho and the trumpets): the Sumerians built walls, as did the Babylonians, Sasanians and Egyptians. Closer to home, the Greeks were dab hands at walls: Leonidas and the Spartans rebuilt the Phocian Wall at Thermopylae to stop the Persians; the Dema Wall stopped Athenian enemies (so, probably Spartans) on the Eleusis plains – in a country where stone was easily available, it's unsurprising that stone should be the main medium. Hadrian was a Graecophile and would have been aware of these and other Greek barriers.

The Romans themselves were known for linear barriers long before Hadrian: Scipio Aemilius built the 150km (c.100-mile) Fossa Regia to separate Carthage from Numidia in 146BC, although this was hardly a defensive barrier. Crassus erected a more solid 60km (c. 40-mile) barrier in 71BC to cut off Spartacus's slave rebellion from Italy. Trajan may have built the first of the palisaded barriers in Germany, the Sibyllenspur or Lautertal *limes*. And, of course, the earlier Flavian emperors had started the ball rolling in Britain with the Gask Ridge line (although some argue this was a protected supply line) and the Stanegate line.

Nevertheless, whether outright innovator or simply building on the ideas of his predecessors, Hadrian started something different: his linear barrier – not just a wall, but a defensive system of ditches, wall, forts and reserve troops – was unparalleled in Europe before then. He would go on to start similar barriers in Germany, Raetia (Switzerland), Dacia and north Africa that would be completed by his successors.

◄ *Roman building techniques were at their peak during Hadrian's time. The wall that carries his name, however, is a utilitarian structure put together by legionary builders.*
Shutterstock

▼ *Aqueducts are a remarkable feats of Roman engineering: the Pont du Gard in France, started by Hadrian, took water to Byzantium.*
Shutterstock

WHY AND WHERE TO BUILD

There has been much scholarly discussion about the rationale for linear barriers per se, and Hadrian's in particular, but there is little consensus and even less documentary evidence. The fact that Hadrian's Wall was altered and ramped up during the building, discarded by Antoninus Pius and the border moved farther north, before, once again, Hadrian's Wall ended up the primary Roman northern defensive line, shows that the Romans felt a border was a necessity and that, ultimately, containment, rather than the conquest, of Scotland was the best strategy.

The wider implications of linear borders – setting limits, awing the locals, and the Augustan view of keeping the empire within sensible lines of communication and logistics – are all very well, but not very Roman: most emperors needed a triumph or two to bolster their power and position. However, in the face of continued raiding, a wall was the logical solution and could act as a jumping-off point for further military action. Added to this, borders certainly helped taxation and import duties, and provided a certain element of control of the movement of people into the empire.

The fact is that an open border like the Stanegate isn't converted into a linear barrier like Hadrian's Wall, with around 160 watchtowers, some 80 milecastles and 25 forts, unless it's to stop something specific – and that specific something was almost certainly bands of raiders who wanted to enjoy the easy pickings south of the wall. On the other hand, if you are trying to control entrance to the south, it may not be a good idea to stud your wall with too many entrances – and it's instructive to note that most of these would be blocked or narrowed in later years.

This was an active barrier where fighting took place regularly and the Romans sustained continued casualties. At times, during major incursions by the tribes north of the wall, these casualties were large enough to require substantial replacements from abroad. Tactically, the Roman Army did not fight from behind barriers: it manoeuvred its enemy into a pitched battle in the open, where its superior training, weaponry and military skills could make mincemeat of most of its enemies – even when seriously outnumbered. But when the enemy isn't an army, it's more difficult to fight and a wall becomes a more practical solution.

So, when Hadrian visited Britain, probably in 122 – although there are few fixed points of reference to make this anything other than conjecture – he may already have decided on a wall. Certainly, the decision to start such a mammoth undertaking is unlikely to have been taken by anyone other than the emperor. Indeed, it's possible that his first governor of Britain (Quintus Pompeius Falco) was sent out to prepare for such an eventuality. Certainly, Aulus Platorius Nepos, the new governor and friend of Hadrian's from an early date, possibly even from his time in Spain, was the perfect person to oversee the building.

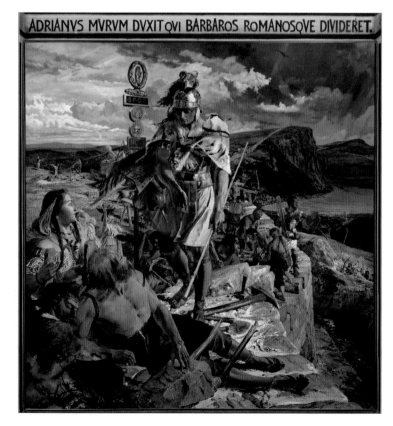

ADRIANVS MVRVM DVXIT QVI BARBAROS ROMANOSQVE DIVIDERET.

◀ *Classic 19th-century view of the wall, complete with characteristic quote 'to separate Rome and the barabarians'. William Bell Scott's 1896 mural at Wallington Hall of the history of Northumbria includes this detail, 'Building the wall'. The centurion is none other than John Clayton, who did so much in the 1930s to preserve the wall, although today his reconstituting of the wall means that little of it is original.* National Trust Photographic Library/Derrick E. Witty/Bridgeman Images

HOW TO DETERMINE THE WALL'S ROUTE

Having decided that a wall was the answer to Hadrian's problem, the first question needing an answer was, where? There are two obvious locations: the Forth–Clyde line, and that between the Tyne and Solway – more specifically, between Wallsend and Bowness, the lowest fording points on each river.

Forth–Clyde was shorter, at only about 60km (37 miles); Tyne–Solway was more than twice that at 140km (90 miles) but it was 160km (100 miles) farther north, through land that, if it wasn't directly hostile, was unfriendly – and much closer to the warlike tribes in the north. Recently, David Breeze (see Bibliography) has suggested that another factor in the placing of the wall is that it was the northern boundary of the territory of the Brigantes.

Then there is the natural advantage of the terrain between the Tyne and the Solway Firth, particularly along the line of the Whin Sill, the central section. Added to this – and even more important – is the fact that this was where the Romans had been since the withdrawal from the north after Agricola's advance. The Romans knew the Stanegate line and country. They had patrolled it, fought over it and trained there for the last 40 years. They would have known the terrain, the people and the resources very well.

The land between the Tyne and the Eden/Irthing is a mixed bag for wall builders. In the east, the land undulates gently towards Cilurnum (Chesters) and beyond, with the only steep slopes being the river valleys – the drops to the Ouseburn in Newcastle and, particularly, to the North Tyne at Cilurnum. The western climb from there to the Whin Sill sees a change in underlying geology as the land rises to the top of the dolerite intrusion that formed the sill. For some 15km (10 miles) or so the landscape is perfect for a defensive wall with sheer north-facing cliffs, the highest section of which rises to 375m (1,230ft) at Winshields.

Stone on the eastern side was plentiful, with limestone outcrops that facilitated building on both sides of the wall and with the Tyne acting as a highway for barges. Only the inaccessibility of parts of the Whin Sill would have caused the Romans any problems.

The western side of the country is very different. After the Whin Sill the wall crosses the Irving at Willowford before rising steeply to Harrows Scar and Birdoswald. From here, the land falls gently to Carlisle, but stone is more difficult to acquire along the Solway Firth – although there are quarries reasonably close at Gelt and Wetherall. This lack of stone to the west may have been the reason for the decision to split the construction style, with stone in the east and turf in the west. Other theses are put forward for this, with the key one being time scale: the implication being that the raiding from the north was continuous and debilitating enough for speed of construction to be essential.

▲ *The wall had to make three river crossings: at Cilurnum (Chesters) it crossed the Tyne; at Willowford, the Irthing; and at Luvogalium (Carlisle) the Eden. This photograph shows the wall slowly descending towards the Irthing. To the right, the abutment of the bridge. Since Roman times the river (visible at the bottom right of the photo) has altered course, leaving Willowford Roman Bridge high and dry.*

THE STANEGATE FORTIFICATIONS

The building of what we call the Stanegate – an old Norse word meaning 'stone road' – probably took place during the period when Agricola was governor or possibly shortly after, sometime between AD80 and AD90. It linked two key Roman roads: the northward extension of Watling Street to Luguvalium (Carlisle) and Dere Street from Eboracum (York) north to Bremenium (Rochester), although there is some evidence that it was extended westwards to Kirkbride and eastwards to at least Washing Wells and possibly Pons Aelius (Newcastle).

The forts protecting the road seem to have four distinct historical phases: first, Flavian: turf-and-timber structures built in the AD80–90 period; second, Trajanic, around the period at the turn of the 2nd century; third, Hadrianic 117–138: it was during Trajan's and Hadrian's reigns that some of the forts were rebuilt in stone; and, finally, post-Antonine when, after withdrawing from the Antonine Wall in the 150–160s, various forts were strengthened or built.

While the Stanegate was not built as a frontier, the fact that it was built and garrisoned meant that the Romans came to know the area well and understood its strategic importance. When Hadrian decided to build a wall it was logical to consider the area around the Stanegate — but to take into account, too, the deficiencies of the existing road and forts as a frontier.

Distances between forts and dates of occupation (E–W)

Washing Wells 24km (c. 15 miles). Probably built around AD85 and abandoned c.125.
Coria (Corbridge) 12km (7.5 miles). Probably built around AD85 and abandoned in the 5th century.
Newbrough 10km (6.25 miles). Evidence lacking for Sidgate site, but thought to be Agricolan and abandoned when Hadrian's Wall built; excavated fortlet in churchyard dates to the 4th century.
Vindolanda 5.6km (3.5 miles). Built around AD90 and abandoned in the 5th century.
Haltwhistle Burn 5km (3 miles). Many local marching camps. Fort built around 105.
Magnis (Carvoran) 3.3km (2 miles). First built from AD80; remaining stone structure dates to around 136–137.
Throp 4km (2.5 miles). Pottery identifies it in use in Hadrianic period and during the 4th century.
Nether Denton 5.2km (3.25 miles). Unexcavated: possibly initially Agricolan.
Boothby 4km (2.5 miles). Pottery discoveries give us an earliest occupation date of late 1st century AD.
Old Church, Brampton 12.5km (7.75 miles). Thought to be Agricolan and abandoned when Hadrian's Wall was built.
Luguvalium 8.5km (5.25 miles). Earliest occupation was before Agricola, probably around AD72–73. The oldest Stanegate location and pivotal in its construction. It survived until at least the 4th century.
Aballava (Burgh-by-Sands) 8.8km (5.5 miles). On the route of the wall, the fort may also have been on a possible extension of the Stanegate to Kirkbride.
Kirkbride. Just south of Bowness, earliest date is probably Agricolan

As well as forts, signal stations have been discovered at Pike Hill, Barcombe Hill, between Vindolanda and Newbrough and at Mains Rigg – almost certainly there are others as yet undiscovered.

▼ *Stanegate milepost at Vindolanda – the only one extant on the road.*
Paul Beston

▲ *The main street in Coria (Corbridge) was the Stanegate. This photograph looks west and shows the road heading towards Newbrough and Vindolanda. Note the granaries in front of the modern museum building.*

▼ *Another aerial view, this of Vindolanda. The Stanegate runs along the bottom of the photograph (the north). The only remaining Stanegate milepost is in the trees to the left.*

SURVEYING

Any society that has developed far enough to have boundary disputes and lawyers requires surveyors – the Roman *agrimensores* and *gromatici*. In an empire as ordered as that of the Romans, surveying was not just an important but an essential requirement. Roman roads were the backbone of the empire and the Romans were past masters at finding the best routes and building roads that lasted. We know quite a lot about Roman surveying through the works of Marcus Vitruvius Pollio and Sextus Julius Frontinus: aqueducts, architecture, canals, city planning, roads and, of course, walls — the Romans were adept at using basic instruments to work out alignments and angles.

Having chosen the rough location of the wall, the first job would have been a detailed survey of the route the wall was to take – not difficult along the Tyne estuary, Solway Firth or Whin Sill; a bit more open to discussion in other areas. This may have been undertaken by senior officers – even, if it happened when he was there, by Hadrian himself, although there is little evidence for this other than the possibility that he visited Vindolanda.

The detailed groundwork would have fallen to the hard practical men of the legions, those who were used to building camps and roads, no doubt often under enemy harassment. They used interlocking squares and lines – castrametation – to form the Roman *castra* or fortified field camp. It is clear from Roman sources that the fieldwork was performed by the *mensores* who orientated the *castra*, and established the main streets and the outer defenses. They worked outwards from the *locus gromae* – the place of the surveyor's cross at the centre of the *praetorium*. The *castra*'s playing-card shape with rounded corners was developed by the mid-1st century AD.

Peter Hill quotes inscriptions from Viminacium in Serbia (by 11 *mensores* from *legio VIII Claudia* in 228) and Lambaesis in Algeria (by nine *mensores* of *legio III Augusta* in the 3rd century) that suggest there were around 10 *mensores* in each legion. There's also a reference (the only one known in Britain) to a *mensor evocatus*, one Attonius Quintianus, on an altar from near Piercebridge. '*Evocatus*' means he had served his time in the army but had stayed with the legion probably because his skills were essential for the job in hand.

The detail work within the *castra* was likely performed by the *metatores*, probably selected from the rank and file of the legion. Indeed, it is possible that each *contubernium* – eight-man infantry squad – provided a *metator*, who, among other duties, would have laid out the position of his own *contubernium* within the *castra*.

The *metatores* were a part of the vanguard of the Roman Army on the march. Just behind the scouts and troops of the van came the engineers, who cleared the path for the rest of the troops (cutting down trees, levelling rough ground and straightening roads) and the *metatores*, 10 men from each century who carried the tools they needed for marking out the camp as well as their personal equipment.

The actual line of Hadrian's Wall, roughly chosen earlier, seems to have been set out using road-planning methods with long-distance alignments – except the central craggy section (Sewingshields and Walltown), which just followed the high ground – between fixed points on the route (primarily the bridges).

The other important consideration was a clear view to the south – fitting in with the original plan that the milecastles and towers should act as a tripwire and be able to signal back to the main troop concentrations in the Stanegate forts. The view to the north, while important, could have been improved in places. Hill quotes as examples of better lines:

'… west of Greatchesters [Aesica] there is a better line only about half a mile to the north, and there is rising ground within half a mile of MCs 9, 10, 13, 16, 20, and 26. It could be argued that the line around MC33 would have been better taken northwards to avoid the dead ground less than half a mile in advance, but the straighter line was chosen … The line in the neighbourhood of Walton is also not good.'

Often, it would appear, the route was chosen to reduce the lengths over broken ground or valleys, but elsewhere there seems scant attention paid to convenience, either to the wall's line (such as west from Sycamore Gap over Steel Rigg) or to the accessibility for carriage of stone, water and other building materials.

Straight alignments were set out using the *groma*, and Hill extrapolates that the detailed survey for the wall, handled by survey parties from each of the three legions involved in the building work, could have taken as little a month to complete.

THE GROMA

This is a very basic tool; it is certainly less accurate than many writers would have us believe. It is composed of the *stellata*, two arms of equal length, crossed at right angles. From the four outer points, the *curnicula*, four plumb lines are suspended, weighted by cone- or pear-shaped weights. The *rostrum* joins the *stellata* to the vertical pole, the *ferramentum*. A fifth plumb line suspended from the *rostrum* ensures the *groma* is centered on the required point. As long as the *ferramentum* is vertical, sighting down the *stellata* provides a useful tool for the surveyors.

Using the groma

By the beginning of the 2nd century, the *groma* was in the hands of the *mensor gromaticus* or *agrimensor*, who dealt with horizontal surveying. The *mensor librator* handled more complicated problems, surveying in both the vertical and horizontal. When building a camp or fort, once the land had been prepared, the surveyors drew the locations of the streets and of the wall, beginning from the centre of the field, possibly using the *groma*. In conjunction with posts (*metae*), the *groma* could provide basic straight lines and right angles. It could also be used in the calculation of

distances as exemplified in the diagram and was of particular use for bridge-making. As Balbus says, 'we were able to fix the width of rivers from the near bank even if the enemy wished to prevent us from doing so.'

With the groma positioned at A, lines were extended to identify points C and D. From the centre of the line A–C a line was extended B–F along the line C–D. As the two triangles so created are congruent, the distance A–B is the same as C–F and can be easily measured. The measurement could have been achieved by using a simple decempeda – as its name suggests, a 10-(Roman) foot long measuring rod. Fitted with iron or bronze end-caps, this staff could be used for measuring distances in 10-(Roman) foot increments.

▼ *Surveyors use the* groma.

▼ *The* groma.

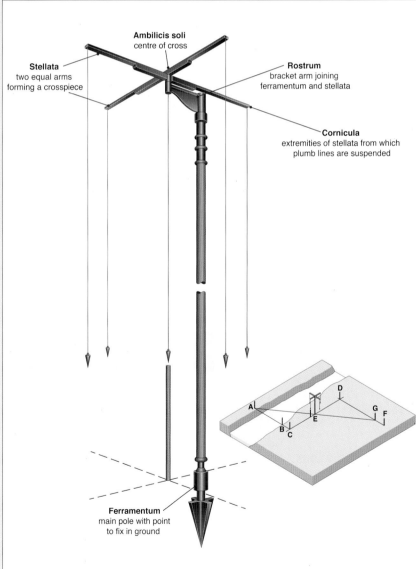

Ambilicis soli
centre of cross

Stellata
two equal arms
forming a crosspiece

Rostrum
bracket arm joining
ferramentum and stellata

Cornicula
extremities of stellata from which
plumb lines are suspended

Ferramentum
main pole with point
to fix in ground

CONSTRUCTION

The Romans were used to building in turf with revetments and gateways in timber: indeed, in 20 years they would go on to build a wall of that construction across the Forth–Clyde line. Unsurprisingly, therefore, the west of Hadrian's Wall – much of the ground alluvial with fewer outcrops of stone – was initially built this way. Turf-and-timber constructions were quicker to build than stone ones and last well, as the replica – now getting on for 50 years old – at Vindolanda proves. It was around 4.9m (15ft) wide, with a walkway on top and a wooden palisade. At regular (roughly one Roman mile) intervals there were 32 milecastles and some 62 turrets between them. During Hadrian's reign, part of this – from the Irving to Milecastle 54 – was rebuilt in stone; the rest later, possibly as late as the early 200s.

In the east, with 49 milecastles and 96 turrets, the wall was built in stone, the first 23 (Roman) miles of it, from Pons Aelius to Cilurnum, on broad – 10 (Roman) feet/3m (9ft 8.5in) – foundations. Building in stone was not unusual for the Romans, but it was slightly unusual for a linear barrier. Nevertheless, it implies permanence and, some 60 years after the invasion, and 15 years after

Mons Graupius, perhaps the Romans felt confident that they were a permanent fixture in the country. Certainly, at the start of the 2nd century a number of other important buildings in Britain were being rebuilt in stone or included stone walls in such locations as Caerleon (Isca – the legionary fortress of II Augusta), Deva Victrix (Chester) and Eboracum (York).

The foundations were laid for what is known as the 'Broad Wall' and much was in place when the decision was made to narrow the wall. Surprisingly, this didn't make the new wall less stable. It rose to about 4.9m (15ft) and may have had a walkway at the top: this is conjecture because there is no evidence to support this, but, on balance, the current view is that there probably was a walkway, but that it would have been fairly narrow on the Narrow Wall and of limited military use. Also undetermined is whether the wall was rendered or whitewashed. There is little evidence that it was rendered, other than the fact that many Roman buildings were, and it would certainly have taken a lot of work. But, as with all armies, the Roman Army needed to keep its men busy, so it's quite possible the wall was finished in this way.

Looking north in front of the wall was a berm leading to a ditch. This berm was about 6m (20ft) in width and possibly studded with pits of sharpened stakes or tree branches – *cippi* or *lilia,* as found at Rough Castle on the Antonine Wall. Pits for *cippi* have been excavated at a number of places on the wall, including Shields Road, Byker, Newcastle and near the fort at Segedunum. However, not all excavations have identified similar pits and there is

◄ *All the stages of construction are shown in this Philip Corke illustration: there's a* groma *top right; cranes to the left, and workers, right, using scaffolding bring stone to the working area; rubble filles the centre after the side walls are created.*
Historic England/Bridgeman Images

THE WORKFORCE

As we have seen, the line of the wall was laid out by surveyors (*mensores*) and took units from all three of Britain's legions to construct the wall: *legio II Augusta* based in Isca in South Wales, *legio VI Victrix* from Eboracum and *legio XX Valeria Victrix* from Deva.

The Clayton Collection, housed in Chesters Roman Fort (Cilurnum), has 53 centurial stones and 11,000 other artefacts, some of which are inscribed. Clayton discovered or purchased them during his long lifetime (1792–1890). As each gang finished its work, it would leave an inscription, some of which have survived. For example, a centurial stone discovered near Milecastle 59 reads:

> '*From the Second Legion Augusta the century of Julius Tertullianus (built this).'*

Another near Milecastle 64 reads:

> '*From the Fourth Cohort the century of Julius Vitalis princeps posterior (built this).'*

[The *princeps posterior* was deputy to the *princeps prior*, a centurion who commanded a *manipulus* (a maniple, i.e., two infantry centuries).]

Master stonemason Peter Hill's analysis of the workmanship of the stonework shows that it was done by soldiers rather than by craftsmen. It's good enough for the job, but the better

stonemasons would have been concentrated on the places where technique was essential: the four gateways in dressed stone needed on the 49 milecastles of the western section.

Surprisingly, there is no sign that slaves were used, although they would have been present, and there is little information pertaining to the use of native assistance.

▼ *The wall was built by legionaries, who were adept at building but were not mastercraftsmen. The best of the builders would have been concentrated on the most difficult tasks: constructing gateways, turrets and milecastles.*
Shutterstock

▼ *Along the course of the wall the builders identified their work with centurial stones. Some of these stones are lost; many are held at Chesters, part of the John Clayton collection now under the careful protection of English Heritage. However, in a farmhouse wall above Willowford Bridge, there is an example identifying* cohors V *of Gellius Philippus's century as the builder. The original was found while ploughing in 1986.*

CHO V
Ɔ G PILIPPI
FROM THE FIFTH COHORT
THE CENTURY OF GELLIVS
PHILIPPUS (BUILT THIS)

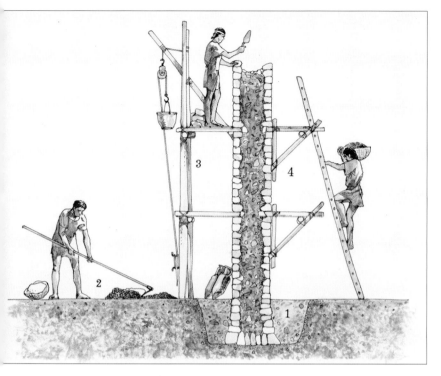

▲ *Building a wall in Roman times. 1 foundations – not as deep as we'd make them today, but sturdy; 2 mixing cement as necessary, usually to make good after a clay-packed wall fell down; 3 scaffolding to support the builders – this needs lots of trees; 4 bringing up rubble and clay: most of the infill was clay.* De Agostini Picture Library/Getty Images

▼ *The Turf Wall and rampart replica at Vindolanda. The wall has undoubtedly sunk over the years – some 1.5m (5ft) – and has been damaged by rabbits – a problem that the Romans wouldn't have had.*

a theory that the holes represent post holes for an altogether larger wooden structure.

Beyond the berm and the pits was a ditch, which ran intermittently in front of the wall for the majority of its course: around 96km (60 miles) of the total – not being present along the crags and parts of the Solway Firth. The ditch was V-shaped, and some 8m (27ft) wide and 2.7m (9ft) deep, although this varied depending on the terrain. At Limestone Corner, for example, the rock precluded this sort of depth.

All this required huge amounts of material: 3.7 million tons of stone. This was limestone initially and then sandstone, ferried along the Tyne. The walls were built with rubble in the centre, set mainly in puddled clay but pointed and mended with lime mortar if they collapsed – and they did.

While clay was the main binding element in the walls, lime needed for mortar was produced in lime kilns that burnt charcoal. There aren't many kilns to be found all along the wall – but there's a big one at Vercovicium. The water for slaking lime and creating mortar came from the many rivers along the wall; sometimes water had to be transported to the wall in barrels. Timber was essential for the charcoal, scaffolding, barrels etc.

TURRETS AND MILECASTLES

The details of these are covered in a later chapter.

Turrets appear along all Roman frontiers: on Hadrian's Wall, in Germany, Dacia and north Africa. The majority were turf-and-timber constructions, although those on Hadrian's Wall were finally of stone. Our knowledge of the ground plans and internal structures of these structures is good, but height and roofing is less understood due to lack of evidence. Trajan's column supplies the basic image for the turrets, which were roofed along the same lines as the reconstructions at Arbeia.

On Hadrian's Wall, turrets were built in pairs between the milecastles; their prime use – it would appear – was as watchtowers. Manned by only two or three lookouts, the turrets were typically 14.5sq m (156sq ft) in area, with two storeys. Should an enemy be sighted, the milecastles or forts could be roused.

The milecastles were bigger than the turrets and centred on a gateway through the wall. Some of these gateways were closed during Roman occupation. They were generally manned by 8–12 men who lived in barracks within the footprint – there were ovens built into the wall. They aren't placed exactly every Roman mile, but this is usually caused by terrain rather than miscalculation. The best-preserved milecastle on the wall is at Poltross Burn (see p94) and provides evidence of a staircase that may have reached a walkway on the wall.

THE VALLUM

The other major component of the wall was the complex earthworks that lay some 18m (60ft) south of the eastern curtain wall and rather further back – nearly a kilometre (around half a mile) around the central section crags. Built after the wall had been erected, around the time the forts were built, the Vallum gained its name from the writings of Bede. It would have been an impressive structure at the time, as it stretched for 112km (70 miles) along the path of the wall. It was some 35m (120ft) across and comprised two earth banks separated by berms and a 6m (20ft)-wide ditch.

Remarkably, no one is quite sure why it was built. The usual theory is that it was to delineate the border zone, creating a space that could only be crossed at the forts' gateways and some milecastles. Others suggest it was the basis for a metalled road that was never finished. Adding credence to this proposal is the suggestion that the Roman military way was built around the time the Vallum fell out of use. Whatever the reason, within a few years of completion it was out of commission.

▲ *The Vallum is some distance from the wall along the Whin Sill, for obvious reasons.*

POSSIBLE ORDER OF CONSTRUCTION

1   In 122 Hadrian comes to Britain. He has probably already decided to build a wall and may have started the planning through his first Governor of Britain, Falco. Falco is followed by Hadrian's friend Nepos to oversee construction.

2   The route is surveyed and delineated.

3   Work commences: building season is April–October, so construction probably starts in 123.

4   In 124 the decision is made to reduce the width of the wall from 3m to 2.1m (9ft 8in to 6ft 6in). By this time, the foundation for the Broad Wall has already been substantially laid and many milecastles and turrets built with Broad Wall joining wings.

5   Before the wall is completed, possibly also in 124, the decision is made to add forts. Turrets already started at Onnum (Halton Chesters), Cilurnum (Chesters), Vircovicium (Housesteads) and Banna (Birdoswald) are dismantled as the forts are built over. There is a dislocation in building work … possibly because of enemy action.

6   Around the same time it was decided to add the Vallum south of the wall. Crossings – cobbled causeways and gateways opposite fort/milecastles entrances – are provided (e.g. Condercum). This controlled zone was relaxed as the *vici* developed.

7   Two extra forts are added, Brocolitia (Carrawburgh) built over the Vallum south of the wall west of Onnum and Congabata (Drumburgh) on the Solway Firth.

8   The wall is extended from Pons Aelius to Segedunum: this section is narrow and has milecastles and turrets but no vallum.

9   Probably before Hadrian's death, stone begins to replace some of the turf wall near the River Irving.

10   It's probable that Fanum Cocidi (Bewcastle) and Castra Exploratorum (Netherby) are built during Hadrian's reign; the third of the northwest outpost forts – Blatobulgium (Birrens) – is probably Flavian.

11   The wall was run down during the advance northwards during Antoninus Pius's reign. This is not to say that it was abandoned.

12   Under Marcus Aurelius the wall is reoccupied and refurbished; the turf wall is replaced by stone with a slight realignment west of Banna.

14   A military road connecting the forts is added.

15   The Vallum is slighted or falls into disrepair during the later 2nd century. *Vici* begin to coalesce around the forts.

16   Doorways of milecastles and forts are blocked and narrowed.

FORTIFICATIONS

The Roman Army built in stone and turf according to availability and time, with the quicker turf-and-timber constructions used for making a temporary camp on campaign when enemy proximity required speed. The more permanent stone replacements came along later, with timber being used in both. Turf was a tried-and-tested technology for the Roman military and was considerably stronger than the modern reader might think. Revetted with timber and huge back-berm earthen banks, which enabled swift mass access to the top rampart, and filled with cores of rubble, a turf wall was just as effective as a stone one, but required rather more maintenance.

Regardless of the difference in size, whether a marching camp, auxiliary fort or legionary fortress, all Roman military installations were called *castrum* (plural *castra*). The very smallest fortlets were known as *castellum*. Army regulations required any major unit on campaign to retire to a properly constructed camp each night – as a precautionary defensive measure.

No Roman *castra* were made to fight from. The Roman Army fought as heavy infantry in the open, where its superior organisation would have the most impact and an outcome could be swiftly reached. Thus, the primary purpose of *castra* was not to withstand attack but to provide a safe staging area for troops to organise and assemble before deployment.

All Roman military installations essentially followed the same basic idealised template, with variations only when demanded by the constraints of time, terrain and materials available. Such a protocol maintained organisation and discipline, for every soldier knew where everything was and where he was supposed to be, whether in a legionary fortress or an overnight marching camp. Marching or night camps on campaign were inevitably slighter and more swiftly erected than their more permanent counterparts. Both were chosen with an eye for a good defensive position, either on high ground or in the open and sited near water. They were marked out in flags and rope lines by a specialist advance squad that was sent on ahead so that the ground plan could be laid out quickly and clearly. When the main body of troops arrived, the visible plan of the camp could then be swiftly realised.

The shape and ground plan of night camps rarely strayed from a rectangular, round-cornered playing-card shape, consisting of a wooden palisade (*vallum*) atop an earthern rampart (*agger*), built up from the earth excavated from the ditch (*fossa*) or ditches in front, with a gate on each side leading to the camp's principal roads. Just behind the vallum a road ran right around the camp and was known as the *intervallum*, enabling swift movement to any part of the defences as well as acting as a safety margin against any incoming missiles.

The inside of the camp was then divided into four quarters by the two roads that bisected each other – the *via principalis* and the *via praetoria*, with the command and supply sections always in the centre. (Sometimes the *via praetoria* did not pierce its walls dead centre, which created three thirds rather than four quarters, but with the middle third still the command and control section.) In the middle of the camp was the *praetorium*, the command centre where the *praetor* (first officer), the unit's standards, pay chests and command staff were housed; the legate's tent with those of the tribunes were ranged in front. The *via principalis* at this central part was used as an assembly area and parade ground. On one side of the *praetorium* there was the hospital and on the other was the *quaestorium* (*quaestor* – supply officer) where the unit's stores and supplies were kept. The cohorts' tents occupied either side of the command section and sometimes part of this space was also left open in which to muster and hold prisoners and booty or horses and supplies. If the unit was especially anxious and expecting imminent attack, more ditches could be dug and the gateways further protected with frontal hemispherical berms. When time was available these ditches could be made more elaborate and deadly, with their backs cut vertically to prevent escape, an ankle-breaker bottom slot and the addition of various sharpened wooden stakes – some huge and obvious while others were more trap-like, hidden in pits covered in brushwood. Wide, deep ditches created a killing zone for the soldiers on the ramparts armed with javelins and supported by artillery.

In the more permanent barracks or forts virtually the same plan was followed but they were made using heavier materials, often over the top of the wooden original. The *praetorium* was built in stone and resembled a Mediterranean Roman villa.

A STANDARD ROMAN FORT

Note the following features:

- *playing-card shape with curved corners and external ditches. Inside the walls a berm helped defenders reach the parapet/palisade.*
- *towers at the corners and gateways – and sometimes interval towers on the walls.*
- *four main entrances (one on each wall). In the early cavalry forts the north, west and east gateways were all north of the wall. To reduce the stress on the south gateway, two smaller gateways in the west and east walls were sometimes opened.*
- *the main streets:*
  two from west to east – the via principalis, *running from the* porta principalis dextra *(right/east) to* porta principalis sinistra *(left/west) and the* via quintana *two from north to south – the* via praetoria *from the* porta praetoria *(north)* to the via principalis; *and the* via decumana *from the southern gate (*porta decumana*) to the* via quintana. *There was also a perimeter road, the* via sagularis *or* intervallum.
- *the three main central buildings: the granaries (*horrea*), headquarters building (*principia*) and commander's house (*praetorium*)*
- *barracks (*centuriae*)*
- *stables (*stabuli*)*
- *workshops (*fabricae*)*
- *latrines (*latrinae*)*
- *ovens (*forni*)*

Where possible, aqueducts brought water to the site, which was saved in water tanks. For safety reasons, bath houses were almost always outside the camps, as they were prone to catch fire.

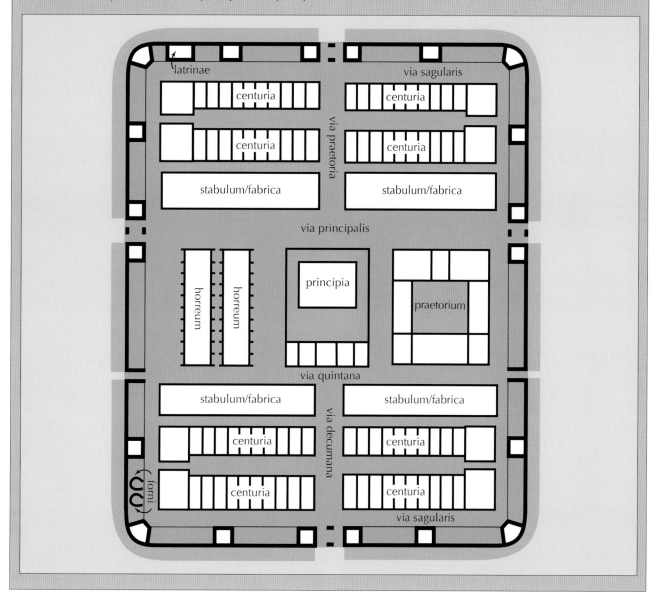

▶*Vercovicium (Housesteads) (see also pp76–77). Note no interval towers on the walls – although the footings for the original watchtower (36B) are visible just before the wall at the lower right of the photograph. There's no water source either, so water tanks were filled from the Knag Burn. Vercovicium has a slightly unusual layout. It includes a hospital. Note the ovens, well-preserved latrines and later corn driers built into the granaries.*

▲ *The* principia *in the early 3rd century.* Historic England/Getty Images

▼ *The hospital in the 2nd century.* Historic England/Getty Images

▼ *The north gate in the 2nd century.* Historic England/Bridgeman Images

▼ *The commandant's house in the 2nd century.* Historic England/Bridgeman Images

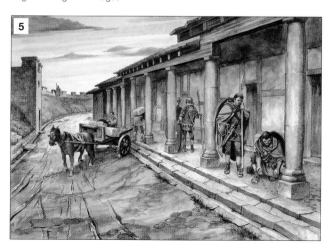

▼ *Barracks block XIII in the 2nd century.* Historic England/Bridgeman Images

▼ *The granaries in the later 2nd century.* Historic England/Bridgeman Images

The *quaestorium* was also constructed in stone and featured the heavy-set *horreum* or granary, with double-skinned walls and a raised floor to aid airflow and prevent vital grain supplies from rotting. Gates in the camp walls were no longer flush with the wall but protruding, often doubled and built of stone, with towers on either side as well as at each corner of the camp, while other watchtowers also studded the walls.

Because of the ever-present danger of fire breaking out, baths were usually built outside the camp, unless the fort was large enough to accommodate them, such as a massive legionary fortress. The vital bread ovens would also be built into the back of the rampart, minimising the risk of fire. Temples, too, were often built close by rather than inside the forts. Deeply superstitious, Iron Age people spent much time and energy trying to placate or beg help from different gods. The Romans were not exempt from these preoccupations and, with their knack of taking what was useful from other cultures, their

acceptance of other gods is quite apparent. They were always perfectly comfortable finding a Roman equivalent to combine with a local deity or even to adopt an attractive exotic import like Mithras, who seemed to have had a particular appeal to soldiers. Other changes or evolutions occurred in camp and fort construction over time and reflected the change of military emphasis away from infantry to different kinds of auxiliary troops – often cavalry or mixed units. Later forts tended to be square.

The day-to-day running of large groups of people in such installations required clockwork precision in order to succeed. Aside from the military duties of guarding the camp itself, other tasks included gathering fuel for the ever-present bread ovens, sourcing and preparing food, gathering water for the baths and latrines and grazing and exercising animals. The supply administration of a permanent camp was run as a business, using money as the exchange medium. Native tribes that supplied many of the army's needs for food, animals, fodder and construction materials accrued considerable wealth in the process. Extra workshops producing building supplies such as tiles, pipes and lime mortar could also be sited outside the defences.

▼ The *Temple of Mithras at Brocolitia went through three main stages taking it from a small shrine to a substantial building with three main altars. It was destroyed and rebuilt at least twice.* Shutterstock

78.

79.

◄ *Roman troops defend a fort in Dacia in a scene from Trajan's Column. Note the attackers' battering ram, the stone walls and crenellations.*
WikiCommons

▼ *The Romans occasionally built smaller camps – castellum – for cohorts or centuries. This is Castleshaw Roman fortlet in the Pennines (possibly Rigodunum). Note wood-and-turf construction, palisade and wooden towers.*
Graham Sumner

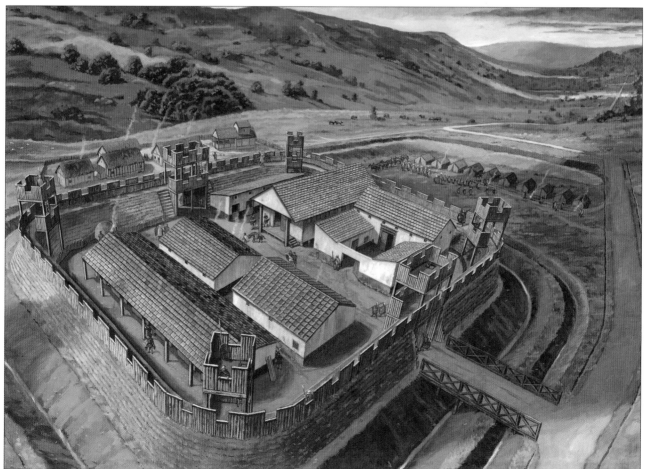

2

THE WALL FROM THE EAST TO WILLOWFORD BRIDGE

Looking towards Crag Lough with Hot Bank Farm behind it.
Shutterstock

THE STONE WALL

Hadrian's decision – for surely only an emperor could initiate such an immense undertaking – to build so much of the wall in stone from the start has left northern England with one of the most remarkable feats of Roman engineering. Stretching across the landscape, it emphasises some 2,000 years later just how powerful the Roman Empire was, and what an impact it made on the history of this country.

The wall in the east was planned to start, appropriately enough, at Pons Aelius where a bridge – named after Emperor Hadrian's family – was built across the Tyne to carry the road northwards. The initial plan for the wall was to build it in stone from the Tyne to the Irthing, and in turf from there to the coast. The geology of the eastern side of the country allowed the legionaries to quarry stone either *in situ* or close by the intended path. We know that the Tyne was navigable to Prudhoe in medieval times, and possibly to Corbridge and Hexham, and would have provided

◄ This aerial view looks along Cawfields Crags towards Cawfield Quarry, showing the use of the natural features in the central section of the wall. The Vallum lies farther down the slope. Even in these remote areas the wall has been plundered.

▼ A reconstruction of Arbeia's west-facing double gate, its size reflecting its strategic importance as a link between maritime supply from the continent and the troops serving in the north and on the wall.

an artery along which building materials could be transported. The road we now know as the Stanegate also provided easy access to the chosen path. In the central section the Whin Sill provided a ready-made natural line for the wall.

The plan developed quickly. The wall was extended from the bridge to the east to meet the river at Segedunum; forts – hitherto held back from the wall – were placed along its length, probably to allow a quicker response in times of trouble: the north certainly enjoyed plenty of these.

The choice of stone construction, however, had one huge disadvantage to us today. The availability of so much easily accessible stone, already quarried and shaped and evenly distributed through the countryside was a resource that was fully appreciated by builders and engineers across the centuries. Castles, churches, houses, roads – more of the wall can be seen in structures along its length than on its course. Nevertheless, although little remains, now the wall is protected, the use of stone ensures that it is more visible than the Antonine Wall farther north.

▼ A diagrammatic representation of the wall runs through the next two chapters, starting from the supply fort at Arbeia to the end of the Western Defences at Maryport. It gives an indication of what has been discovered of the wall and what can still be seen today.

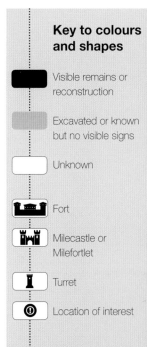

Key to colours and shapes

■ Visible remains or reconstruction

▨ Excavated or known but no visible signs

□ Unknown

⌂ Fort

⌂ Milecastle or Milefortlet

Ⅰ Turret

◎ Location of interest

ARBEIA

▲ *Reconstructed commander's quarters in the centre of Arbeia Fort, built around a small colonnaded garden.*

ARBEIA (SOUTH SHIELDS)

The name Arbeia – The Place of the Arabs – is thought to be a Romanised name from Aramaic, the native language of the last presumed unit stationed there. The furthest east of the garrison forts along Hadrian's Wall, Arbeia was built on the south bank of the River Tyne estuary near the outlet to the North Sea.

Arbeia was first built in c. 129 by *legio VI Victrix* some, 6–8km (4–5 miles) from Segedunum, overlooking and protecting the mouth of the River Tyne where it enters the North Sea. Originally configured in the standard layout of an auxiliary cavalry fort, this substantial and strategically important stone-built edifice was used by the Roman military for almost 300 years with various changes of design, use and personnel according to need. At times it was virtually on the frontier itself and vital; at others it became of secondary importance. However, it never lost its strategic position as a guard fort of the harbour at the mouth of the river.

On initial completion it began as a garrison fort for an *auxilia* cavalry *ala* of 500 horsemen. Following the Antonine advance to the new line some 160km (100 miles) to the north, the fort underwent modification to became a supply base. Even later, c. 208, during the Severan campaigns against the Caledonian tribes of the far north, the auxilary cavalry were withdrawn and replaced by an auxiliary infantry cohort, while undergoing extensive rebuilding to become a major supply base for the northern campaigns.

In c. 222–235, when the border was once again pulled back to Hadrian's Wall, it became the

Granaries
Barracks
HQ
1 Original HQ
Footprint of CO's house reconstruction
Original south wall
Ditches

◀ *Arbeia was enlarged until it was eventually filled for the most part with 24 granaries, with new barracks and* principia *built in southern section of the extended fort. In the 4th century, however, the fort burnt down, the granaries were returned to use as barracks and the commander had a grand house in the southeastern corner.*

pre-eminent supply base for the wall, where ships from the *Classis Britannica* (the Roman British fleet) could download grain supplies that were then shipped up the Tyne to supply the garrison forts. At this time only the original *horreum* (granary) was kept. Everything else inside the walls was rebuilt with the addition of a further 18 stone-built granaries. Subsequently, there were further repurposings. Around 300 the granaries became barracks and a luxurious new centurions' block and commander's house were built at the southern end. These have been reconstructed in the fort.

Arbeia was abandoned when the Romans withdrew from Britain and, without their skill in maintenance and engineering, it fell into disrepair.

The fort has been extensively excavated and many major finds have been made. Epigraphic evidence attests the building by the Sixth, the occupation by *ala I Pannoniorum Sabiniana* – an auxiliary cavalry unit recruited from Pannonia (now part of modern Hungary); the *ala I Hispanorum Asturum* – another auxiliary cavalry unit, this one from Spain; the *cohors V Gallorum* – the Fifth Cohort of Gauls (a 1,000-man infantry unit); and finally *numerus Barcariorum Tigrisiensium* – a company of bargemen from the River Tigris in the Middle East, whose origins gave the fort its final name.

Other finds include dedications to a variety of Roman, Greek and British gods (Aesculapius, Brigit, Mars, Ansus Vitiris, Numinibus Augusti); perhaps the best-preserved ringmail armour found in the UK; tombstones to freed slaves who then married Roman soldiers and citizens; as well as many other everyday artefacts and jet jewellery.

Today, much of the original foundations and outline of the defences and interior buildings are visible and the *praetorium*, a barracks and the western gate with its guard towers have all been reconstructed to give contemporary visitors an idea of the fort's appearance when in Roman use.

Classis Britannica

Not natural seamen, the Romans nevertheless had to come to terms with the requirement for naval power in their struggles, firstly to dominate the Mediterranean and then later to expand into northern Europe. In order to achieve this they used similar methods to their development of cavalry (another mode of warfare in which they did not naturally excel): they recruited from peoples who had the necessary skills they lacked. This meant their navy had a heavy Greek presence and was never accorded the importance equal to that of the legions.

The *Classis Britannica* was formed in the early 40s AD at Gesoriacum or Bononia (Boulogne) for the Claudian invasion of Britain and following

▲ *A touching tombstone found at Arbeia dedicated to the freedwoman Regina of the Catuvellaunian tribe from southeast Britain, who died in childbirth aged 30. She was freed, married and mourned by Barates, a Syrian originally from Palmyra.*

its success was then based at Rutupiae (Richborough) until around AD85, when it relocated to Dubris (Dover). It remained in the Channel area until the Flavian expansion from AD69–96, when it was used by Agricola to aid and supply his progress northwards. During this period it is said to have completed a circumnavigation of the entire island of Britain. The fleet certainly attacked the coast of Caledonia, even reaching the Orkney Islands around AD84. The fleet then continued to supply Roman forces in the north of Britain, with the base at the mouth of the Tyne supporting Hadrian's Wall during the 2nd and 3rd centuries.

In the late 3rd century Carausius was appointed its commander, with the added task of suppressing piracy. When he was accused of treachery c. 287 he seceded from Rome and declared himself Emperor of Britain and northern Gaul, but by 300 the fleet was back on side. Its final role before the Roman withdrawal from Britain was the defence of the eastern and southern coasts against Saxons.

Arbeia Fort
Location: South Shields
Status: Visible remains; reconstructed buildings; museum
Fort: Separate from wall
Built: 129, by *legio VI Victrix*; enlarged 208
Dimensions: 189m (620ft) long (N–S) by 97.5m (320ft) (E–W) after enlargement as supply base
Gates: N, E, S and W
Vallum: None
Vicus: to E

Segedunum Fort
Location: Wallsend
Status: Visible remains; reconstructed bath house and wall; museum
Fort: First from E; 5.6km (3.5 miles) from Pons Aelius
Built: 127
Dimensions: 138m (453ft) long (N–S) by 120m (394ft) (W–E) covering 1.65ha (4 acres)
Gates: N, E, and W to N of wall; SW and S inside wall which ran to river
Vallum: None
Vicus: to S and SW inside wall; also outside

Conjectured milecastle beneath the fort

Turret 0A: Nothing known

Turret 0B (St Francis): Covered over

Milecastle 1 Stott's Pow
Status: Remains covered over
Type: Short axis
Builder: *Legio II Augusta*

Turret 1A: Nothing known

Turret 1B: Nothing known

Milecastle 2 (Walker)
Status: Covered over
Type: Short axis
Builder: *Legio II Augusta*

Turret 2A: Nothing known

Turret 2B: Nothing known

FROM SEGEDUNUM TO PONS AELIUS

▲ *An aerial view of Segedunum Fort with its viewing tower and the reconstructed Roman bath house in the left-hand corner of the site. The river's path has changed since the Romans built their fort.*

SEGEDUNUM (WALLSEND)

A later (AD127) 5km (3.5-mile) eastward extension of the wall from Pons Aelius (Newcastle) to the low-tide level on the north side of the River Tyne, this sealed off the last strategically relevant part of the land as well as the wall itself. Most of the wall here is buried under the modern A187 road.

Segedunum was built at the eastern end of the extension of the wall, close by the river, approximately 8km (5 miles) upstream from Arbeia on the opposite bank. Originally four milecastles would have punctuated this extension to the wall but all have vanished beneath the five modern metropolitan boroughs of Tyne and Wear, although excavations have revealed that parts of it collapsed back in the time it was in use.

Perhaps being built to a much narrower gauge

than the wall to the west of Pons Aelius – 2.30m (7ft 6in) on a foundation of 2.4m (8ft) – made it more susceptible in certain places. With the river so close behind, no Vallum was deemed necessary. The fort itself was aligned NNW, with three of its five double gateways north of the wall acting as sally ports for swift offensive action. The wall entered midway on its southwestern side and exited from the southeastern corner tower down to the River Tyne. Between the fort and the river there was a small *vicus* with a quay.

Originally, only the walls and command buildings were built in stone and the barracks in wood, but the whole fort was upgraded c. 160, during the Severan period, and rebuilt in stone with additional buildings, including a hospital (*valetudinarium*). It was garrisoned by an auxiliary *cohors equitata* of 120 cavalrymen and 480 infantry and so had six infantry and four cavalry barracks, a *praetorium* and a double granary.

The first unit's identity remains unknown, but in the 2nd century *cohors II Nerviorum civium Romanorum* – the Second Cohort of Nervians from an area of Gallia Belgica (modern Belgium) – was stationed there. It was replaced in the 3rd and 4th centuries by *cohors IV Lingonum equitata*. The Lingones were also from Gallia Belgica, as attested in the 4th-century *Notitia Dignitatum*.

The fort was finally abandoned c. 400, when the last Roman troops left Britain and the civilian settlement relocated upriver, farther away from the growing danger from sea raiders. In the 18th century

▶ *Layout of the main features of Segedunum Fort, showing its four double gateways and where the wall entered and exited.*

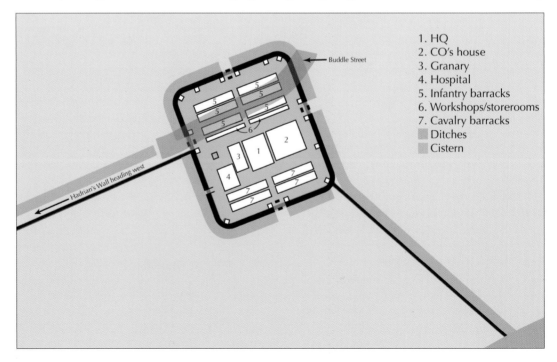

Buddle Street

Hadrian's Wall heading west

1. HQ
2. CO's house
3. Granary
4. Hospital
5. Infantry barracks
6. Workshops/storerooms
7. Cavalry barracks
Ditches
Cistern

▶ *An artist's impression of Segedunum Fort at the time when it was active, with its* vicus *and a quay behind it and the wall falling to the river.*
English Heritage/ Heritage Images/Getty Images

a colliery was started in the area; it closed in 1969. In the early 20th century the site was buried under a housing estate and remained hidden until the estate was demolished in the 1970s.

Today's Segedunum Roman Fort is located in Buddle Street at Wallsend. It opened in 2000 as a museum and visitor centre, with an imposing 34m (111ft 6in) viewing tower that reveals the delineated plan of the fort during the Severan period and includes an excellent computer-generated animation covering its entire lifetime. This is just as well, for, being buried under the modern town, and with its industrial antecedents, little of the original fort survives beyond outlines. The site also includes the only reconstructed Roman bath house in Britain and a reconstructed section of wall, which overlooks a short stretch of the original wall's

foundations across Buddle Street opposite the site.

Outside the museum stands an imposing steel sculpture of a Roman centurion: Sentius Tectonicus, a real name sourced from an original inscription found nearby.

Roman baths

Influenced by the Greeks, the Romans embraced bathing and expanded it to become a focal point of their recreational culture, to be used by all in a social, rather than private, context. The Romans' advanced hydromechanical engineering skills enabled them to pipe in water and build extensive bathing complexes or simpler bath houses all over their empire. Some were built by emperors as a gift from the city and people of Rome; others were by the army or the civil administration of a province. All were founded on the same basic principles: a series of progressively hotter rooms with the heat supplied from a central furnace guided through an underfloor chamber known as a *hypocaust*, although they also enclosed existing hot springs to achieve the same effects. According to the size and complexity these *balnea* (baths) might also contain elaborate changing rooms, places for exercise, lavatories and refreshment areas, but at their core the essential elements were an *apodyterium* (changing room), a *frigidarium* (cold room), a *tepidarium* (warm room) and a *caldarium* (hot room). All would have basins of running water with which to cool or wash. As soap was a very expensive luxury, oil was used and then scraped off with a metal tool known as a *strigil*. Although expensive to run and always a fire hazard, baths were deemed essential for a civilised life and virtually everyone had access to them.

◀ *Layout of the bath house at Segedunum, which was excavated in 2014.*

Milecastle 3
(Ouseburn)
Status: Remains covered over
Type: Unknown
Builder: Unknown

Turret 3A: Nothing known

Turret 3B: Nothing known

Pons Aelius Fort
Location: Newcastle (under castle)
Status: Positions of buildings (granaries, headquarters building, commanding officer's house) marked on the ground
Fort: Second from E; 4.8km (3 miles) from Segedunum
Built: 122 by *legio VI Victrix* or *XX Valeria Victrix*
Dimensions: Unknown; covering 0.6ha (1.53 acres)
Gates: Unknown
Vallum: None visible (first record a couple of kilometres to W)
Vicus: Unknown

Milecastle 4
(Westgate Road)
Status: Remains exist beneath the Newcastle Arts Centre
Type: Long axis
Builder: *Legio VI Victrix* or *XX Valeria Victrix*

Turret 4A: Nothing known

Turret 4B: Nothing known

Milecastle 5 (Quarry House)
Status: Nothing known
Type: Unknown
Builder: Unknown
Vallum starts close to the milecastle

Turret 5A: Nothing known

Turret 5B: Nothing known

Milecastle 6 (Benwell Grove)
Status: Nothing known
Type: Unknown
Builder: Unknown

Turret 6A: Nothing known

FROM PONS AELIUS TO CONDERCUM

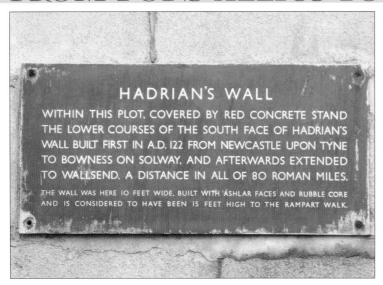

▲ *A plaque at 21 Westgate Road in Newcastle city centre recording the discovery of some lower courses of the original wall.*

PONS AELIUS (NEWCASTLE)

Very little remains to be seen of Roman Newcastle as the modern city has been built over the top. Occasionally, Roman remains are excavated or dredged up from the River Tyne. The wall here passes just north of the mid-Victorian Roman Catholic cathedral in the centre of the city and is hidden beneath the A6115 running westwards and the A187 that runs eastwards.

Apart from the reconstructed segment and the original foundations across Buddle Street from the Segedunum Museum, nothing of the wall is visible, buried beneath Shields Road. Somewhere near

Byker Bridge it angled slightly to the left and then proceeded straight towards where the Tyne Bridge and the medieval castle – the New Castle – are now situated, with the castle being built directly over the fort of Pons Aelius, obliterating almost all trace of it.

The wall originally began here with a small fort on a promontory giving excellent observation and protecting the important river crossing, over which a bridge was built c. 122. Some of the 16 stone piers, 6m (20ft) wide and 5m (16ft) long, have been found, indicating a substantial structure more than 213m (700ft) in length, with caissons constructed from iron-shod oak piles filled in with stone rubble. However, despite the bridge, Pons Aelius was not particularly important among the northern Roman settlements and remained relatively small.

Seven altar stones and 11 other building inscriptions have been found in the vicinity, now housed in the Great North Museum: Hancock. Two dredged from the Tyne are dedicated to the powerful water gods Oceanus and Neptune and mention *legio VI Victrix*; two are dedicated to Jupiter Best and Greatest; and one to Silvanus and one to the Mother Goddess from Across the Sea. Other epigraphic evidence attests the arrival of reinforcements of German origin for *legio II Augusta* and *legio XX Valeria* c. 150 after their losses during a revolt by the northern British tribes.

In the 3rd century, during the governorship

▶ *An aerial view of Newcastle city centre showing the the area where Pons Aelius Fort was sited, now covered by the medieval castle's keep, at the top end of the High Level Bridge on the left.*

of Gaius Julius Marcus, the fort was manned by an approximately 500-man *cohors quingenaria equitata*, a mixed auxiliary cohort of infantry and cavalry (*cohors I Ulpia Traiana Cugernorum*) from the Cugerni tribe, who inhabited the Lower Rhine area of Germany, attested by a stone dedicated to the Emperor Hadrian's mother dated 213. Unusually, in the late 4th century the *Notitia*

▼ *A layout plan of Pons Aelius Fort at Newcastle, showing the amount that has been discovered, with the rest having to be surmised due to the extensive construction on the site.*

▲ *On the pavement below Newcastle's medieval castle are the outline of parts of the Roman fort – the* principia, praetorium *and* horreum. Paul Beston

Dignitatum records the fort garrisoned by *cohors I Cornoviorum*, recruited from the Cornovii tribe whose tribal lands are now in Shropshire, Cheshire, Staffordshire, and Hereford and Worcester. It is the only native British unit ever known to have been stationed on the wall.

▼ *Newcastle's keep sits on the site of the Roman fort.* Hans Peter Schaefer/WikiCommons (CC BY-SA 3.0)

Granary　**Probably barracks**

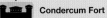

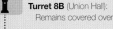

FROM CONDERCUM TO HEDDON

◄ *Benwell Temple today. Sited just outside the southeastern defences of the now-vanished Condercum Fort.*

CONDERCUM (BENWELL)

Much of the fort lies underneath later buildings and, to the north, a Victorian reservoir. Built astride the wall, its unique features are the mention of Antenociticus, possibly a native British deity, and, south of the fort, the only permanent crossing of the Vallum anywhere along the wall.

Condercum was a larger fort than Pons Aelius, covering some 2ha (5 acres), with three of its four gates opening to the north to allow swift troop

deployment. It was first built by *legio II Augusta* and repaired c. 122–126 by *legio XX Valeria*, with a granary added at the same time by a detachment from the Roman British Fleet, *Classis Britannica*. In the 2nd century, it was garrisoned by a part-infantry part-cavalry *milliaria equitata* of 1,000 men, the *cohors I Vangiorum* (the Vangiones were from Upper Germania). The *Notitia Dignitatum* then lists the 500-man cavalry unit *ala I Asturum* (First Wing of Asturians from northern Hispania) as resident 207–367.

Unusually, altar stones and dedications furnish the only evidence for the worship of a god unknown anywhere else: Antenociticus. Although nothing of the fort remains, a small 4.5m by 6m (15ft by 20ft) apsidal temple dedicated to this god has been found 100m (330ft) outside the southeastern defences (just off Broomridge Avenue), where there are traces of an extensive *vicus*. Other altars found are dedicated to Jupiter, Mars, Minerva and Vheterus.

Another rare survival just to the south in Denhill Park is the fort's Vallum crossing – the only one to have been discovered along the entire length of the wall, although a similar head has been found in Binchester Roman fort. This causeway cuts across the Vallum directly in line with Condercum's

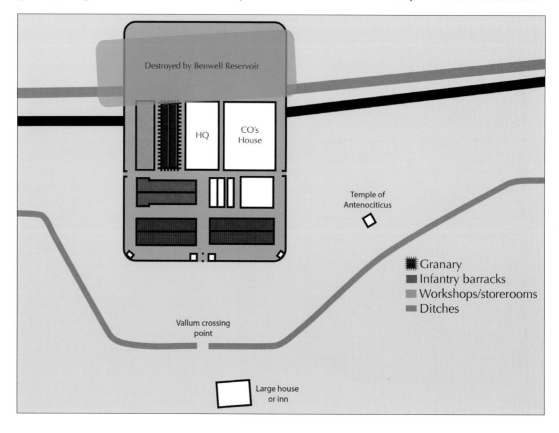

Destroyed by Benwell Reservoir

HQ

CO's House

Temple of Antenociticus

▨ Granary
▬ Infantry barracks
▬ Workshops/storerooms
▬ Ditches

Vallum crossing point

Large house or inn

◄ *Plan of Condercum and surrounding area, showing the position of the possible mansio (official visitors' accommodation), Temple of Antenociticus and Vallum crossing.*

southern gate, some 50m (165ft) away. Halfway across it there was a gate supported on massive uprights that controlled access from the south to the fort and military zone. The causeway's surface had been remetalled three times, with the top layer dating to the 270s.

DENTON TURRET

The first turret visible along the wall, Denton Turret has foundations up to six courses high in places, sitting with some 60m (200ft) of wall just beside the A69. Discovered in 1928 and built of unusually large masonry, the turret was recessed 1.5m (5ft) into the Broad Wall (which was over 2.7m/9ft thick)

▶ *Graham Sumner's reconstruction of a Vallum crossing point shows a border post like any passport control system in use today.* Graham Sumner

▼ *The causeway cuts across the Vallum directly in line with Condercum's southern gate, approximately 50m (160ft) away. Halfway across it there was a gate supported on massive uprights that controlled access from the south to the fort and military zone.*

▲ *An artist's impression based on known archaeology of how the Benwell Temple might have looked at its time of use.* Getty Images

and measured 4m by 4.25m (13ft by 14ft), with its entrance at the east end of its south wall and the remains of a stepped-stone platform that led to an upper level. Three periods of occupation have been identified and attributed to the 2nd, 3rd and 4th centuries.

FROM HEDDON TO VINDOBALA

▲ *An aerial view of the wall at Heddon-on-the-Wall. A small segment of fighting ditch, wall and Vallum are visible.*

VINDOBALA (RUDCHESTER)

After Denton Turret, apart from a few indentations and lumps, for some kilometres there is no sign of the wall other than periodic lengths of the frontal fighting ditch and the vallum. The milecastles are the vaguest suggestions, for the most part hidden under grass. At Heddon-on-the-Wall a small segment of fighting ditch, wall and Vallum are visible, but no trace of the milecastle that would have been just beyond it. This is where General Wade's 209km (130-mile) Northumbrian Military Road runs west to Greenhead. Built in 1746

▼ *Ground view of the wall at Heddon-on-the-Wall. This is a fine section of Broad Wall, roughly 10 Roman feet wide (3m/9ft 8.5in).*

during the suppression of the Jacobites, when Bonnie Prince Charlie evaded Wade's forces in Newcastle and instead attacked Carlisle, the road underlined the need for a modern east–west route, although it was not built until after the rebellion had ended. Wade's road now follows the line of the wall for some 48km (30 miles), literally obliterating the original Roman remains, since much of the stone used in constructing the road was robbed from the wall itself in what has since been called one of the most damaging single operation to Hadrian's Wall in recorded history.

The next fort – Vindobala, now Rudchester Roman Fort – was situated about 11km (6.8 miles) to the west of Condercum and 12km (7.5 miles) east of Onnum (Halton Chesters) and was built to guard the valley of March Burn. It apparently lasted until the 18th century, when it also was destroyed by Wade's road builders, although some stone had already been plundered to build Rudchester Manor and various surrounding farm buildings. Probably built by *legio VI Victrix*, the fort was laid out in the conventional Roman military fashion. It was designed to house a combined infantry and cavalry force (*cohors quingenaria equitata*) of 500 men. The wall enters and leaves the fort below the main gates: the two lesser gates would probably have been aligned with the military way.

The Vallum passed about 220m (656ft) south of the fort, and there was a *vicus* to the south and southwest. Excavations carried out in 1924 and 1972 have revealed that the fort took the brunt of the attack from the north and was destroyed by fire late in the 2nd century, then partially rebuilt c. 370. It was finally abandoned at the beginning of the 5th century, when the Roman troops left.

The names of the original and subsequent units stationed there are unknown. The only formation that is attested by the *Notitia Dignitatum* is the late 3rd/4th-century garrison, *cohors I Frisiavonum* (the First Cohort of Frisiaovones, originating from part of what is now the Netherlands). It is thought that this unit came over with the Governor Petilius Cerealis in AD71 and perhaps was stationed continuously at Vindobala.

In the 1760s a full-sized statue of Hercules was unearthed and in 1844 five altars were discovered. They came from a Mithraic temple that was situated 140m (450ft) to the west of the fort, with dedicatory inscriptions to Mithras and his Graeco-Roman counterparts, Apollo and Sol Invictus. Oriented east to west, the temple was first constructed in the late 2nd/early 3rd centuries, then later modified, losing its antechamber, before being decommissioned and deliberately destroyed by fire in the 4th century.

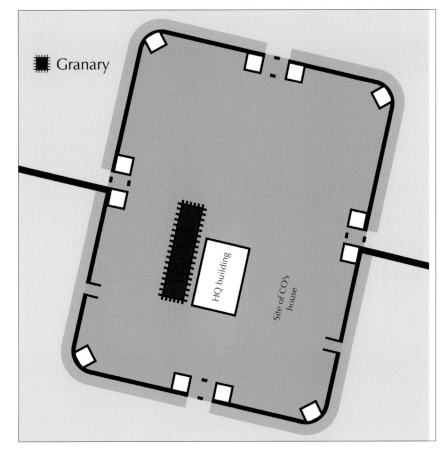

▶ *Ground-plan of Vindobala Fort. Archaeology exposed a* hypocaust *associated with the* praetorium *(commander's house).*

■ Granary

HQ building

Site of CO's house

Turret 13B (Rudchester West): No remains

Vindobala Fort
Location: Rudchester
Status: Remains covered over; Mithraeum to S
Fort: Fourth from E; 11.2km (7 miles) from Condercum
Built: 122, probably *legio VI Victrix*; burnt end 2nd century and rebuilt
Dimensions: 157m (515ft) long (N–S) by 117m (384ft) (E–W); covering around 1.8ha (4.5 acres)
Gates: N, E and W double-portal N of wall; S double-portal and two single-portal S of wall
Vallum: 220m (720ft) away
Vicus: to S and SW

Milecastle 14 (March Burn)
Status: No remains
Type: Short axis; unknown (possibly Type I) N gateway
Builder: Possibly *legio II Augusta*
Dimensions: 18.3m (60ft) across; walls broad

Turret 14A (Eppies Hill): No remains

Turret 14B: Nothing known

Milecastle 15 (Whitchester)
Status: Robbed walls, platform only; traces of ditch
Type: Long axis; unknown gateway
Builder: Probably *legio VI Victrix* or *XX Valeria Victrix*

Turret 15A: Remains covered over

Turret 15B: Possible remains covered over

Milecastle 16 (Harlow Hill)
Status: Slight earthworks
Type: Unknown
Builder: Unknown

Turret 16A: No remains

Turret 16B: No remains

FROM VINDOBALA TO ONNUM

▲▶ *A Roman auxiliary cavalryman re-enactor gives a good idea of what one of the soldiers living in Onnum would have looked like. Note the shield shape, as seen on Trajan's Column. However, it's worth pointing out that most auxiliary cavalry shields were hexagonal rather than curved and the one on Trajan's Column probably belonged to an infantryman.*

Ermine Street Guard; WikiCommons

ONNUM (HALTON CHESTERS)

Much of the importance of Onnum lies in the fact that it guarded the Portgate, where Dere Street crosses the wall. This hugely strategic road was built by governor Gnaeus Julius Agricola in around AD80 and used as an important highway to get soldiers up and down to Scotland quickly. It is one of only three Roman roads to cross the wall.

Due north of Coria (Corbridge), the fifth fort on the wall, Onnum, is now known as the Roman Fort at Halton Chesters, although, other than a few earthworks, nothing remains to be seen today, for it is buried beneath Halton Castle. It once guarded Dere Street 800m (half a mile) away in the valley below, as it passed through the wall northwards. Onnum was constructed c. 122–126, primarily by *legio VI Victrix* (although later modifications were also undertaken by *legio II Augusta* and *legio XX Valeria Victrix*) and followed the usual pattern for a fort, housing an auxiliary 500-man mixed infantry and cavalry *cohors quingenaria equitata*.

Straddling the wall, it was almost square and had only four gates, with three to the north outside it. Some time between 208 and 211, during the Severan campaigns, an extension, which unusually included a new bath house within the walls, was added to the southwest corner of the fort, giving it an L-shaped appearance. At the end of the 3rd century, along with other alterations, the baths were replaced with barracks and stables and relocated to the northwest corner of the fort, but they still remained within the camp itself – because of the fire hazard, this was not normal Roman practice. The fort had a *vicus* that extended from outside its southern gate past the Vallum for some 300–400m (320–440yd).

Three legible altar stones have been found dedicated to Fortuna, the Mother Goddess and the Living Spirits of the Emperors. The first *auxilia* occupants are unknown, but epigraphic evidence records the presence of the 500-man cavalry *ala I Pannoniorum Sabiniana* (First Sabinian Wing of Pannonians, coming from part of what is now modern Hungary) coincidental with the 3rd-century modifications to the fort. The *Notitia Dignitatum* recorded this unit as still present at Onnum in the 4th and early 5th centuries.

▼ *Two ground plans showing the development of the fort at Onnum (Halton Chesters) over a period of almost 200 years.*

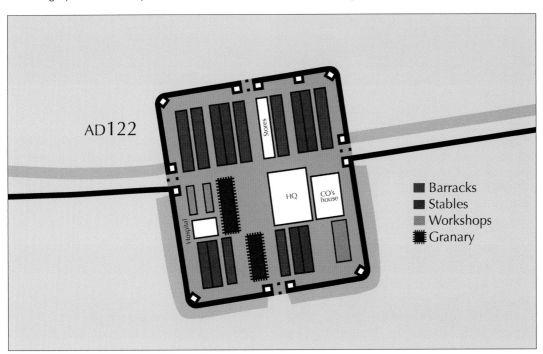

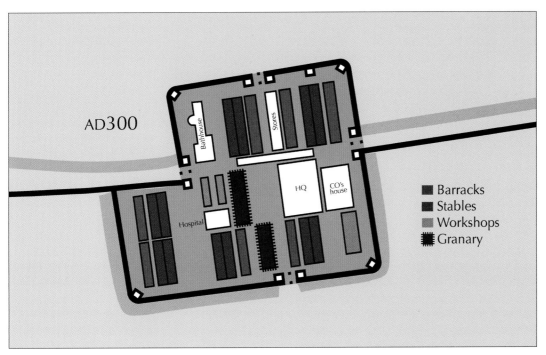

Milecastle 17 (Welton/Whittledean)
Status: Slight earthworks
Type: Short axis; Type I gateway
Builder: *Legio II Augusta*
Dimensions: Platform is 16m (53ft) (E–W) by 15m (49ft) (N–S)

Turret 17A (Welton East): Remains covered over

Turret 17B (Horsley): Remains covered over

Milecastle 18 (East Wallhouses)
Status: Remains covered over
Type: Short axis; Type I gateway
Builder: Mixed – gateway associated with *legio II Augusta*; layout *legio VI Victrix* or *XX Valeria Victrix*. Perhaps started by one and finished by another?
Dimensions: 16.36m (53ft 8in) (E–W) by 18.14m (59ft 6in) (N–S); walls 2.36m (7ft 9in) thick

Turret 18A (Wallhouses East): Remains covered over

Turret 18B (Wallhouses West): Remains covered over

Milecastle 19 (Matfen Piers)
Status: Remains covered over.
Type: Long axis; Type III gateway
Builder: *Legio VI Victrix*
Dimensions: 16.25m (53ft 4in) (E–W) by 17.2m (56ft 5in) (N–S)

Important altar discovered, dedicated to a mother goddess by men from the *cohors I Varduli*.

Inscribed

'MATRIB TEMPL CVM ARA VEX COH I VARD INSTANTE P D V VSLM'

('To the Mother Goddesses the detachment of the *cohors I Varduli* erected the temple with this altar, and willingly and deservedly fulfilled its vow, under the direction of Publius D[omitius?] V[?]')

Causeway used to be visible across the vallum to the south

FROM ONNUM TO CILURNUM

▶ *The wall remains at Planetrees on a bright frosty morning. This is where the wall changed from broad to a narrower gauge.*

DERE STREET

The main Roman road heading north into Scotland, Dere Street started from the legionary fortress base of Eboracum (York) and is the first route listed in the Britannic section of the Antonine Itinerary – a list of the empire's roads dating from the time of the Emperor Antoninus (138–161).

Just 800m (half a mile) from Onnum, Dere Street met the wall at the Portgate, a purpose-built fortified gateway – one of only three such gateways that were not inside forts or milecastles but pierced the curtain wall as discrete entities in themselves. The other two were Lugavalium (Carlisle) in the east and at Knag Burn near Vercovicium (Housesteads) – the latter is of a much later date and must have served a more local purpose.

Dere Street (its original Latin name is unknown) was built by Agricola as he campaigned northwards in AD70s–80s. Its northernmost point is at Veluniate (Carriden), the eastern end of the Antonine Wall – a distance of almost 364km (230 miles). Initially it went as far as Camelon near Falkirk. Approximately 7.7m (25ft) wide and metalled to a depth of 30cm (12in), it crossed the River Ure at Isurium Brigantum (Aldoborough), the Swale at Caractonium (Catterick), the Tees at Morbium (Piercebridge) and the Wear at Vinovium (Bishop Auckland). All were equipped with their own guard forts, with the addition of two more at Longovicium (Lanchester) and Vindomora (Ebbchester), before it crossed the Stanegate line near Coria, which was built around the same time.

Some 50 years later, with the construction of Hadrian's Wall, it was given its own gateway (the Portgate), close by Onnum. The next fort after the wall – Habitancum (Risingham) – guarded the

crossing at the River Rede. Between Bremenium (High Rochester) and Trimontium (Melrose) there is evidence only of marching-camp remains and the exact route is unknown, although traces exist beyond the Tweed through Lammermuirs over Soutra Hill and on to Edinburgh. The northern campaigns of Agricola, Antoninus and Severus were all brief and no land beyond Hadrian's Wall was held by the Romans for long (although there were some periods when a Roman would have felt more comfortable there than others).

The Portgate was located in 1966 when the gateway's huge masonry foundations were exposed, projecting 3.6m (12ft) forward of the wall, indicating its substantial and impressive size. Nothing remains to be seen now and no details of its architecture and construction have emerged, having been obliterated by the building of modern roads and a roundabout.

BRUNTON TURRET

A little farther on from the Portgate is one of the best-preserved turrets of the wall, along with some 64m (210ft) of wall itself. Built by *legio XX Valeria Victrix*, it is recessed 1.2m (4ft) into the wall, with a nearly 1.2m (4ft)-wide doorway and side walls 0.85m (2ft 10in) thick. Each turret was built with short wings on either side to be joined to, yet on the Brunton Turret's eastern side there is a small bit of additional wall linking to what had become the Narrow Wall in order to match up the angles of both. This proves that the turret was built first with the wall then being built up to it from either direction. Deep grooves in the door jambs and floor show where the hinged doorway worked and within the turret there is a free-standing altar.

▶ An artist's impression of what Brunton Turret might have looked like when it and the Wall were operational. The height, wooden superstructure and roof are all conjectural. English Heritage/Heritage Images/Getty Images

▼ Brunton Turret is well preserved and is recessed 1.2m (4ft) into the stonework.

Turret 19A (East Clarewood): Remains covered over

Turret 19B (West Clarewood): Remains covered over

Milecastle 20 (Halton Shields)
Status: No visible trace
Type: Long axis; Type III gateway
Builder: *Legio VI Victrix*
Dimensions: 17.7m (58ft) by 16.3m (53ft 5in)

Turret 20A (Carr Hill): Remains covered over

Turret 20B (Downhill East): Remains covered over

Temporary camps: Two possible, approximatedly 350m (380yd) S of Milecastle 20

Milecastle 21 (Down Hill)
Status: No visible trace, but fine views of vallum from this area
Type: Unknown
Builder: Unknown

Turret 21A (Red House): No visible trace

Onnum/Hunnum Fort
Location: Halton, 4km (2.5 miles) N of Coria (Corbridge); guards Dere Street crossing wall
Status: Some slight earthworks; bath house not visible
Fort: Fifth from E; 11km (7 miles) from Vindobala
Built: 122, by *legio VI Victrix*; enlarged after 208
Dimensions: 140m (460ft) long (N–S) by 120m (410ft) (E–W); later S wall extended to 170m (570ft) long and making L-shaped appearance. Area covered: N – 1.7ha (4.3 acres); S – 1.9ha (4.8 acres)
Gates: N, W and E double-portals north of wall; S double-portal
Vicus: S of vallum

CORIA

Pre-dating the wall by almost 40 years, Coria was a town that grew up on Dere Street where it crossed the lowest fordable point of the River Tyne. It was also the easternmost fort on the east–west line, now called the Stanegate, that ran from Coria to Lugavalum. Over the course of its life, this intersection – combined with its river crossing – underwent a sustained and complicated development from an early turf-and-wood fort to a bustling legionary supply base and then a mixed civilian and Roman Army garrison town. Today, the site includes a museum containing many recovered altar stones and epigraphic dedications, as well as items from the Corbridge Hoard and the extensive visible remains of the fort and its *vicus*.

Originally Agricola had built a supply fort, Red House Farm, for his northward advance. But c. AD86 it was moved around 400m (0.25 miles) to its current location. It is thought the name 'Coria' traces its origin to an original local settlement by a tribe of the Brigantes that was eventually

appropriated to build a turf-and-wood ramparted fort following Agricola's campaign. It was garrisoned by a 500-man cavalry unit – perhaps the *ala Petriana*. This first fort was levelled by fire c. 105 and another was built on a different plan in stone. It was modified around the same time as Hadrian's Wall was built – c. 120–126 – and was again beefed up c. 139–140 during the governorship of Quintus Lollius Urbicus, as the main supply base for the army of Antoninus Pius as it advanced into Scotland.

With the next Stanegate fort, Vindolanda, 25km (16 miles) east and the wall 4km (2.5 miles) away, Coria's importance only further inreased as a supply base for all units in the northeast. By 163 it was a thriving military and colonial settlement housing detachments of *legio XX Valeria Victrix* and *legio VI Victrix*. It had a stone bridge and a series of civic buildings, seven temples, precincts and houses were erected, along with still more granaries for the military depot in the centre of the

▼ *An aerial view of Coria (Corbridge) on the Stanegate, an important supply depot for the troops on the wall that grew to become a civilian town that sprawled over its defensive boundaries.*

town, with the defensive walls being built over.

Burnt remains indicate trouble from across the frontier c. 185 and the early 3rd century saw another round of military construction to support the Severan campaign of 222–224. The supply depot, supporting *legio II Augusta* and *legio VI Victrix*, was further enlarged and more elaborate civic and civilian building then followed. There is also evidence for the growth of metal and mineral industries: lead, iron, coal and clay besides the market agriculture, making Coria sprawl over its defensive boundaries.

Cohorts or vexillations from all three British legions – II, VI and XX – were stationed at Coria at different times; the last one (VI) dated to the end of the 3rd century. The 1,000-man mixed infantry and cavalry unit (*milliaria equitata*) *cohors I Vardullorum* – the First Cohort of the Vardulli from Guispuscoa northern Hispania – was stationed there 216–241. Auxiliary units included the *ala Petriana*, which was later transferred to the major command fort on the wall: Uxelodunum (Stanwix), which became known as Petrianum after the unit stationed there.

More than 20 altar stones have been discovered at Coria: four dedicated to the Romano-British composite god Apollo-Maponus, three to the Germanic Veterus, and two each to Jupiter and Discipline (a military deity). Others from the Graeco-Roman pantheon include Astarte, Concordia, Diana, Hercules, Mercury, Minerva, Panthea, Silvanus, Sol Invictus and Victory. Details of the the town after the Roman Army left are sparse. Almost certainly it was still partly inhabited and the vital bridge, presumably, still standing when the Anglo-Saxons, unable to maintain the crumbling infrastructure, began building their Corbridge a little farther downstream, using stone from Coria in the process, for it is the only Roman town on the Stanegate to yield Anglo-Saxon artefacts. Its strategic location thus ensured its survival, regardless of who was in overall control of the area.

▼ *Map of the Coria area showing the fort as a key crossroads between the W–E Stanegate and N–S Dere Street. The fort was redeveloped a number of times until it was absorbed into a bustling town.*

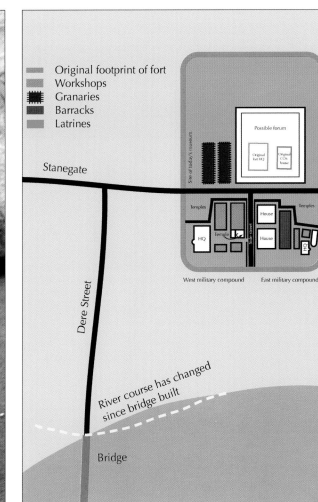

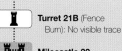

Turret 21B (Fence Burn): No visible trace

Milecastle 22 (Portgate)
Status: Some slight earthworks: good views of vallum
Type: Probably long axis; Type III gateway; north gate apparently blocked in Severan reconstruction
Builder: *Legio VI Victrix*
Dimensions: 16.76m (55ft) between walls; walls 2.45m (8ft) thick

Port Gateway: Remains covered over. Dere Street crosses vallum. Square gateway (compare Arbeia reconstruction) projecting 3.6m (12ft) N and similar distance S of wall.

Turret 22A (Portgate): Remains covered over

Turret 22B (Stanley): Remains covered over

Milecastle 23 (Stanley)
Status: Some slight earthworks
Type: Probably long axis; unknown gateway
Builder: *Legio VI Victrix*
Dimensions: 15.24m (50ft) across

Turret 23A (Stanley Plantation): Remains covered over

Turret 23B (Wall Fell): No visible trace

Milecastle 24 (Wall Fell)
Status: Slight earthworks showing ditch, robber trenches
Type: Probably long axis; unknown gateway
Builder: Probably *legio VI Victrix*
Dimensions: 15.24m (50ft) across

Turret 24A (Green Field): Remains covered over

Turret 24B (Tithe Barn): Remains covered over

CILURNUM

The next fort running westwards is Cilurnum, now known as Chesters Roman Fort, guarding the strategically important crossing-point bridge over the North Tyne. Cilurnum is perhaps the best-preserved cavalry fort of them all, almost certainly built by *legio VI Victrix* c. 123.

Built in the usual playing-card shape, Cilurnam straddles the wall with three gates to the north. Very little excavation has been carried out since the 19th-century owner's time. Newcastle town clerk and antiquarian John Clayton (1792–1890), who became known as the 'Father of the Wall', inherited the family home of Chesters, in whose grounds Cilurnum is now situated. He ensured its survival (his father previously buried it in landscaping).

It was John Clayton who began to buy and conserve the wall for prosterity, as well as conducting his own careful archeological examinations of this fort and others on the wall from 1843 until his death in 1890. Most of Cilurnum and its *vicus* have since remained unexcavated, but aerial photography and geophysical scans continue to reveal more about this relatively unspoilt structure.

The originally Hadrianic *principia* had five entrances, a colonnaded forecourt and hall as well as five back administrative rooms. The central one for the standards had stairs leading down to a well-preserved vaulted strong-room/treasury beneath. Although there was a small internal bath house at one stage, the main well-preserved bath house was built close to the river and the bridge, whose massive stone abutments, dating from the Severan period, can be seen on the eastern side. Within them are smaller Hadrianic abutments indicating the slighter wooden-piered original. The later bridge was built to take the Roman military way across the

▼ *An aerial view of Cilurnum (Chesters) Fort and the family home of 19th-century antiquarian John Clayton in whose grounds Cilurnum is now situated. 1 The Roman bath house was built outside the fort close by the river. 2 Remains of the stonework abutments of the bridge that was built to take the Roman Military Way across the North Tyne, using three large masonry piers built on the river bed for support.*

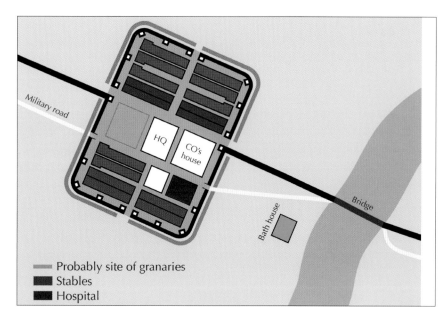

▶ *Map of Cilurnum, which housed a cavalry regiment that guarded the strategically important crossing-point bridge over the North Tyne. The abutments of the bridge are still in place. The fort was built over the Broad Wall foundations, which run under the* via principalis.

Military road

HQ

CO's house

Bridge

Bath house

■ Probably site of granaries
■ Stables
■ Hospital

North Tyne, using three large masonry piers with upstream cutwaters built on the river bed to support the large timbers, and great stone abutments supporting the bridge ends on either bank.

There was an extensive *vicus*, with side streets on this southern side linking the camp, the bridge and the river, while the road from the southern gateway also linked the fort with the old Agricolan Stanegate. We know the fort was inserted into the wall after it was realised that those on the Stanegate were too far away to respond quickly enough, as some of the original Broad Wall foundations and the forward fighting ditch were found beneath its principal east–west street. The Sixth, although never stationed here other than when first building it, returned periodically to carry out attested alterations and renovations.

Probably the first unit to garrison Cilurnum was the 1,000-man mixed infantry and cavalry *cohors I Vangionum* (First Cohort of the Vangiones, from the Upper Rhine area of Germania) in 122–138, although the men might well have been split between Cilurnum and Condercum, where there is also epigraphic evidence for them. The first recorded cavalry wing at Cilurnum (c. 130s) was the mysteriously unnumbered *ala Augusta*, who, apart from another 2nd-century inscription found in Lugavalium, are not known. Next, between the 130s and 223, came the *cohors I Delmatarum*, who guarded the still-important bridge during the time of the Antonine Wall, when the border had been pushed 160km (100 miles) farther north, with the consequent decline in importance of various Stanegate and Hadrian's Wall installations. From the late 2nd century *ala II Asturum* – the Second Wing of Asturians (from northern Hispania) – took over the fort and remained there according to the

Notitia Dignitatum. Twelve altars, votive stones and building inscriptions ranging from AD122 to 223 have been unearthed, dedicated to emperors (Hadrian, Caracalla and Antoninus) and gods – four to the Germanic war-god Veterus, three to Jupiter Best and Greatest, and single ones to Bona Dea, Fortuna, Disciplina and the Mother Goddess.

BRIDGING THE TYNE

There have been at least two Roman bridges at Cilurnum. The first was probably built at the same time as the wall and spanned the river with at least eight hexagonal stone piers about 4m (13ft) apart for a length of about 60m (200ft). It is thought that it supported the wall itself, as its width was 3m (10ft) – the width of the Broad Wall. One hexagonal pier survives and shows traces of dovetailed iron cramps set in lead to hold the stones tightly together.

The second Roman bridge dates from the early 3rd century and was built of stone with possibly a timber superstructure. It was even larger and more imposing, but a little shorter, at 57m (189ft) long. It boasted massive rectangular stones held together with long iron ties channelled into the masonry on the front face. It had four arches supported on three substantial piers 10m (34ft) apart and probably supported the Military Way across the Tyne and over the wall, where it was defended by a cavalry fort. A male fertility symbol was carved into the north face of the eastern abutment. This second bridge was discovered in 1860 and held some of the most massive masonry structures on the wall. Only the eastern abutment remains, as the western side disappeared when the Tyne shifted course. The earliest-known garrison here was the *ala Augusta ob virtutem appellata*.

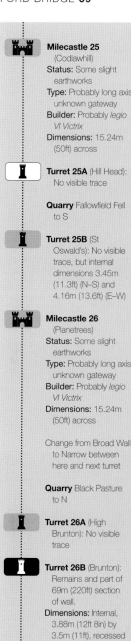

Milecastle 25
(Codlawhill)
Status: Some slight earthworks
Type: Probably long axis; unknown gateway
Builder: Probably *legio VI Victrix*
Dimensions: 15.24m (50ft) across

Turret 25A (Hill Head): No visible trace

Quarry Fallowfield Fell to S

Turret 25B (St Oswald's): No visible trace, but internal dimensions 3.45m (11.3ft) (N–S) and 4.16m (13.6ft) (E–W)

Milecastle 26
(Planetrees)
Status: Some slight earthworks
Type: Probably long axis; unknown gateway
Builder: Probably *legio VI Victrix*
Dimensions: 15.24m (50ft) across

Change from Broad Wall to Narrow between here and next turret

Quarry Black Pasture to N

Turret 26A (High Brunton): No visible trace

Turret 26B (Brunton): Remains and part of 69m (220ft) section of wall.
Dimensions: Internal, 3.88m (12ft 8in) by 3.5m (11ft), recessed 1.22m (4ft) into the wall; doorway is 1.22m (4ft) wide. The eastern wall is narrow (8 Roman feet wide = 2.37m/7ft 9in), the western broad (10 Roman feet = 3m/9ft 8.5in); within the turret is a free-standing altar

Milecastle 27 (Low Brunton)
Status: Some slight remains
Type: Probably long axis; unknown gateway
Builder: Probably *legio XX Valeria Victrix*
Dimensions: 18m (60ft) (N–S) and 15m (50ft) (E–W)

FROM CILURNUM TO BROCOLITIA

▼ *An aerial view of the wall, its front fighting ditch and Vallum in the area of Black Carts Turret, which is visible at right.*

INSET 1 – A detail of Black Carts Turret. During periodic archaeological investigations in the 19th and 20th centuries coins from Vespasian, Trajan, Hadrian and Constantine were found, indicating a considerable timescale of occupation.

INSET 2 – Although severely robbed out on its southern side, some of the masonry from Black Carts Turret stands up to 11 courses high in the recess. Its broad-gauge wing walls prove that the turret must have been constructed before the wall itself.

LIMESTONE CORNER

The inappropriately named Limestone Corner (its geology consists not of limestone but Whinstone Dolerite) has the distinction of being the most northerly point of Hadrian's Wall. It also marks the spot where the wall kinks to retain the defensive high ground of Tepplemoor Hill. Another unusual feature is the failure to complete the excavation of the forward fighting ditch, which is cluttered with some massive dolerite blocks, one bearing chisel marks. Iron wedges were discovered within

the wall core of the nearby milecastle – aptly illustrating the process used for their removal. This unfinished section does prove that this part of the ditch was completed from west to east: other sections were cut in the reverse. The remains of a construction camp are to be found on the hilltop, with the foundations of several buildings indicating its occupation over more than a single season. Pottery has been excavated dating from the 2nd to the early 4th centuries.

BLACK CARTS TURRET

With its 457m (1,500ft)-long stretch of narrow-gauge curtain wall Black Carts Turret is an impressive sight. It's another consolidated survival and although severely robbed out on its southern side, some masonry stands up to 11 courses high in the recess. Once again, broad-gauge wing walls prove that the turret must have been constructed prior to the wall itself. With a 1m (3ft)-wide entrance located in its southern wall, it is of a type thought to have been built by the *legio XX Valeria Victrix*, for each legion built with slight variation. During periodic archaeological investigations from 1873 to 1971, coins from Vespasian, Trajan, Hadrian and Constantine were found, indicating a considerable timescale of usage.

▲ *Another view of the consolidated stretch of narrow-gauge curtain wall of the Black Carts section.* Shutterstock

▼ *Limestone Corner has the distinction of being the most northerly point of Hadrian's Wall and marks the spot where the wall kinks to retain the defensive high ground of Tepplemoor Hill. It is unusual in that it is not made of limestone. Another unusual feature is the failure to complete the excavation of the forward fighting ditch, which is cluttered with massive dolerite blocks, one of which bears chisel marks that illustrate the process used for their removal.*

Coria Town
Location: Corbridge; 4km (2.5 miles) S of Onnum on Stanegate
Status: Many visible remains
Fort: First, 12km (7.5 miles) to Newbrough
Built: By AD80 at Red House Farm; Corbridge site around AD86; rebuilt after fire in 105
Dimensions: Huge site
Gates: N, W and E double-portals north of wall; S double-portal
Vicus: Major Roman town surrounds fort

Bridge Built in the Hadrianic period over River North Tyne, rebuilt in the Severan period; 60m (190ft) long

Turret 27A (Unnamed): Demolished after construction; remains under the fort

Cilurnum Fort
Location: Chollerford, guards river crossing
Status: Extensive remains, including bath house and museum
Fort: Sixth from E; 10km (6 miles) from Onnum
Built: 122, by *legio VI Victrix*; enlarged after 208
Dimensions: 140m (582ft) long (N–S) by 120m (434ft) (E–W); area covered: 2.3ha (5.75 acres)
Gates: N, W and E double-portals north of wall; S double-portal and two single-portal gateways
Vicus: S of fort along road to Stanegate

Turret 27B (Unnamed): No visible trace

Milecastle 28 (Walwick)
Status: Unknown
Type: Unknown

Turret 28A (Unnamed): No visible trace

Turret 28B (Unnamed): Some stonework

FROM BROCOLITIA TO VERCOVICIUM

▼ *Today, there's little to see of Brocolitia except for the outlines of the fort. Clayton's excavations found a bath house outside the west gate and a shrine known as Coventina's Well. INSET – In 1949 a temple to Mithras was discovered. It had been destroyed during the Carausius rebellion (286–296).*

BROCOLITIA (CARRAWBURGH)

Nothing remains of Brocolitia except the ditch earthworks measuring out a site of 1.4ha (3.5 acres), postdating the wall and the vallum, both of which it was built over by the redoubtable *legio VI Victrix*. The wall here was narrow gauge, built on a Broad Wall foundation. The fort stood in open moorland 1.6km (1 mile) west of milecastle 30 and the wall's most northern point.

Almost 50 inscriptions have been unearthed at the site, which provide a good record of the auxiliary units that served there and the gods they called upon. Excavations by John Clayton in 1873–1876 revealed a bath house outside the western gate, the gateway itself and the southwestern corner tower foundations. He also discovered a shrine and centre of worship to the Romano-British water goddess Coventina at the source of Meggie's Dene Burn, which still runs close by the remains of the fort. A substantial 12.2m by 12.2m (40ft by 40ft) temple housed the source itself and 10 altar stones to the

goddess were found dedicated by various serving auxiliary units. Between the stream and the fort was a small *vicus*, and it was here that two other sanctuaries were also discovered and excavated later in the 1950–1960s – a Mithraeum and another open-air water-based shrine to the Nymphs and Genius Loci – the local spirit of the place.

The Mithraeum was found well preserved with its three later altars intact – each one dedicated by the same 3rd-century Batavian Cohort commander. It showed three clear phases of use, the first building measuring 5.5m by 7.9m (18ft by 26ft) with an anteroom and a nave with raised side seating. The second building lasted almost the whole of the 3rd century and had an expanded nave of 11m (36ft) and was much more elaborately furnished. Sometime around 296–297 it was looted and burnt, but the stone structure and monuments survived and the temple was rebuilt shortly afterwards, and would enjoy a renaissance, especially with the dedication of

▶ *This plan shows the line of the north edge of the wall which is now under the B6318. The fort was built later than most of the wall's structures, running over the Vallum.*

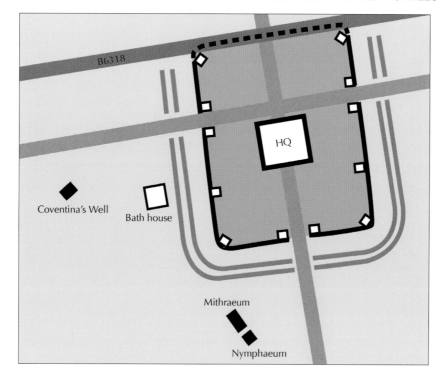

cohors I Batavorum. Coins found were dated up to 308 but not thereafter, suggesting a decline and demise – certainly of the temple, if not the cult – and the final version was at some point deliberately decommissioned and shut down.

The shrine to the Nymphs and Genius Loci was built c. 213 in a period when the Mithraeum was not being used, for parts of it were then used in

the Mithraeum's second version and both share the destruction layer of 296–297. Other deities receiving dedications at Brocolitia include Fortuna, Minerva, Veterus, Mercury and Belatucader.

Auxiliary units at Brocolitia: *cohors I Tungrorum, cohors I Aquitanorum, cohors I Cugernorum, cohors I Frisiavonum, cohors II Nerviorum, cohors V Raetorum* and *cohors I Batavorum*.

▼ *Turret 33B was consolidated to a height of 1.1m (3ft 6in), its walls are 90cm (3ft) thick. It has an entrance at the east end of the south wall, with a platform in the southwest corner, and a hearth in the centre. It was built with broad wing walls prior to the narrow-gauge wall.* Richard Wood

▼ *An aerial view of Turret 34A at Grindon West, just to the east of Sewingshields farm. Its walls are 90cm (3ft) thick, with a mortar core and it has unusually short wing walls, suggesting a late construction. The door is on the eastern side of the south wall with its pivot hole still visible.*

▲ *A view looking towards the beginning of Sewingshields Crags in the distance, with the fighting ditch to the right and the Vallum clearly visible ahead of the road. Milecastle 34 is contained within the tree enclosure on the right.*

▼ *When Milecastle 35 was excavated, at least four separate phases of internal buildings were detected. The site was reoccupied in the late-medieval period, when two longhouses were built.*

THE GREAT WHIN SILL

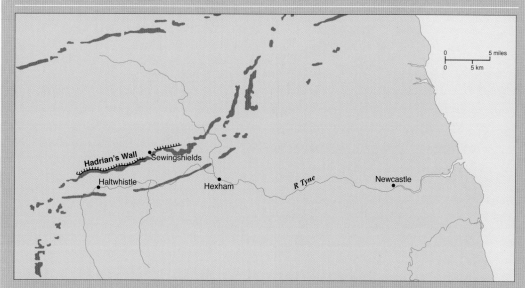

This is a natural outcrop of tabular igneous dolerite rock – hard, dark, crystalline stone – that appears almost midway along Hadrian's Wall in the North Pennines.

The sill itself formed 295 million years ago, when magma rose from deep beneath the Earth's crust and forced its way up between the layers of shale, sandstone and limestone but didn't break the surface. It ended up hidden underground as a vast sheet almost 800m (half a mile) thick lying under much of northeast England. As it cooled over a period of 50 years it contracted and produced long vertical cracks that broke into rough columns: these form the dramatic cliff face in many places along its length. Through the action of weather and erosion, many millions of years later the

▲ *Map showing the Sewingshields Crags of the Whin Sill with dolerite in green. The Romans appreciated and exploited its geology, taking advantage of the natural defences of the dolerite crags between Walltown and Sewingshields.*

formation became partially exposed in long lines of impressive crags roughly 70m (230ft) thick, that runs generally east–west, with a steep northern cliff face and a gentle fall away on the southern side.

With typical ingenuity, Roman surveyors took advantage of the impenetrable structure of Whin Sill and incorporated the imposing features as part of the wall's defences. But they did not use the stone to build the wall, as it is far too hard and difficult to work.

Limestone

Sandstone

Shale

Whin Sill

Molten rock

▶ *The creation of the Whin Sill: the intrusion of igneous rock between layers of limestone. Erosion left the dolerite on top.*

Brocolitia Fort
Location: Carrawburgh
Status: Earthwork remains; Mithraeum to SW outside fort
Fort: Seventh from E; 5.6km (3.5 miles) from Cilurnum; first infantry fort
Built: After 130, by *legio VI Victrix*; Mithraeum built in three stages from 1st to 3rd centuries; Nymphaeum in front of Mithraeum built during the 3rd century; Coventina well
Dimensions: Area covered: 1.5ha (3.5 acres)
Gates: W (blocked soon after construction), E and S double-portals S of wall; N unknown (demolished for Wade's road) but almost certainly N of wall
Vicus: W of fort

Turret 31A (The Strands): Remains covered over

Turret 31B (Carraw East): Slight earthworks

Milecastle 32 (Carraw)
Status: Slight earthworks showing robber trenches
Type: Long axis; unknown gateway
Builder: Probably *legio VI Victrix* or *XX Valeria Victrix*
Dimensions: Roughly 20m (65ft 6in) (N–S) and 16.5m (54ft) (E–W)

Temporary camp: Brown Moor to S

Turret 32A (Carraw West): Remains covered over

Temporary camp: Brown Dikes to S

Turret 32B (Brown Moor): Nothing known

Milecastle 33 (Shield on the Wall)
Status: Some remaining stones
Type: Long axis; Type II gateways
Builder: *Legio XX Valeria Victrix*
Dimensions: External 24m (78ft) (N–S) and 21m (68ft) (E–W)

Turret 33A (unnamed): No remains

FROM VERCOVICIUM TO CASTLE NICK

▲ *The remains of the Knag Burn Gateway – a very rare occurrence since it was not part of a milecastle or fort. It seems that it was a later addition from some time in the 4th century and was probably just for local traffic.*

▼ *An aerial view of Vercovicium Fort. With all the foundations of its curtain walls and its double gateways intact, as well as most of its interior core of original Hadrianic buildings, it is the best-preserved fort on Hadrian's Wall. It lies on the eastern end of a mile-long stretch of undulating steep crags on the Whin Sill, stretching between the Knag Burn (1) in the east and the Bradley Burn to the west.*

VERCOVICIUM (HOUSESTEADS)

For 150 years, this stone fort has been revealing the secrets of its past as archaeologists dig farther into its foundations. Set in a bleak landscape, it lies near the halfway section of the wall and only a short march from Vindolanda. Originally built around 122, it supported a substantial *vicus* and was rebuilt at least twice in Roman times. To the north lies the formidable Whin Sill dolerite ridge that also accounts for the fort's unusual structure lying alongside the wall. Vercovicium is exceptionally well preserved and includes all the features of a long-standing Roman frontier fort, including curtain wall and four gates, ancient latrines, granaries, barrack blocks, cisterns and water channels. Further excavations have unearthed an extensive collection of inscribed stones that reveal detailed insights into the military and religious life of the garrison.

Vercovicium, now called the Housesteads Roman Fort, lies on the eastern end of a mile-long stretch of undulating steep crags on the Whin Sill, stretching between the Knag Burn in the east and the Bradley Burn to the west. The site was one of the five wall farms that John Clayton bought up and is now owned by the National Trust and run by English Heritage, with a small museum on the footprint of a house that was in the *vicus*. Being so remote, the fort is one of the best preserved on the wall, with all the foundations of its curtain walls and its double

▶ *An artist's impression of the Knag Burn Gateway in operation, with a group of native Celts and their packhorses being checked by auxiliary troops.*
Historic England/ Bridgeman Images

gateways intact, as well as most of its interior core of original Hadrianic buildings – and it boasts the best-preserved Roman latrines in Britain.

Given its location on steep ground, it runs parallel with the wall rather than straddling it and has only

▼ *A view of Vercovicium Fort from the south, showing its position descending the hill. Given its location on steep ground, it runs parallel with the wall rather than straddling it and has only one gate opening north.*

one gate opening north. Its northern wall was built over the original wall foundation and incorporated a turret, with the wall itself joining up to the fort on either side. In fact, the north wall and gateway proved something of a problem and suffered from subsidence, having to be rebuilt a number of times.

Built c. 120–125 Vercovicium takes up 2ha (4.25 acres), with walls 6m (20ft) thick revetted in 1.5m (5ft) of stone, with a 4.5m (15ft) clay bank at the back. It had four arched double gateways with built-in guardrooms. The interior was divided

 Turret 33B (Coesike): Visible stone remains; walls 0.9m (2ft 11in) thick; turret was abandoned and reoccupied following withdrawal from the Antonine Wall

 Milecastle 34 (Grindon)
Status: No remains
Type: Long axis; Type II gateways
Builder: *Legio XX Valeria Victrix*

 Turret 34A (Grindon West): Visible stone remains; internal dimensions, 3.9m (13 ft) (E–W) by 2.3m (7ft 7in) (N–S)

Temporary camp: Coesike East to S

Temporary camps: West Coesike 1 and 2 to S

Temporary camp: Grindon School to S

 Turret 34B (Unnamed): Remains covered over by farmhouse built of Roman stone

 Milecastle 35 (Sewingshields)
Status: Complete foundations
Type: Long axis; Type IV S gateway (no N)
Builder: Probably *legio XX Valeria Victrix*
Dimensions: Internal, 18.3m (60ft) (N–S) and 15.2m (50ft) (E–W); walls 3.2m

 Turret 35A (Sewingshields Crag): Complete foundations; internal dimensions 3.7m (12ft 1in) by 2.4m (7ft 11in)

 Turret 35B (Busy Gap): Earthworks; internal dimensions 3.8m (12ft 6in) by 5.5m (18ft)

 Milecastle 36 (King's Hill)
Status: No remains, robbed
Type: Long axis; unknown gateway

 Turret 36A (Kennel Crags): Some earthworks

▼ *An artist's impression of Vercovicium Fort and its* vicus *during its heyday. A view looking towards the beginning of Sewingshields crags in the distance, with the fighting ditch to the right and the Vallum clearly visible ahead of the road. Milecastle 34 is contained within the tree enclosure on the right.* English Heritage/Heritage Images/Getty Images

▲ *The main southern gateway of Vercovicium Fort with houses from the* vicus *nestling almost up against its walls. By the end of the 3rd century the* vicus *had been abandoned for the security of the fort.*

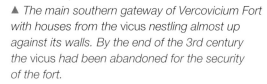

▼ *An artist's impression of the latrines at Vercovicium (Housesteads) – which has the honour of possessing the best-preserved Roman Army toilets in Britain.* English Heritage/Heritage Images/Getty Images

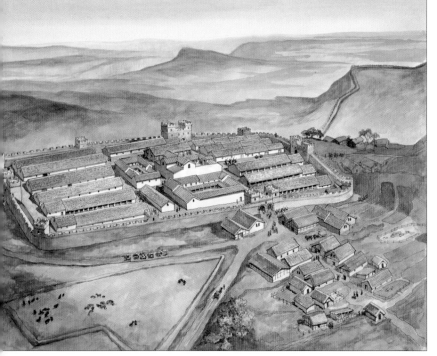

VERCOVICIUM FORT

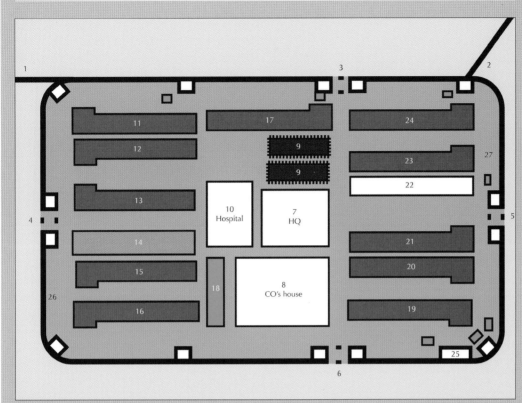

Blue = water cisterns. Vercovicium did not have the benefit of a well.

1 Continuation of Hadrian's Wall towards Magnis.

2 Continuation of the wall towards Chesters.

3 North Gate. Blocked in the later Roman era, it is likely the eastern gate at Knag Burn was used instead. The wall of the fort to the east of the gate was liable to subsidence and had to be rebuilt numerous times.

4 West Gate. Also blocked in the later period.

5 East Gate. Main entrance to the fort.

6 South Gate. The vicus lies just outside, spreading around both east and west sides. Just to the left at the entrance are the remains of a fortifed 'bastle' house, which was home to the notorious Armstrongs, a family of Border reivers – horse thieves and cattle rustlers. The road went to nearby Vindolanda.

7 The principia (headquarters building) has a later corn drier built into it.

8 The praetorium (commanding officer's house). This magnificent building shows the important status of the family who lived here.

9 The horrea (granaries) are placed at the highest point of the fort, taking full advantage of the flat ground.

10 This large courtyard building was probably a valetudinarium (hospital). A farmhouse was built over the area in the 18th century, using robbed stone.

11–13, 15–16, 19–21, 23–24 10 barrack blocks.

14 Probably a workshop.

17 Probable barracks, built over the remains of Turret 36B, which was destroyed when the fort was built.

18 Possibly a bath house for the commander.

22 Building 15, close to the east gate, was extensively rebuilt in the late 3rd century as a massive storehouse. Later, a small bath house was inserted into its east end, most likely replacing a bath house outside the fort in the valley to the east.

25 Southwest corner contained the communal latrines.

27–28 Bakeries.

Knag Burn Gate: Some earthworks and foundations built possibly in 4th century.
Dimensions: Gateway – 3.7m (12ft) wide; guard chambers (?) – 4.65m (15ft 4in) by 3.25m (10ft 8in), with entrances 0.95m (3ft 1in) wide

Turret 36B (Housesteads): Some earthworks; demolished when fort built

Vercovicium Fort
Location: Housesteads
Status: Extensive remains, including hospital and museum; faces E
Fort: Eighth from E; 8km (5 miles) from Brocolitia
Built: c. 124–128, rebuilt after destruction in 197, 296 and 367
Dimensions: 186m (610ft) (W–E) by 112m (367ft) (N–S); area covered: 2ha (5 acres)
Gates: W, E (main gate) and S all double-portals S of wall; N double-portal to N of wall, but very steep (possibly leading to building of Knag Burn Gate)
Vicus: S and E of fort

Milecastle 37 (Housesteads)
Status: Walls and remains of buildings; altars
Type: Short axis; Type I S gateway (no N)
Builder: Probably legio II Augusta

Turret 37A (Rapishaw Gap): Slight earthworks

Turret 37B (Hotbank Crag): Slight earthworks

Signal tower
Barcombe A to S

Signal tower
Barcombe B to S

▲ *An artist's impression of Milecastle 37, which has been partly reconstructed and consolidated and is now in the care of English Heritage.* DeAgostini/Getty Images

▼ *An aerial view of Milecastle 37. Excavations in 1988–1989 showed three distinct periods for the north gate, which was firstly built, next blocked, then later partly demolished.*

into three parts, in classic Roman Army style, with the central command and supply section flanked by barrack blocks. Outside the fort, the outlines of field systems and the extensive *vicus* are visible, where various Romano-British temples (including a Mithraeum) and shrines have been excavated, then back-filled, along with shops, taverns and houses. In one of the houses two skeletons were found – one murdered by a knife in the ribs.

Vercovicum underwent various repairs and alterations during its use, being enlarged in c. 200 to accommodate a biggger auxiliary unit. Partly because of its location on a hill, its northern defences were prone to collapse. It also had no internal water supply and relied upon large rainwater-collection cisterns and Knag Burn just below it to the east.

Attested units include *legio II Augusta* and *legio VI Victrix*, no doubt doing the building work and later alterations. As regards garrison troops, the first auxiliary cohort is unknown, but there is much epigraphic evidence for the 1,000-man unit *cohors I Tungrorum* (the Tungri of Gallia Belgica) which was resident from the late 2nd through to the 4th centuries, when regular renovation work took place and the *vicus* was at its largest. Although part of this unit moved to the Antonine Wall when

it was operational, it seems part of it remained and the rest returned. Over time, its strength slowly diminished and additional auxiliary units also served at Vercovicium. *Cohors I Hamiorum sagittariorum* was made up of bowmen from Syria, who are also attested at nearby Magnis Fort farther along the wall to the east. Also present were the Germanic (Frisian) horsemen of the *cuneus Frisiorum* (the *cuneus* was the unit's wedge-shaped battle formation) and, later, another Germanic warband, the *numerus Hnaudifridi,* composed of men who were not part of the regular army but hired mercenaries.

By the end of the 3rd century the *vicus* had been abandoned for the security of the fort, whose walls were renovated and west and north gates blocked; it was manned by a now much smaller garrison. The *Notitia Dignitatum* records the Tungrians still at Vercovicium in the 4th century – by now a substantially smaller unit of around 300 men. By 409 the Roman Army had withdrawn. Vercovicium's position no doubt made it an asset in the dangerous times of the unrecorded Dark Ages that followed the Romans' departure, and it aquired an infamous reputation as a lair for an outlaw gang and border reivers. By the south gate are the remains of a late-medieval defended farmhouse, known as a bastle.

One of the most popular lengths of the wall today, the section from Vercovicium to Milecastle 39 is craggy and spectacular, with views to north and south. To the south, just visible from the wall, lies Vindolanda: not on the wall but very much part of it. Farther along is a modern icon: Sycamore Gap, popularised by its use in 1991's *Robin Hood: Prince of Thieves.* The tree is destined to be a permanent feature as a replacement sapling grows nearby to replace the original when necessary.

▲ *Ground view of Milecastle 37 looking north. The wall achieves a maximum height of 2m (7ft) internally, and the single barrack block on the eastern side survives to about 1m (3ft). There is much excavation spoil on the escarpment north of the milecastle, blocking what would have been a difficult but possible descent to the base of the crag.* Paul Beston

VINDOLANDA

Vindolanda is on the Stanegate and pre-dates the wall by some 30 years, dating back to the Flavian period when the conquest of Britain was prosecuted under the Emperor Domitian and his governor of Britain, Gnaeus Julius Agricola. The need for reinforcements in Dacia around AD87–88 saw the Romans pull back from the Highlands of Scotland that they had garrisoned under Agricola. Today, with centuries of delineated ownership and hard borders, it's too easy to fall into the trap of assuming the Stanegate was similar – but Vindolanda's position in the centre of the Solway–Tyne line ensured its importance, and it's no surprise that it's believed that Hadrian may have stayed there when he visited England to initiate the building of the wall. Vindolanda played a significant role during the construction of the wall, and its long Roman occupation would continue on to the 5th century.

Above Vindolanda on Barcombe Hill are two signal stations. The more defined of the two is 17m by 13m (56ft by 43ft), with a rampant and ditch. There's a limestone flagged area that would have acted as foundations for turf ramparts. Flavian pottery found there shows it pre-dates the wall but it's difficult to know whether it was used to signal with locations on the wall such as Vercovicium (invisible from Vindolanda). There are also signs of quarrying.

FROM CASTLE NICK TO CAWFIELDS

▶ *An aerial view of the famous Sycamore Gap with Milecastle 39 – Castle Nick – above it. Such gaps along Hadrian's Wall in the Whin Sill are channels worn away by vast amounts of meltwater flowing beneath the ice sheets that once covered the area.*

CAW GAP

It seems that stones were robbed from Hadrian's Wall since antiquity. Fearing that the wall would disappear altogether under the wholesale robbing, John Clayton bought up some land on which the wall still stood. His purchase included Housesteads and Caw Gap. He had his workmen consolidate the wall by retrieving fallen stones and digging them out of the ground, then reconstructing them as coursed dry-stone walling on top of the surviving courses – they were thus 'Claytonised'. The estate was broken up in 1883 to pay his son's gambling debts. Much of the land was bought by the National Trust.

Due to the popularity of the wall and the number of visitors who flock there to see these remnants of Roman Britain for themselves, the footpath alongside the wall is being severely eroded, which has had an impact on the wall. In October 2017 the National Trust had to set about repairing part of the footpath at Caw Gap, a particularly popular tourist spot. They helicoptered in 35 tonnes of stone to repair a 76m (250ft)-long section of path.

PEEL GAP TURRET

Positioned where there is a natural defile between turrets 39A and 39B, this turret was a later addition to the wall – making it unique as a third turret. It is much more roughly built with boulders than other turrets, which suggests non-fighting men unaccustomed to building work – perhaps built in a hurry while the experienced soldiers were fighting. A ballista bolt was found here, leading to the suspicion that turrets also contained attack weaponry.

▲ *The Sycamore Gap tree is one of most photographed in the country and in late 2016 it won the English Tree of the Year in the Woodland Trust's awards. The circular wall in front protects a small replacement sycamore sapling from the local sheep.* Shutterstock

▼ *An aerial view of Turret 39A on Peel Crag and the Peel Gap Tower. 39A was abandoned, dismantled and its recess built up at the end of the 2nd century. In its northwest corner was found a later burial of a man and a woman. The Peel Gap Tower was constructed after the wall was completed and was built abutting it, rather than recessed into it like other turrets.*

 Turret 39A (Peel Crag): Abandoned and dismantled in the 2nd century

Peel Gap Turret
Status: Complete foundations; built after wall completed 345m (1,130ft) from Turret 39A
Type: Rectangular, no gateway
Builder: Unknown
Dimensions: 4m (13ft) (E–W) by 3.6m (11ft 10in) (N–S); walls 0.9m (3ft) thick

Temporary camp: Twice Brewed to S

Temporary camp: Seatsides 1 and 2 to S

Temporary camp: Bean Burn 1 and 2 to S

Turret 39B (Steelrigg): Abandoned and dismantled in the 2nd century

Milecastle 40 (Winshields)
Status: Turfed rubble banks
Type: Long axis; Type II gateways later reduced for pedestrians only
Builder: Unknown
Dimensions: Unknown

Turret 40A (Winshields): No visible remains

Turret 40B (Melkridge): No visible remains; 2.7m (8ft 11in) wide

Milecastle 41 (Melkridge)
Status: Turfed banks, robber trenches
Type: Short axis; gateways unknown
Builder: Unknown
Dimensions: Unknown

Turret 41A (Caw Gap): Some stone remains; demolished in Roman times

Temporary camp: Milestone House to S

Turret 41B (Thorny Doors): No visible remains

FROM CAWFIELDS TO AESICA

▲ *A view of Cawfields from the south showing the top of the crags and the Vallum.*

▼ *Milecastle 42 situated on a steep south-facing slope, 10m (32ft) south of Cawfield Crags, overlooking Hole Gap to the west.*

MILECASTLES

When the wall was planned there were no forts on the wall, just milecastles and turrets: essentially watchtowers positioned up to 3km (2 miles) north of the Stanegate to look out for and warn of impending trouble coming from the north. Virtually every milecastle and turret is in direct line of sight with a fort or other relay tower. The larger milecastles had more men who were also there to regulate and control civilian movement across the wall. When trouble was spotted, a runner or signal (using lighted flares or semaphore) would be sent back to the nearest fort on the Stanegate.

Originally it seems that 77 milecastles were planned to span the length of the wall. But plans changed: new forts, such as Maia (Bowness) and Aesica (Great Chesters), replaced milecastles (namely 80 and 43), and then the wall was extended and at least three more were added. The final total may never be known.

The milecastles were gateways across the north–south divide. They were a method of regulating trade and traffic across the wall. Milecastles varied a little in design, but the basic structure had a north and south gateway linked by a central road that ran through the fortification. It is not known but thought probable that the gateways each had a tower. Inside the perimeter were one or two internal buildings on either side of the road; a stairway in another corner led to the rampart walk. The external curtain wall was probably much the same height as the nearby wall.

Again, it is not known how many men would garrison a milecastle. The soldiers were probably on a rota system from the nearest fort. A minimum of six men were needed to keep a constant watch on the horizon, so if six were on duty at any one time then their relief would be resting or sleeping: this gives a working minimum of 12 men needed for each milecastle. Hearths in the turrets and ovens indicate that the men cooked there, but their accommodation was altogether smaller.

▶ *Cawfield's dolerite crags and lough. The lough is in fact the flooded former quarry.*

The provision for living on the frontier were small barrack blocks in the milecastles, only later, when the forts were built on the wall itself, were soldiers actually garrisoned there full time. It seems that some milecastles accommodated eight men while others (maybe the busier crossings) held up to 32 men. This only changed when plans for the wall were revised to include forts directly on the frontier.

Civilians could cross the wall at these points and while the restrictions for Hadrian's Wall are not recorded, if the same regulations applied as for the Rhine crossings in Germany, then civilians were allowed through the gate on payment of a fee and/or customs dues, but they had to be unarmed and escorted by soldiers.

HALTWHISTLE BURN

The area around the Haltwhistle Burn is chock full of Roman remains. The burn is a tributary of the South Tyne, and creates a gap that needed to be carefully protected. The fortlet is located on gently sloping ground before the steep drop into

▶ *Milecastle 42 was excavated in 1847–1848 and again in 1936, when a dedication slab was found indicating that its builders were the redoubtable legio II Augusta.* Shutterstock

◀ *Philip Corke's impression of Milecastle 42 when it was operational. Whether the wall had an upper rampart walkway is a much-discussed mystery.* English Heritage/Heritage Images/Getty Images

▲ *The remains of a forward fortlet built at the same time as the Stanegate, before Hadrian's Wall, to guard the area around Haltwhistle Burn.*

Haltwhistle Burn, guarding the Stanegate crossing. Built around AD105 – so earlier than the wall – it included a barrack block and officers' quarters still visible as earthworks. Externally, it had a stone-faced rampart backed by an earthen bank and fronted by two ditches. The defences to the west of the fort have been eroded by the Burn and 19th-century quarrying operations.

There were four temporary camps south of the wall, all alongside the Stanegate. Haltwhistle Burn 1 was an east-facing camp on the north-facing slopes of a low ridge, which extends west towards the Haltwhistle Burn.

Haltwhistle Burn 2 was later divided in two by a rampart and ditch to form Haltwhistle Burn 3.

Haltwhistle Burn 4 lies 20m (65ft) south of the Vallum. There are two opposed gateways, one in the east and one in the west, each 3.5m (11ft 6in) wide. Because of its weak defensive position the camp is unlikely to pre-date Hadrian's Wall.

TEMPORARY MARCHING CAMPS

Remains of marching camps are found all around the Roman landscape although they leave little evidence behind and almost no artefacts. Originally found through perimeter traces such as earthern ramparts or ditches, most recently these camps have been identified through aerial photography, which records crop markings that highlight unusual shadows and lines.

The camps were only occupied in marching season – roughly March to October – and are thought to have been built to house soldiers while on manoeuvres, but also when they were reconnoitering the layout of the land, campaigning or policing an area possibly while building Hadrian's Wall. They could be occupied for anything between a single night and a number of weeks and were laid out in typically Roman standard formations (depending, of course, on the topography of the land on which they were built).

Camps were usually protected by turf ramparts, a ditch and a stake palisade (stakes were carried by every Roman soldier). Some camps were of considerable size and would have provided temporary shelter for thousands of soldiers living under leather hide tents (*sub pellibus*), plus their servants, baggage, horses, pack animals and wagons. When a camp was occupied for a period of time it is probable that 'camp followers' would have pitched up outside the confines of the camp. These would include suppliers and traders, as

▶ *An aerial view of a temporary Roman marching camp, set up each night and deliberately slighted when no longer required. This one's near Poltross Burn Milecastle.*

well as soothsayers and prostitutes and general hangers-on. Contemporary military manuals do not allow provision for camp followers (although they were undoubtedly a fact of life) but it seems most likely that civilians were allowed on to camp confines during the day but expelled at night.

Estimates about the density of marching camps varies. *De munitionibus castrorum*, probably written in the 2nd century and possibly referring to Marcus Aurelius's campaigns on the Danube, gives detailed specifics for such camps. For example, a century of 80 men has eight tents (eight men per tent and 16 on guard duty) that take up 120 by 30 Roman feet (35.2m by 8.9m/115ft by 29ft). This extrapolates to 120 by 180 Roman feet (35.2m by 53.3m/115 ft by 175ft) – 21,600 sq Roman ft – for a complete cohort of 480 men. In modern terms this means 1,890sq m or almost half an acre. But none of this provides for the headquarters tents, the commanding officers' accommodation, the horses and wagons, cookhouse, latrines and so on, which would have at least doubled the required space. Modern scholars tend to agree that the camps would have accommodated around 480 men per hectare (or 200 men per acre).

▼ *Map of Hadrian's Wall in the area of Caw Gap, Cawfields Crags, Burnhead and Aesica Fort (Great Chesters). Temporary construction camps and the Stanegate are also included.*

Furthermore, cavalry units would have required up to four times the space of infantry units for their horses, grooms, feed, stabling etc.

All such estimates are speculation, but won't be far from the truth. Roman land surveyors used the *actus* – a unit of length of 120 Roman feet (35.2m/115ft). It is now widely thought that the square *actus* was also applied to marching camps (it was for some forts). So, a cohort of 480 men needed 8 square *actus* (1 hectare), plus space for the ramparts and *intervallum*.

The Roman marching camp at Moss Side (White Moss) near Crosby-on-Eden, east of Carlisle, was studied in the late 1990s. Archaeologists concluded that it covered 1.2 hectares (almost 3 acres) and possibly accommodated two cohorts (judging by the number and position of the pits). These men may have been involved in constructing the wall, but equally might have been campaigning in the area or training there.

Milecastle 42
(Cawfields)
Status: Extensive stone remains
Type: Short axis; Type I gateways
Builder: *Legio II Augusta*
Dimensions: Internal, 17.8m (58ft 3in) (E–W) by 14.4m (11ft 10in) (N–S); walls 2.8m (9ft 2in) thick

Temporary camp: Cawfields to north

Fortlet (Haltwhistle Burn): Visible earthworks

Quarry Haltwhistle Burn to S

Temporary camps: Haltwhistle Burn 1–4 to S

Turret 42A (Burn Head): Unknown; destroyed by quarrying

Temporary camp: Burnhead to N

Temporary camp: Chesters Pike to N

Turret 42B (Great Chesters): Visible earthworks

Temporary camps: Markham Cottage 1 and 2 to N

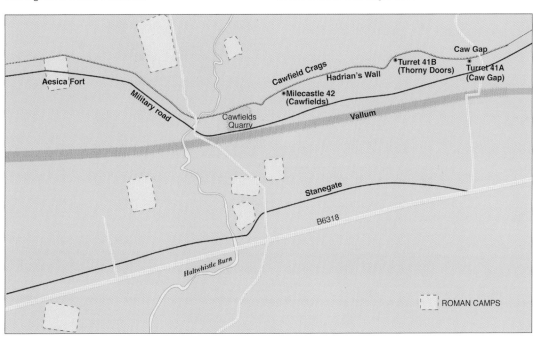

ROMAN CAMPS

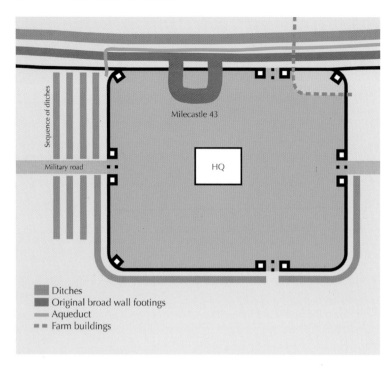

Ditches
Original broad wall footings
Aqueduct
Farm buildings

Sequence of ditches

Milecastle 43

Military road

HQ

▲ *Aesica fort was constructed over Milecastle 43 as shown in this plan. Note the aqueduct that headed off north of the wall.*

AESICA (GREAT CHESTERS)

Aesica guards the gap where the Haltwhistle Burn runs across the wall. The fort was probably completed in 128. Its entirety lies south of the wall and covers an area of roughly 1.2ha (3 acres). Milecastle 43 was demolished to make way for the interior buildings and its footings now rest under the northwest corner of the fort. This suggests that the fort was decided on after the wall was built.

Interestingly, the foundations for the wall here are for the Broad Wall, but the edifice that was constructed was narrow gauge. The Narrow Wall footings were built immediately behind the Broad Wall foundations, and were later incorporated into the fort's northern defences. The fort was supplied with water via

▼ *An aerial view of Aesica (Great Chesters). Under the northwest corner of the fort lie the footings of Milecastle 43, which had to be levelled in order to accommodate the fort's interior buildings. It had only three main gates – south, east and west – each with double portals with towers. At some point the west gate was completely blocked up.*

▲ *The* sacellum *of Aesica. The* sacellum *was a vaulted underground strong room and the spiritual centre of any Roman Army camp where the unit's sacred flags and its treasury were kept.* Paul Beston

▲ *Part of the defences and internal structures of Aesica. Its purpose was to guard the Caw Gap, where Haltwhistle Burn crosses the wall. A 10km (6 mile) acqueduct supplied the fort with water from the head of the burn north of the wall.*

▲ *An altar filled with modern coins sits in the guardroom of the southern gateway of Aesica Fort (Great Chesters). Eleven altar stones are identified in RIB as being found at Aesica – three to Jupiter and three to Vheterus.*

a twisty 9.5km (6 mile)-long shallow-channelled aqueduct from the head of the Haltwhistle Burn (it's actually only 3km/2 miles distant but follows the contours of the hills). This also supplied the water for the bath house.

There were three double-portal gates with towers at each corner: east, west and south. The Military Way entered by the east gate and left by the west gate, but over the years the latter was successively narrowed until the decision was taken to completely block it up. The Vallum was built before the fort and a branch of the Stanegate crosses over it to enter the fort by the south gate. A single ditch protects the south and east side but the flatter western approach is guarded by four external ditches.

The *vicus* lay south and west of the fort with a burial ground towards the Stanegate. Near the south gate a jewellery hoard dated to the 3rd century was found in the 19th century, including a gold and bronze ring, silver collar pendant, a gilded bronze brooch and a hare-shaped enamel brooch.

An inscription suggests that the fort was originally built by *legio XX Valeria Victrix,* who

wintered at Cilurnum and was responsible for much of the wall building hereabouts.

In 1897, 90m (300ft) to the south, a bath house was discovered. It includes a latrine, cold room with cold bath, dry-heat room, warm-steam room, hot-steam room and dressing room.

In total, 31 inscribed stones have been found, including 11 altar stones (with three to Jupiter and three to Vheterus), seven tombstones and six building inscriptions.

Inscriptions indicate that the fort was garrisoned by *legio XX Valeria Victrix,* then *legio VI Victrix.* They were possibly followed by the *cohors II Gallorum,* then the 500-strong infantry *cohors VI Nerviorum.* Another 500-strong infantry unit, *cohors VI Raetorum,* followed, and then *vexillatio Gaesatorum et Raetorum.* The latter was an irregular detachment of spearmen from what is now Switzerland; they are not known serving anywhere else in Britain. Thanks to a partial hearth stone found nearby in Milecastle 42, it is thought that *cohors I Pannoniorum* may have garrisoned the fort for a time. In the 3rd century the 500-strong mixed infantry and cavalry *cohors II Asturum* provided the garrison.

Aesica Fort

Location: Great Chesters

Status: Earthworks and stone remain, including only altar stone left *in situ* on the wall; infantry fort facing E to defend the Caw Gap, extensive W ditches; bath house to SE fed by aqueduct (N of wall, roughly 1m by 1m/ 3ft by 3ft runs for 9.5km/6 miles)

Fort: Ninth from E; 8.8km (5.5 miles) from Vercovicium

Built: After 128 by *legio XX Valeria Victrix*

Dimensions: 128m (419ft) (E–W) by 108m (355ft) (N–S); area covered 1.2ha (3 acres)

Gates: N, W (first one and then both portals blocked), E (main gate) and S all double-portals S of wall

Vicus: S and W of fort

Temporary camp: Lees Hall to south

Milecastle 43 (Great Chesters)

Status: No visible remains; built over by Aesica

Type: Short axis; Type I gateways

Builder: Legio II Augusta

Dimensions: Unknown

FROM AESICA TO GILSLAND

▼ *Turret 44B with Walltown Crags in the background. A centurial stone found here identified the builders as the first cohort of Flavius Crescens' century. It is unusually set into a right-angle of wall.*

INSET – Turret 45A is similar to Pike Hill signal station near Turret 52A (Banks East) and is probably a watchtower pre-dating the wall. This is surmised because it is separate from the wall, which buts up against it rather than being joined in.

QUARRIES FOR THE WALL

As far as possible Hadrian's Wall was built from stone sourced from local quarries, of which a number have been found. The locations were chosen for their proximity to the wall and for the quality of their stone: Fallowfield Fell near Collerton; Chesterholm, where in 1837 a small bronze purse containing three gold and 60 silver

Hadrianic coins was found; Busy Gap; Chollerford; Haltwhistle Burn; Coombe Crag (3km/2 miles west of Birdoswald); Lanerton; Crawfields; Wetheral; Gelt near Brampton (for sandstone); Pigeon Crag (sandstone); Irthington; Blatearn; Grinsdale (north of the wall); Shawk; and a quarry north of the Solway near Bowness. Where quarries were not close or quarried out, stone had to be sourced and transported from farther afield.

Rubble used to fill the core of the wall was sourced locally all along the length of the wall, supplemented by clay and soil. Limestone for the lime was gathered from Irthing near Newcastle and a pit has been found near Housesteads. Despite using Great Whin Sill as part of the defences, the dolerite stone of the long outcrop was too hard to cut for stones. However, the sandstone of Firestone Sill was ideal for lining and making hearths. The gritty sandstones of Gridstone Sill made ideal millstones for grinding grain and the slabby sandstones of Slate Sills split easily into roofing tiles.

Temporary camps:
Sunny Rigg 1–3 to S

 Turret 43A
(Cockmount Hill): No visible remains

 Turret 43B (Allolee East): No visible remains

 Milecastle 44 (Allolee)
Status: Earthworks
Type: Long axis; unknown gateways
Builder: Unknown
Dimensions: Internal, 20.3m (67ft) (N–S) by 17m (55.8ft) (W–E)

Turret 44A (Allolee West): Turf bank remains

Turret 44B (Mucklebank): Visible stone remains

 Milecastle 45 (Walltown)
Status: Robber trenches remain; wall here disappears into Greenhead Quarry
Type: Unknown
Builder: Unknown

Turret 45A (Walltown): Visible stone remains; external
Dimensions: 5.8m (19ft) by 5.5m (18ft). It isn't linked to the wall and may be an earlier watchtower linking in to the Stanegate system

Turret 45B (Walltown West): Destroyed by quarrying; internal
Dimensions: 3.8m (12ft 6in) by 4m (13ft 1in) with .1m (3ft 3in) walls

  Milecastle 46 (Carvoran)
Status: No visible remains
Type: Unknown
Builder: Unknown

▲ *MC45 has been robbed, unfortunately. Between the milecastle and Turret 45A the wall disappears into Greenhead Quarry. The dolerite quarried from here was used for road building.*

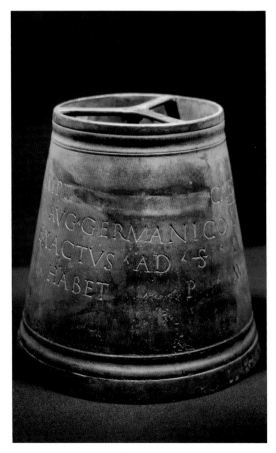

► *Carvoran does not appear to have been abandoned during the Antonine Wall period (c. 140) – rather it seems to have played a crucial role in the supplying of goods and personnel northwards. The most important find from the site is the Carvoran* modius, *a bronze vessel for measuring corn dating from the reign of Domitian (ruled AD81–96).*
Historic England/ Bridgeman Images

The soldiers themselves would do the quarrying and the cutting of the stone into square blocks and almost (if not all) of the building, both of the wall itself and of the forts and other buildings within. They would carefully choose the stone, which, where possible, was a hard quartzite grit that would hold mortar well, but local sandstone was most extensively used. The soldiers were also charged with operating the limestone kilns.

After the Romans left Britain and Hadrian's Wall fell into disuse, the forts and walls were systematically robbed for stone for houses, churches, dry-stone walls, farm buildings and so on. Consequently, much of the wall still survives locally, but scattered about the landscape rather than in its original location.

MAGNIS/MAGNA (CARVORAN)

Magnis was a Stanegate fort with a sizeable *vicus*. It was placed on the junction of the Stanegate and the Maiden Way. Little remains to be seen except a turf-covered platform surrounded by a ditch and some stonework at the northwest angle of the fort. Owned by the Vindolanda Trust, it is the site of the excellent Roman Army Museum.

The first earth-and-timber fort at Carvoran was built at the same time as the Stanegate, c. 80. Unusually, the Vallum runs to the north of the fort, separating it from the wall. The fort was rebuilt several times before 120 – with each version levelled for the subsequent fort. When the Hadrianic frontier was constructed, the fort was rebuilt and it seems to have been regularly improved to as late as 136, only a few years before the wall was temporarily abandoned. However, Magnis appears to have remained in use while the Antonine Wall was active and probably played a crucial role in supplying the garrisons there.

The visible remains date to the early Antonine period, around 136–137, when the fort was rebuilt in stone. The *vicus* lay to the south of the fort and the tombstones that have been recovered from the area indicate that it was occupied by the extended families of the garrison.

The most significant find at Magnis is the 1st-century *modius*, a bronze bucket-shaped vessel for measuring corn made during the reign of Emperor Domitian. It could hold 17.5 *sextarii* (3 litres/16.8 pints).

The site has yielded 34 altars and votive stones, nine tombstones, 18 different building inscriptions, plus eight unidentifiable inscriptions. It seems that legionaries built the fort but it was occupied by Roman citizens, who were artisans, engineers and manufacturers, and who were charged with planning and maintaining the fabric of the frontier and all its associated infrastructure.

The garrison most associated with Carvoran is *legio XX Valeria Victrix,* but the original unit is thought to have been the 500-strong mixed infantry and cavalry *cohors I Batavorum aquitata.* The late Hadrianic garrison was *cohors I Hamiorum sagittariorum*, bowmen from Syria who probably were participants in the Claudian invasion in AD43

▲ *Atop Walltown Crags, the consolidated wall stretches across an undulating surface.*

and were the only regiment of archers known to have been billetted in Britain. The 3rd-century garrison was the mixed infantry and cavalry *cohors II Delmatarum* (from Dalmatia).

Twelve altar stones here were dedicated to the cult Celtic warrior god Vheterus – who may have embodied three gods. Three stones have been found dedicated to the war god Belatucader.

▼ *Reconstruction of how the living quarters of a Roman frontier soldier might have looked.* Alamy

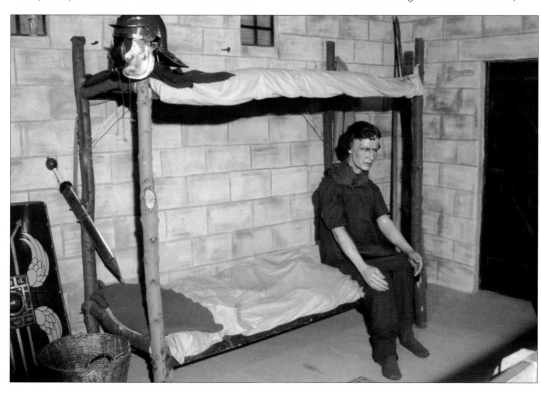

 Magnis Fort
Location: Carvoran; important Stanegate fort guarding the crossroads with the Maiden Way – wall and vallum are to the N
Status: Earthworks, NW corner turret but little to see; excellent museum (Carvoran Roman Army Museum)
Fort: 10th from E; 5km (3.25) miles from Aesica
Built: Geophys shows layers of occupation from about AD80; stone wall from c. 136–138
Dimensions: 110m (360ft) (W–E) by 132m (435ft) (N–S); area covered 1.45ha (3.5 acres)
Gates: Fort faced S; N, W (first one and then both portals blocked), E (main gate) and S all double-portals S of wall
Vicus: Extensive to W, S and E of fort

◄ View down the Vallum, east of the village of Gilsland. The steep groundworks are still clearly visible after nearly 2,000 years, yet no accepted purpose for the existence of the Vallum is generally supported other than as the definition of a military zone around the wall.

MAIDEN WAY

Running almost 32km (20 miles) down the Pennines north to south, connecting Magnis on the wall with Bravoniacum (now Kirkby Thore) – where it meets the important highway of Watling Street – the Maiden Way was probably constructed to help access to the important lead and silver mines near Epiacum on Alston Moor and other places around the North Pennines. It also facilitated the supply of men and goods to the central and eastern wall areas from the south.

The exact route of the road is unknown, but a lot of archaeological work is currently being undertaken (aerial photography is proving invaluable for this): the last and only comprehensive survey was in 1855. Medieval ridge-and-furrow agriculture and later enclosures, for which much of the stone was robbed, has helped to obliterate its track The road clearly changed in construction and dimensions along its length according to the terrain it was traversing. For example, when the Maiden Way was described in 1845, the stretch on Melmerby Fell was reported as being 6.4m (21ft) wide, up to 1.2m (4ft) high with ditches on either side and crossed by many conduits. Along the sides the stones were 0.6–0.9m (2–3ft) long and up to 0.6m (2ft) wide, with smaller stones in the middle. Over wet ground the stones were thicker. More recently the 9.5m (6 mile)-long stretch between Birdoswald to Bewcastle was surveyed: at Highstead Ash part of the original road was examined and found to be built on subsoil with a packed layer of cobbles and stone (the *agger*), between 4.9–5.2m (16–17ft) wide, edged with squared kerbstones and flanked by side ditches.

POLTROSS BURN MILECASTLE

Located on the southwest edge of Gilsland village, Poltross Burn is one of the best-preserved and best-studied milecastles. Known locally as the 'King's Stables', it sits on a steep slope that falls away sharply on the east side. It was first excavated in 1886, when parts of the structure were revealed, and over the years and subsequent excavations (principally in the mid-1960s) has provided most of our current knowledge about milecastle structure and layout.

The interior of the fortlet is one of the largest on the wall. It had gates with two pairs of responds (the remains of the northern gateway are visible), and two barrack blocks large enough to house a garrison of 64 soldiers on either side of the road that ran north–south through the fortification. One of the blocks contains an oven.

Its most important feature, however, is the three steps in the northeast corner, the remains of a wide flight of steps leading up – it is surmised – to a walkway. If extrapolated correctly, they give the height of the inside top wall at around 3.7m (12ft), which would make the outside parapet over 4.6m (15ft) high. As vertical dimensions are the main feature lacking on all the remaining structures along the wall, this is important evidence. However, what it doesn't prove is whether there was a walkway all along the wall – something that's lacking in other Roman linear boundaries such as the German barrier.

▼ Poltross Burn's foundations show two barrack blocks for the soldiers on either side of the north–south road that runs through the stronghold. From their size it is surmised that a garrison of 64 soldiers manned the milecastle.

▶ *Poltross Burn is part of the Broad Wall (3m/9ft 8.5in wide) and contains what may be evidence of a staircase in the northeast corner (at right) that would have taken the soldiers up to a walkway on the wall, an estimated 4.5m (15ft) above the ground.*

ROBBING THE WALL

Much of Hadrian's Wall still exists – but not on the wall itself. Its cut stones have been arbitrarily robbed and reused the length of the wall. Over the centuries, stone from the wall has been taken away and repurposed into castles, farmhouses, towns, roads and endless dry-stone walls. Much of the older parts of Newcastle benefit from the stone. This was particularly so in the west, as local stone is not readily available. Some of the greatest damage was done in the mid-18th century when stone was robbed to make the Military Road in Northumberland – constructed to help quell the Jacobite rebellion in the Highlands. Construction gangs attacked the wall and broke up the stone

for road surfaces and the flanking field walls, and even 20th-century road-constructors were guilty of robbing the remnants of the wall for their projects.

Studies have been made that show that over 91 percent of the wall has disappeared, between 1–2 percent was destroyed in the 19th and 20th centuries, 2 percent of the visible remains are Victorian restoration and 5 percent are 20th-century consolidations.

▼ *Thirlwall Castle was most likely built in the middle of the 14th century with stone robbed from Hadrian's Wall, wiping out all traces of the curtain wall for miles around.*

 Thirlwall Castle:
Hadrian's Wall reused

 Turret 46A
(Holmhead):
Unknown

Temporary camp:
Glenwhelt Leazes
to S

 Turret 46B (Wallend):
Unknown

 Milecastle 47 (Chapel
House)
Status: No visible
remains
Type: Long axis
Builder: Possibly *legio
XX Valeria Victrix*

 Turret 47A (Foultown):
No visible remains

 Turret 47B (Gap):
No visible remains
but excellent views
of ditch

Temporary camp:
Crooks to S

 Milecastle 48
(Poltross Burn)
Status: Extensive
remains – one of
the best-preserved
milecastles on the
wall – including
staircase to wall
walkway estimated
at 3.7m (12ft) and an
upper wall height of
4.6m (15ft)
Type: Long axis; Type III
gateway
Builder: Possibly *legio
VI Victrix*
Dimensions: 18.5m
(60ft 8in) (E–W) by
21.3m (69ft 10in)
(N–S)

 Fortlet (Throp)
Status: Turf ramparts;
sited to protect the
Stanegate crossing
over the Poltross
Burn, a tributary of
the River Irthing.
Built: Early 2nd
century; second brief
occupancy in 4th
century
Dimensions: Internal,
55m by 55m (180ft
by 180ft) and
enclosing an area
of about 0.3ha
(0.75 acres)

WILLOWFORD BRIDGE

▼ *Aerial view of Willowford Bridge eastern abutment and length of wall, with Harrows Scar Milecastle and Vallum in the foreground. The heavily wooded River Irthing gorge separates the ruins but clearly shows their alignments.*

INSET 1 – The consolidated remains of Willowford Bridge abutment. The bridge was built in three phases: the first was round-arched and was built 122–160; the second, built 160–80, had added sluices; the third, built 205–7, was widened and strengthened to carry a military road.
INSET 2 – Looking down the hill towards Willowford bridge.
INSET 3 – Turret 48B, like its companion Turret 48A, was found to have had four superimposed floors composed of clay or flagstones. After being abandoned, neither seems to have been demolished like other turrets in the central section.

WILLOWFORD BRIDGE

Hadrian's Wall crossed three major rivers along its length and consequently required three important bridges: across the Tyne at Chesters, the Irthing at Willowford and the Eden at Carlisle. Remains of the bridges at Chesters and Willowford are still visible. The river has changed its course since Roman times.

Although the bridge itself is long gone, the east abutment that carried the wall itself over the River Irthing is still visible. The original bridge had stone piers and was wide enough to take a walkway (although almost certainly not the wall itself): the watercourse was probably protected by a boom between the arches. At either end of the bridge were Turrets 48A and 48B guarding

the passageway. It was built c. 122–125, and the first three or four courses show that this was a continuation of the Broad Wall at 3m (9ft 10in) wide. But while being built, quite when it is impossible to tell, the decision was taken to reduce the width of the wall and it can be seen here where the width drops to 2.2m (7ft 2in) wide. The eastern-end remains show that access to the bridge was through a tower that was partly recessed into the wall.

The Irthing is prone to flooding and the Romans did their best in the mid-2nd century to protect the bridge by revetting the eastern river bank and adding sluices. However, this didn't stop the eastern river pier being swept away sometime before the end of the 2nd century (after 160). The bridge was rebuilt: a new timber span replaced the fallen arch and a bigger tower was built slightly farther east.

Little is known about the detail of the bridge except that in the late 2nd or early 3rd century it was widened to accommodate a road (as was Chesters bridge). Also, a ramp was built behind the wall to take the Military Way up to the road level across the bridge. The rebuilt eastern abutment comprised a thin wall of stone blocks to contain the riverbank. The first river pier was a rectangular foundation separated from the abutment by a narrow channel.

The turrets contained four levels, each floored with flagstones or clay tiles. No pottery has been found dating from later than the start of the 3rd century, so it is presumed that the towers were abandoned but not demolished (like others in the central sector). In the 4th century, stone was robbed from the bridge to repair the east wall of Birdoswald fort.

CONSTRUCTION TECHNIQUES

The Romans used stone to build bridges with arches to strengthen the structure. According to Vitruvius, the Romans constructed curved, watertight barrels of wood bound with metal and then lined these with pitch or clay, putting them together to form something like a modern coffer dam. If they could, they diverted the water flow and lowered these vessels on to the river bed so they could dig down to establish the foundations. Where possible the foundations would comprise hard rock, otherwise they drove wooden piles deep into the river bed. The lack of oxygen in the wet mud prevented the wood from being destroyed by bacteria. With the foundations in place, the supporting pillars were built up inside the barrels using clay and stone, and then concrete was poured in to set the whole together.

The Romans had discovered a natural underwater cement – they called it *pozzolana* (also *pozzolan/pozzuolana*)– which was used particularly for bridges. *Pozzolana* is made by grinding natural volcanic or artificial blast-furnace slag with powdered hydrated lime. This was mixed by weight of one part lime to two parts *pozzolana* to strengthen mortar and concrete. In the 3rd century this was used instead of sand in concrete and mortared rubblework. When it was mixed with an aggregate such as broken stone or brick it was incredibly strong and resilient and useful for bridge construction. Scaffolding was erected and the arches would be supported by trusses until they were fully constructed.

Turret 48A (Willowford East): Visible stone remains; broad- to narrow-gauge switch; 4.1m (13ft 6in) across

Temporary camp: Willowford to S

Turret 48B (Willowford West): Some stone remains

Bridge (Willowford): Extensive stone remains of bridge over River Irthing

Milecastle 49 (Harrows Scar)
Status: Extensive stone remains
Type: Short axis; Type I gateways
Builder: *Legio II Augusta*
Dimensions: Internal, 17.8m (58ft 3in) (E–W) by 14.4m (11ft 10in) (N–S); walls 2.8m (9ft 2in) thick

3

THE WALL FROM WILLOWFORD BRIDGE TO THE WEST

The Turf Wall was replaced by stone in two tranches, the first during Hadrian's reign (to Milecastle 54); the second later – possibly during Septimius Severus's reign (193–211). This is the section at East Banks turret (52A). Shutterstock

THE TURF WALL

The northwest of England is very different to the other side of the country. The Solway Firth is a much bigger estuary than that of the Tyne. Fed by the Eden, Esk and Nith, the firth is flanked by low-lying country that floods easily, but mudflats in the estuary allow easy access from the Scottish Lowlands.

The first bridge may be at Carlisle, but there are a number of fording points – *waths* in the local dialect – farther west, with the Bowness Wath the most westerly. It is unsurprising, therefore, that the Romans should have started the western end of the wall here, with the terminal fort named Maia. As Scotland and Ireland are so close here, defences continued down the Cumbrian shore at least as far as Maryport, perhaps farther: there are Roman remains at Flimby, Siddick and Moresby.

◄ *For a feeling of the original substance of Hadrian's Wall, the length from Harrows Scar through Birdoswald and then west provides a considerable continuous length.*

▼ *Leahill Turret was constructed to abut the curtain wall as shown by the butt joints on either side. The remains were discovered in 1927, under the road that ran behind the wall. It was two storeys high, with living quarters on the ground floor.*

No one knows why the wall between the Eden and the Irthing was built from turf instead of stone. Some point to the lack of availability of stone; others that it was erected quickly because of an actual threat by local tribes. It was not unusual for the Romans to build in turf – they did so 20 years later when they built the Antonine Wall and did so every time they made camp. The experiment at Vindolanda, where a turf wall and rampart was built in 1973, shows the practicalities of such a design. One of the advantages of turf is that it takes less effort than stone – no quarrying, fewer problems of transport and fewer resources – but its impermanence meant that when the Antonine line was abandoned and Hadrian's Wall became the de facto border, the turf was replaced by stone.

Today, little remains of the Turf Wall, even along the stretch where the replacement stone wall was realigned to the north. Indeed, little remains of any of the forts or any other sign of the wall between Banks and the sea.

FROM HARROWS SCAR TO BANNA

▼ *The walls at Harrows Scar butt against Hadrian's Wall. This indicates that the wall was built first and then the milecastle afterwards. Much of the interior of the building has been long removed by the farm track that runs right through it.*

INSET 1 – Harrows Scar was a fortified gateway on Hadrian's Wall on the western side of the River Irthing gorge. It was originally part of the turf rampart and was later rebuilt in stone around the end of the 2nd century. In the 17th century a small cottage and garden were built within the ruins near the south gate.

INSET 2 – Harrows Scar (Milecastle 49) was excavated in 1898 and 1953 and is the best-preserved milecastle on Hadrian's Wall. The most exciting find was a Roman altar dedicated to Silvanus, the Roman spirit of the woods.

INSCRIPTIONS ON THE WALL

An altar, dedicated to Silvanus, was found at Harrows Scar in 1953. The inscription read:

'[Deo sancto Si]L[v]AN[o] [F]LAVIUS MARCELLINUS DEC(urio) V(otum) S(olvit) L(ibens) M(erito)'
('To the holy god Silvanus, Flavius Marcellinus, decurion, willingly and deservedly fulfilled his vow')

Much of our knowledge about Hadrian's Wall comes from the numerous inscriptions carved on stones found on the wall itself and on the buildings associated with it. In fact, until the mid-19th

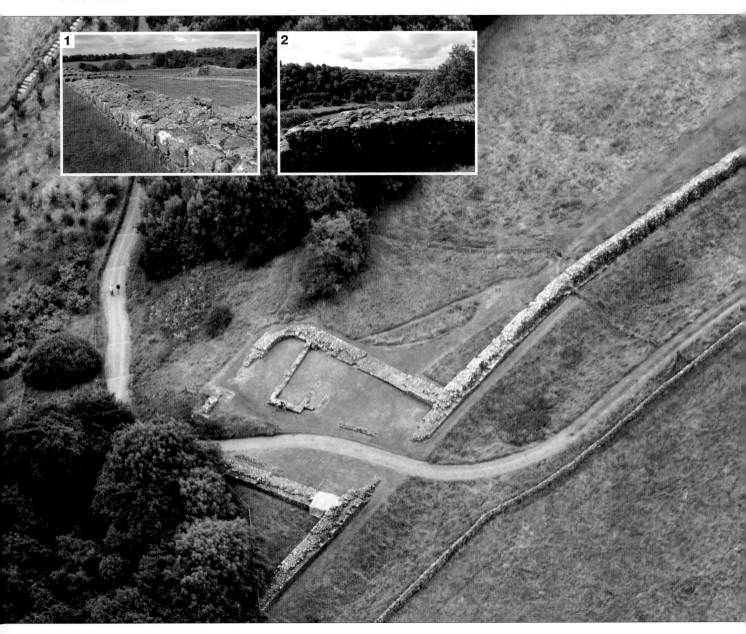

century, the inspiration for the wall was ascribed to the 20th emperor, Septimus Severus, until an inscribed stone was found stating that emperor Hadrian had built it.

Luckily the Romans liked to leave their names carved on stone to record their achievements. Inscriptions are found on altar stones, tombstones and building dedications. Unfortunately, and inevitably, many of these stones are damaged or incomplete, but enough still survives for scholars to be able to interpret them. On Hadrian's Wall they say who built which bits, the names of the garrisons that lived there, their emperor and who they worshipped, and on tombstones they mark the dead's status, his (usually) family and any important relationships and achievements.

Stating the obvious, these inscriptions are in Latin and can be tricky to read for various reasons. Inscriptions usually used capital letters. The words don't always have spaces between them, although often they have dots or triangular incisions; sometimes the letters get smaller to squeeze them in and the stonemasons regularly split words between lines. They also used abbreviations so the words could fit on the stone but without punctuation. Another way of squeezing in letters was by linking letters together using ligatures. Also, perhaps surprisingly, words could be misspelt.

The Roman alphabet had 21 letters and is very much the same as ours but excluding J, U (they used a V) and W. However, the numbering system is completely different, although very familiar.

On official stones was listed the name of the person or unit dedicating the stone and to whom – often a favourite god. Usually, the name of the current emperor was added and the legion. The inscriptions are rarely dated, so the best way to date them is through the emperor.

Along the wall, local stones were used, so many of the inscriptions are carved into sandstone. The words of the script would be decided on, then the stonecutter (*lapicida*) would select a slab of stone and smooth the relevant surfaces. The quality of the stone depended on the importance of the dedication and the finished result depended on the skill of the stonemason (*lapidarius*), which in the provinces like Britannia was not always top quality. Guide lines were drawn across the stone and then the letters themselves drawn on in chalk, charcoal or paint, sometimes making important names (like the emperor's) bigger than others. This whole process is called *ordinatio*. The man who actually inscribed the letters was a *sculptor* or *scriptor titulorum* (writer of texts). He used a chisel (*scalprum*)

ROMAN NUMERALS

1	I	20	XX
2	II	21	XXI
3	III	30	XXX
4	IV	40	XL
5	V	50	L
6	VI	60	LX
7	VII	70	LXX
8	VIII	80	LXXX
9	IX	90	XC
10	X	100	C
11	XI	101	CI
12	XII	120	CXX
13	XIII	150	CL
14	XIV	200	CC
15	XV	300	CCC
16	XVI	400	CD
17	XVII	450	LD
18	XVIII	500	D
19	XIX	1000	M

and hammer (*malleus*). When the stone was complete, it was generally painted, with the letters themselves picked out in red using cinnabar (*minium*). Other details could be painted in a variety of colours.

The Roman love of dedicating inscribed stones seemed to decline after the 3rd century across the length of Hadrian's Wall and without them our knowledge similarly declines.

BANNA (BIRDOSWALD)

The wall is very impressive here, running to the horizon eastwards and westwards. Unfortunately, no interior building elements remain – although it had a fort, granaries, gates, drill hall, towers and *vicus* and was extensively excavated – but the fort defences are still impressive, with large double gateways. Inside the northern end a big house and farm buildings have been converted into tourist facilities.

Banna, now Birdoswald, was a naturally strong site with the fort built on a prominent ridge to guard the important River Irthing crossing 800m (half a mile) to the east. To the south were steep cliffs overlooking Irthing Gorge towards the Stanegate; westwards lay a perilous bog and northwards was a view over Midgeholme Moss to Bewcastle fort. Birdoswald has proved a rich source of archaeology: yielding 44 altars/votive stones, 10 building inscriptions, four tombstones, plus various other inscriptions. In 1929, 51 coins were unearthed (more have been found since).

Banna Fort
Location: Birdoswald
Status: Extensive remains; museum
Fort: 11th from E; 5.2km (3.25 miles) from Magnis
Built: Cavalry fort 125; stone fort after 130
Dimensions: 177m (580ft) (N–S) by 122m (400ft) (W–E) and covered an area of almost 2.2ha (5.5 acres)
Gates: Turf Wall – N, W and E all in advance of wall; S and secondary W and E behind wall; stone wall replaced N wall. Main gates double-portal (E and W gate later half-blocked); secondary gates single-portal)
Vicus: Extensive all round fort, especially W and E

Turret 49A: Original turret built with Turf Wall was removed when fort built

Turret 49B (Birdoswald): Replacement for Turf Wall turret further S; visible stone remains

Signal Station Mains Rigg to S

Milecastle 50 (High House) (Stone Wall)
Status: No visible remains; no remains of Turf Wall milecastle 200m (655ft) S
Type: Long axis; Type III gateways
Builder: Possibly *legio VI Victrix*
Dimensions: Stone – 18.3m (60ft) (E–W) by 23.2m (76ft 1in) (N–S); turf –16.76m (55ft) by 20.1m (66ft)

▼ *The excavated granary of Banna Fort, looking north, can be seen in front of the (17th-century) bastle farmhouse. Right, a reconstructed depiction by Philip Corke of how it would have appeared in the mid-3rd century.* Bridgeman Images

INSET 2 and 3 – The east–west gateways opened out on to the vicus that grew up around the fort. Both the east (2) and west (3) gates, reconstructed by Philip Corke, were half blocked after construction. Bridgeman Images

The first fort was built of turf and timber on the Turf Wall to hold 500 cavalry soldiers. In time, the garrison changed to an infantry cohort around the era when the turf was replaced with stone (c. 130s) and the wall was realigned to incorporate the northern defences of the fort. This is the only place that the line of the wall was substantially altered, possibly because the Romans were worried about the stability of the escarpment. The beneficial consequence for us today is that about 4km (2.5 miles) of the Turf Wall still remains west of Birdoswald.

The footprint of the Vallum bows out around the south side in such a way as to suggest an earlier fort on the wall, of which there is now no trace. The later Hadrianic fort is much bigger and seems to have been built soon after the vallum, part of which had to be back-filled to accommodate it. The fort covered some 2.2ha (5.5 acres).

The recorded builders of Birdoswald are *legio II Augusta*, who are mentioned on two stones, and *legio VI Victrix,* who are mentioned on three others. The known garrisons are *cohors I Thracum Civium Romanorum* at the start of the 3rd century, which was perhaps helped to repair the fort by *cohors I Aelia Dacorum* just before it left. The next unit in residence was *Venatores Banniensis* (The Hunters of Banna) who arrived during the 4th century. Another inscribed unit named for the 3rd and 4th century is the 1,000-strong infantry *cohors I Aelia Dacorum,* which is attested on 31 inscribed stones (24 with altars inscribed to Jupiter Best and Greatest).

The large *vicus* started to grow east of the fort, with its associated burial ground a little farther south. Then, possibly because of threatening landslip, the *vicus* moved (maybe by direct military order) to southwest of the fort, where it grew to become one of the largest settlements along the wall. Historic England's Pastscape records that a geophysical survey, 'identified an extensive area of buildings, hearths, pits, and ditches'. Evidence has also been found of the *vicus* extending east and west along the Military Way.

COHORS I AELIA DACORUM

Emperor Trajan campaigned in Dacia (present-day Romania) in 101–2 and 105–6 and finally conquered and claimed the territory. The achievement is celebrated on Trajan's Column (completed 113), where Roman auxiliaries are shown brandishing Dacian heads in triumph. Rome organised Dacia as an armed province

into the Roman Empire and, like the other subjugated lands, the new province supplied men for the Roman Army, always serving well away from their homeland.

The 1,000-strong *auxilia* cohort – *cohors I Aelia Dacorum* – was raised by Hadrian some time before 125 and immediately sent to serve on the far-flung frontier of Britannia. It is likely it first went to Bewcastle, where the men were put to digging the Vallum but then, and seemingly for most of their service, they deployed and became most closely associated with Banna (Birdoswald), where the cohort remained throughout the 3rd century and into the early 4th century, with sons following fathers into service.

The Dacians almost certainly took part in the numerous campaigns against Caledonia, and over the course of their service the regiment won five imperial titles for showing loyalty to the empire and emperor: *Antoniniana*, *Gordiana*, *Postumiana*, *Tetriciana* and *Probiana*.

I Aelia Dacorum's presence is recorded on 23 altar stones at Birdoswald (dedicated to Iovi Optimo Maximo), a building stone, a tombstone to the infant son of the tribune Aurelius Julianus, and five stones with religious inscriptions (to deified emperor Augustus, Mars, Neptune, Fortuna and one to the British god Cocidius). One of the stones shows a distinctive curved Dacian sword and palm frond.

Around 400 of *I Aelia Dacorum* were sent to Camboglanna (Castlesteads), by which time it was a much smaller unit. They stayed until the general Roman withdrawal from Britain in around 410. After Dacia was relinquished by Aurelian in the late 3rd century, the *cohors* was no longer recruited there and the unit probably ceased to exist.

▶ *Found near Banna, this gilded copper figure of Hercules is said to be a likeness of Emperor Commodus (ruled 177–192).* Universal History Archive/UIG/ Bridgeman Images

▲ *RIB (Roman Inscriptions of Britain) translates this inscription as, 'Under Modius Julius, emperor's propraetorian legate, the First Aelian Cohort of Dacians (built this) under the command of Marcus Claudius Menander, the tribune'.*

Turret 50A (High House): Slight earthwork remains; no sign of Turf Wall turret to S

Turret 50B (Appletree): Slight earthwork remains; no sign of Turf Wall turret to S

Nether-Denton Fort
Location: Chapelburn
Status: Unexcavated
Fort: Three overlaid forts: Stanegate fort; 4km (2.5 miles) from Throp
Built: First, Flavian; second, probably c. 103; final, Trajanic
Dimensions: Second, largest, version 225m (740ft) (N–S) by 205m (675ft) (W–E) and covered an area of almost 4.6ha (11.5 acres)
Gates: Stanegate enters through S and exits through E
Vicus: To SW

Milecastle 51 (Wall Bowers)
Status: No visible remains; where turf rejoined the stone wall, the stone milecastle overlaid the dismantled turf version
Type: Long axis; Type III gateways
Builder: Possibly *legio VI Victrix*
Dimensions: Unknown

Quarry Coombe Crag to S

Turret 51A (Piper Sike): Stone overlaid turf; visible stone

Turret 51B (Lea Hill): Foundations visible
Dimensions: 4.2m (13ft 8in) (N–S) by 4.4m (14ft 6in) (E–W)

FROM BANNA TO PETRIANA

▲ *A replica section of turf-and-stone walls, built in 1973, was controversial but has since been appreciated as an educational tool.*

▼ *The original fort of Banna was on the Turf Wall. When the wall was rebuilt in stone it was diverted to link with Banna's northern wall.*

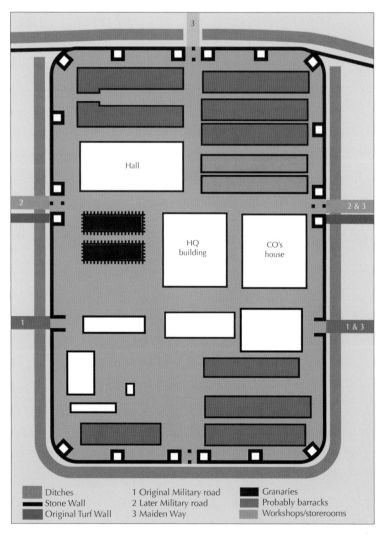

Hall

HQ building

CO's house

Ditches	1 Original Military road	Granaries
Stone Wall	2 Later Military road	Probably barracks
Original Turf Wall	3 Maiden Way	Workshops/storerooms

THE TURF WALL

The first plan for the north British frontier was for a stone curtain wall to run from Newcastle to the River Irthing, after which a turf rampart would run to the west coast at Bowness. This decision may have been because the Romans wanted the wall constructed quickly and the western section ran over country that had little suitable stone building material for such a rapid construction project. Depending on what raw materials were available, the wall was constructed on a base about 20 Roman feet wide (roughly 6m/19.5ft), without dug foundations, but using either turves or cobbles for the base. The front face was constructed to rise vertically, then may have sloped at the top. The rear face sloped at an angle of around 67 degrees. The whole was covered with soil and turves and in front of its length on the north side ran a parallel ditch.

At regular intervals the wall was punctuated with turf-and-timber milecastles and stone turrets. The free-standing turrets were abutted with the turf rampart. No proof has been found to show that a walkway ran its length; the only possible indication is that the new stone wall was slightly set back from the front of the turrets, which was sufficient to allow for a walkway. When the wall was rebuilt in stone, the turrets were incorporated into the whole.

TURRETS

Very little is known about how the turrets actually looked as none is complete. Most have disappeared altogether, but sufficient remain for archaeologists to be able to draw some conclusions, and there is general evidence from other sources, such as Trajan's column.

Construction and occupation of the line of turrets started around 122. Two were built between each pair of milecastles all along the wall, with an average of 495m (1,625ft) between the turrets. They were positioned to have as large a panorama of the surrounding landscape as possible, both to the north, to spot trouble, but also down into the valleys. It seems they were abandoned during the period of the Antonine Wall when some of them were robbed of their stone – quite probably by the remaining garrisons repurposing the stone. Around 162, when the Antonine Wall was abandoned, the turrets were rebuilt and reoccupied with the exception of those on the western defences along the Cumbrian coast. Around 180, a number of further turrets were abandoned and their doors blocked up. Then, around the turn of the 3rd

▶ *Turret 51B – Leahill – was built around 122 on the lower slope of Allieshaw Rigg. It was demolished in the early 3rd century under Emperor Severus (ruled 193–211) before being refurbished and briefly reoccupied in the 4th century.*

▶ *A few hundred metres west of Banna sits Turret 49B, aka Birdoswald Turret. This replaced the earlier Turf Wall turret and was excavated in 1911 and consolidated for display in 1953–1954. Unusually in this stretch of wall, the turret is bonded to the curtain wall.*

▶ *Another view of the Vallum and Turf Wall near Birdoswald. Some of the dents in the wall were made by local farmers for ease of moving their livestock across the pasture.*

 Milecastle 52
(Bankshead)
Status: No visible remains; replaced Turf Wall predecessor
Type: Short axis; Type III gateways
Builder: Possibly *legio VI Victrix*
Dimensions: 27.5m (90ft) (E–W) by 23.4m (76ft 8in) (N–S)

 Signal Station Pike Hill
Status: Partial remains; most destroyed by roadbuilding
Type: Square and tall (has deep foundations) but at 45-degree angle to the wall
Builder: Unknown; Stanegate period
Dimensions: 6.1sq m (c. 20sq ft)

 Turret 52A (Banks East): Walls visible; replaced nearby turf turret

 Turret 52B: Unknown

 Milecastle 53 (Banks Burn)
Status: No visible remains; turf milecastle underneath/nearby
Type: Long axis; Type III gateways
Builder: Possibly *legio VI Victrix*
Dimensions: 21.9m (71ft 10in) (E–W) by 23.3m (76ft 5in) (N–S)

 Hare Hill curtain wall: Tallest piece of wall; narrow gauge, 2.3m (7ft 6in) wide. Facing stones are a Victorian reconstruction.

 Turret 53A (Hare Hill): Earthworks

Turret 53B (Craggle Hill): Earthworks

◄ *View from Pike Hill Signal Station along the line of the wall to Banks East Turret (Turret 52A), with a short length of wall on either side. It is one of the best-preserved turrets on the wall.*

century, turrets 33B to 41B in the centre of the wall were abandoned and demolished. Others along the line were slowly abandoned as the century progressed.

Because of the existence of broad wing walls on the east and west elevations, it is surmised that the turrets were built before the curtain wall and then incorporated into it using the wings to lock in when the wall was built. Turrets were built of stone to a square plan and rose to a height of around 9m (30ft). The north wall was thickest at about 1m (3ft 3in), with the others around 0.75m (2ft 6in) thick. Entrance was through a ground-level doorway, usually but not always in the south wall, into a room that may have had a shuttered window, although a few glass shards have been found in five turrets. Access to the level above was probably via a ladder. Many turrets have been found to have a stone floor on the upper level although they probably all started with a clay floor and only subsequently improved. Many contain hearthstones for fires and various cooking implements have been found, but no ovens for baking. No evidence has been found for soldiers actually living at the turrets; most likely they were deployed from the nearest fort on a rota to man the turret for a short period. It is thought – judging by the size of the turret – that between four to six men would be standing watch at a time.

The roof shape above the viewing platform is a mystery: some evidence of both roof tiles and slates have been found at a few locations, but it is even possible that a form of thatch was used.

Following excavations at Peel Gap turret (39A) in 1987, theories about the purpose of turrets have changed. It was obvious that this turret was placed between two pre-existing turrets to add line-of-sight views over what before had been dead ground. This points to the logic that the turrets were vital look-out defences and part of the early warning and control system that ran the length of the wall.

PIKE HILL SIGNAL STATION

Signal stations were a remarkably efficient concept for transmitting basic information from the wall. Originally the Romans built two for every (Roman) mile of wall and each was manned by a minimum of six soldiers whose job was to watch for trouble coming from the north and warn the forts of any brewing trouble. The first signal towers were built

▶ *Interior of Banks East Turret. It would have supported two storeys, with the first floor reached by a ladder. Another ladder would have led up to the roof-top observation platform. Soldiers were likely deployed on a rota system from the nearest fort, to man the turrets for a short period of time.* Shutterstock

to communicate along the Stanegate in the early 2nd century. From excavations, it seems that they were turf-and-timber rectangular buildings, with a central timber watch tower, all established on a firm stone foundation. They were surrounded by a wide turf rampart that, in turn, was fronted by a wide ditch.

Lying between Turret 51b and Turret 52a, Pike Hill signal station pre-dates Hadrian's Wall and probably also the Turf Wall, but was later incorporated into the former. It was originally a square tower, 6m by 6m (20ft by 20ft), with deep foundations and, when incorporated into the wall, stood at a 45-degree angle to it. There was a ditch to the north following the line of the

tower. The building of the nearby modern road has, unfortunately, destroyed most of the remains. Now only a 2m (6ft 7in) length of the southeast wall is visible. The tower signalled to Barrock Fell and Gillalees Beacon. It is supposed that it was manned by soldiers garrisoned at Milecastle 52, which was 20 percent larger than other milecastles – one assumes to accommodate extra men for Pike Hill.

▼ *Reconstruction of Banks East Turret – the crenelations are likely but unconfirmed. The turret has an excellent view south but to the north would have relied upon the nearby signal tower mounted atop Pike Hill.* Heritage Images/Getty Images

Milecastle 54
(Randylands)
Status: No visible remains; turf milecastle underneath
Type: Long axis; gateways unknown
Builder: Unknown
Dimensions: 19.3m (63ft 4in) (E–W) by 23.3m (76ft 5in) (N–S)

Turret 54A (Garthside): Turf Wall visible nearby; older collapsed turret

Turret 54B (Howgill): No visible remains

Milecastle 55 (Low Wall)
Status: No visible remains; Turf Wall nearby
Type: Unknown
Builder: Unknown
Dimensions: 22m (72ft 2in) (E–W) by unknown (N–S)

Turret 55A (Dovecote): No visible remains

Turret 55B (Townhead Croft): No visible remains

Milecastle 56
(Walton): Location unknown
Status: Unknown
Type: Unknown
Builder: Unknown

Turret 56A (Sandyside): Unknown

Turret 56B (Cambeck): No traces visible

Camboglanna Fort
Location: Castlesteads; detached from wall
Status: Unexcavated; bath house to NW; parade ground to N near turret 56B; robbed to build Lanercost Priory
Fort: 12th from E; 12km (7.5 miles) from Banna
Built: c. 128
Dimensions: 122sq m (400sq ft) and covered an area of about 1.5ha (3.75 acres)
Gates: NE, NW, SE, SW double-portals
Vicus: Causeway across vallum to SE

CAMBOGLANNA (CASTLESTEADS)

Camboglanna is the only garrison fort to lie between the wall and the Vallum. Situated a short distance south of the wall, it was located on rising ground on a platform overlooking the Cam Beck valley and was probably built by the *legio II Augusta* and *legio VI Victrix* at the same time that the Vallum was constructed.

There has been some debate over the years as to whether this fort is the one known as Banna by the Romans. Currently historians have fixed on Birdoswald as Banna and Castlesteads as Camboglanna. Evidence from coins points to the fort being abandoned by the middle of the 3rd century.

It was probably built over the foundations of an earlier turf-and-timber fort (discovered in the 1930s), but slightly realigned along its northern defences to mirror the new wall. Originally square in plan and covering about 1.5ha (3.75 acres), the fort now appears rectangular thanks to erosion of the river cliff-edge of the platform on the northwestern side.

A military bath house was discovered and excavated in the mid-18th century, some 200m (660ft) north of the fort. Another 100m (330ft) farther north lies ground that is thought to constitute the fort's parade ground – this is surmised from the number of martial altarstones discovered there.

The nearby Vallum passed close to the southern defences. It was accessible from the fort via a causeway opposite the southeast gateway. The *vicus* was nearby on the southern slopes of the hill. Surveys made at the end of the 20th century showed Roman field boundaries to the east.

▼ *Camboglanna Fort is thought to have been built at the same time as the Vallum and is placed between it and the wall. It was the only garrison fort that was not attached to the wall. The stone was robbed by Augustinian monks to build Lanercost Priory, seen here.*

In 1732, an altar stone dedicated by the *legio VI Victrix* was discovered near the eastern gateway. A slab recovered from the *hypocaust* proves that the *cohors I Aelia Dacorum* (Gordian's Own) was at the fort for a period and was aided by the garrison unit *cohors II Tungrorum*.

Altar stones dedicated to Jupiter Best and Greatest state that the mixed infantry and cavalry *cohors Quartae Gallorum* (the Fourth Cohort of Gauls) recruited from central France was probably the first garrison posted here in Hadrian's time. It was later posted on to Vindolanda. The 2nd-century garrison was probably the 1,000-strong mixed infantry and cavalry *cohors I Batavorum* (Batavians). However, the entire cohort cannot have been located here, as the fort is far too small. In turn, it was followed by the 1,000-strong part-mounted *cohors II Tungrorum Milliaria*

Equitata (Tungrians) who left an inscription here dated 1 January 241.

Twenty-one altar stones and inscribed stones have been found around the site. Dedications include seven altars to Jupiter Best and Greatest, and others to Neptune, God of the Sea; three to the Sol Invictus and Mithras; two to the Mother Goddesses of All Nations; and two to Sanguine (Bloody) Mars.

The stone from the fort and for many miles around the wall was robbed to build the Augustinian Lanercost Priory in 1169. All remaining stone was used for Castlesteads House in 1779, while at least 50 percent of the footprint of the fort was used for the walled gardens. Some defensive earthworks hidden in woodland are just discernable, and some scarp along the southeast boundary of the walled garden and a scrap of more obvious scarp in the rose garden.

 Milecastle 57
(Cambeckhill)
Status: Unknown
Type: Unknown
Builder: Unknown

Old Church Fort
to S on Stanegate;
probably dismantled
when Hadrian's Wall
built
Dimensions: 125m
(410ft) (N–S) by
121m (396ft) E–W
occupying 1.5ha
(3.75 acres)

 Turret 57A (Beck): No
traces visible of this
turf turret
Dimensions: 6.1m
(20ft) by 6.9m (22ft
7in)

 Turret 57B: Unknown

 Milecastle 58
(Newtown)
Status: Unknown
Type: Unknown
Builder: Unknown

 Turret 58A: Unknown

 Turret 58B: Unknown

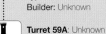 **Milecastle 59** (Old
Wall)
Status: No visible
traces
Type: Unknown
Builder: Unknown

 Turret 59A: Unknown

 Turret 59B: Unknown

Milecastle 60 (High
Strand)
Status: No visible
traces
Type: Unknown
Builder: Unknown

Temporary camp:
Watchclose to S
(under Carlisle Airport
runway)
Dimensions: 0.5ha
(1.4 acres)

 Turret 60A: Unknown

 Turret 60B: Unknown

FORTS NORTH OF THE WALL

▲ *Found on the Maiden Way just south of Bewcastle, this buff sandstone-coloured altar is known as the Annius Victor Fanum Cocidi. It was found in the late 19th century and translates as, 'To the holy god Cocidius, Annius Victor, legionary centurion'. Cocidius is the Germanic god of war.*

A number of forts were built and maintained north of the wall for reasons that are not completely clear. They certainly served as an advanced early warning system, and staging posts for units advancing deeper into Scotland. They could also have protected friendly locals from raids. All were about half a day's march northwards from Hadrian's Wall. These forts include Bewcastle and Netherby in the west and High Rochester and Risingham on Dere Street in the east. It appears the forts remained active until the early 4th century, when they were abandoned. This has been concluded from the fact that the last coins found there all date from the early 4th century.

This withdrawal may be due to one of several reasons: Emperor Constantine was expected to visit Britain in 312 – a special coin was even issued – to garner soldiers for his battles closer to Rome, so troops were removed from the outposts to support him. Alternatively, it has been suggested that the lords of the Scottish Lowlands became Romanised and provided buffer states between Roman Britain and the hostile northern tribes, rendering the outposts unnecessary, although very little evidence supports this theory.

BLATOBULGIUM (BIRRENS)

Originally built around AD80 and sited to control the northern approaches to the Solway, this was one of the earliest Roman outposts. Blatobulgium was constructed under the direction of governor Gnaeus Julius Agricola by *legio XX Valeria Victrix*. It appears to have been rebuilt in the Antonine period by men of the *legio VI Victrix* (borrowed from Eboracum) at which time it had a turf rampart, timber buildings and a central stone range. Some time later, this was demolished and replaced with a much larger stone fort that had extensive ditches and a turf rampart laid over stone foundations. It was destroyed then rebuilt in 158.

The first garrison billeted here was probably the 1,000-strong mixed infantry and cavalry *cohors I Nerviorum Germanorum milliaria equitata*. It was followed by the 1,000-strong part-mounted *cohors II Tungrorum milliaria Equitata* (attested here on nine inscriptions), who also served at Castlesteads.

The fort remained manned after the Antonine Wall was abandoned. Pottery evidence suggests that the Romans left in 184 after Ulpius Marcellus quelled the native rebellions in the north and consolidated his strength around Hadrian's Wall. However, finds of 3rd-century pottery point to a reoccupation.

FANUM COCIDI (BEWCASTLE)

Situated about half a day's march from Hadrian's Wall, the outpost fort at Bewcastle was built during the Hadrianic period. It is shaped as an irregular hexagon, with no two sides or angles the same and covers roughly 2.4ha (6 acres). Originally built of turf and timber, the fort was revetted with stone cladding in the mid-2nd century. It was in direct communication with the wall fort at Banna via two signal stations. Inscriptions found around the site claim that the fort was built or renovated by *legio VI Victrix*, *legio XX Valeria Victrix* and *legio II Augusta*.

Nine Roman altars have been found here, with six of them dedicated to Cocidius, the Germanic god of war. Excavations have unearthed a number of coins that imply that the fort was occupied until the late 4th century. The only identified unit known to have been stationed here is the 1,000-strong infantry *cohors I Dacorum* (Dacians) who dedicated an altar to Jupiter Best and Greatest. It was probably occupied by *cohors I Nervana Germanorum* in the 3rd century. The fort was abandoned in 367.

CASTRA EXPLORATORUM (NETHERBY)

Also about half a day's march north of Hadrian's Wall and situated roughly 30km (18 miles) between Birrens in Dumfries and Galloway and Carlisle in Cumbria, the first Castra Exploratorum (Camp of the Scouts) was probably a pre-Hadrianic fort before the authenticated fort and was likely situated to look northwest across the Esk and into hostile territory. This outpost was manned by part-mounted auxiliary units comprising men recruited from tribes noted for their hunting and tracking abilities. Their task was to scout enemy territory and probably to act as protection for the constructors of the wall itself.

No physical evidence of the c. 3ha (7.5 acre) fort remains, it having long since disappeared underneath the gardens and house of Netherby Hall; the 15th-century tower house is thought to have been constructed from the fort's material. However, it seems that there were a minimum of two military encampments on the site and possibly two more. The first known garrison was the 500-strong infantry *cohors I Nervanorum*, stationed c. 125. It was followed later by the 1,000-strong *cohors I Aelii Hispanorum Milliaria* with 300 horses.

The builders of the first Hadrianic fort were *legio II Augusta*. Both of the other legions (*legio VI Victrix* and *legio XX Valeria Victrix*) were also involved at different dates, and later still, *cohors I Hispanorum*,

▶ *Today, the site of Fanum Cocidi (Bewcastle) shows only the shape of its irregular outline, as the stone has been entirely robbed for nearby buildings. Situated half a day's march north of the wall, it was in contact with the fort at Banna (Birdoswald) via two signal stations.*

who left inscriptions recording their work at intervals between c. 213 and 222. A number of altar stones have been found here, with about half of them dedicated to gods of Germanic origin (Cocidius, Huetirus, Moguntus and Belatucader) as well as to the more usual Roman deities (Jupiter, Fortune, Apollo, Silvanus and Mars).

BREMENIUM (HIGH ROCHESTER)

On Dere Street, some 38km (23.5 miles) north of Coria, Bremenium dates to the Flavian period. Occupied during Trajan's reign, it was empty as the wall was built, but reoccupied during the Antonine period when it was garrisoned by *cohors I Lingonum Equitata* – a part-mounted unit mainly from the Bourgogne region of central France.

Bremenium was extensively rebuilt from Severus's reign, including the addition of *ballistaria* (catapault platforms). Within the ramparts, the fort covered a little over 1.6ha (4 acres) but outside this were 26 ditches, 13 of which were to the north.

The fort's later garrison was *cohors I Fida Vardullorum Antoninianae Equitata Milliaria Civium Romanorum* (The First Faithful Cohort of Antoninus's Own Vardulli, part-mounted, 1,000-strong, citizens of Rome). Other inscription attest that *cohors I Delmatarum* (from Dalmatia) was here for a period of unknown duration and mention *numerus exploratorum Bremenio* – the Bremenium scouts.

HABITANCUM (RISINGHAM)

Dere Street crosses just east of the fort, which lies in open farmland about 25km (15 miles) north of Coria. A number of the foundations are still visible in turf outline and the surrounding defensive ditches are still very present – the fort covered almost 1.5ha (4 acres).

For such a relatively unknown Roman outpost, an astonishing 56 stone inscriptions have been found. Thanks to these, we know more than usual about the names of the units that served here. One of the stones says that *legio VI Victrix* built it. Another stone claims that *cohors I Vangionum* (a Germanic tribe) built here. Other stones name the various garrisons as *cohors IV Gallorum Equitata*, *cohors I Vangionum milliaria equitata,* and mention the *numerus exploratorum Habitanco* – the Habitancum scouts. There are few signs of occupation before the 2nd century, but it is likely to have been built then. The fort was rebuilt during the Severan period and continued in service until mid-4th century, with the 367 attacks the final blow.

The gods worshipped at Risingham were Jupiter Best and Greatest, Jupiter Dolichenus (venerated especially by Syrian auxiliaries, this was a cult of Jupiter linked to the eastern god Doliche), Hercules, Victorious Mars, Fortuna the Homebringer, Moguns, the Overseas Mother Goddess, Diana, Cocidius, the Gods of the Locale and the Spirit of the Emperor.

▶ *This sand-stone altar was discovered built into the foundations of Bewcastle Church. Its inscription reads: 'To the holy god Cocidius, Quintus Peltrasius Maximus, tribune, promoted from cornicularius to their Eminences, the Praetorian Prefects, willingly and deservedly fulfilled his vow.'*

 Milecastle 61
(Wallhead)
Status: Unknown
Type: Unknown
Builder: Unknown

Temporary camp:
Moss Side 2 3.9ha
(9.7 acres)

Temporary camp:
Moss Side 1ha
(2.4 acres)

 Turret 61A: Unknown

 Turret 61B: Unknown

 Milecastle 62 (Walby East)
Status: No visible remains
Type: Long axis
Builder: Unknown
Dimensions: Internal, 17.8m (58ft 5in) (E–W) by 14.6m (78ft 8in) (N–S)

 Turret 62A: Unknown

 Turret 62B: Unknown

 Milecastle 63 (Walby West)
Status: Unknown
Type: Unknown
Builder: Unknown

 Turret 63A: Unknown

 Turret 63B: Unknown

 Milecastle 64
(Drawdykes)
Status: No visible remains
Type: Short axis
Builder: Unknown
Dimensions: Internal, 16.5m (54ft 1in) (E–W) by 24m (78ft 8in) (N–S)

 Turret 64A: Unknown

 Turret 64B: Unknown

 Milecastle 65 (Tarraby)
Status: No visible remains
Type: Short axis
Builder: Unknown

 Turret 65A: Unknown

 Turret 65B: Probably demolished when Uxelodunum/ Petrianum built

UXELODUNUM AND LUGUVALIUM

▶ *Statue in a car park in Uxelodunum (Stanwix) marking the location of the wall and fort. The largest fort on the wall, it was also sometimes known as Petrianium after the ala Petriana (a Gaulish cavalry unit), that was probably stationed there.*

UXELODUNUM AND LUGUVALIUM

These two important Roman forts almost face each other on either side of the River Eden and it was across this divide that the third and final bridge across the wall was constructed. Uxeldodunum was the largest and probably most important fort on the entire wall, as it was the military administrative centre for the frontier. Uxelodunum may have been the original western terminus of the wall, meaning that the extension of the wall to Bowness was added later, when it became apparent that it was needed – perhaps after the river had proved too fordable nearer the sea.

UXELODUNUM/PETRIANUM (STANWIX)

It seems that Uxelodunum was generally known as Petrianum among contemporary Romans, a name adapted from the *ala Petriana*, the garrison first known to us at Stanwix.

The first fort was a turf-and-timber building that had its long axis parallel to the Turf Wall, with the wall itself forming its northern defences. This indicates that it likely housed an infantry garrison. The next fort was built in stone and was probably built when the Turf Wall was rebuilt.

At a somewhat later date, and maybe in Rome itself, the workings of Hadrian's Wall were

▼ *View from Uxelodunum back over the River Eden. Rivers were substantial obstacles hindering cross-country movement and so good fords and bridges were important strategic locations.*

▲ *Carlisle Castle sits directly over most of the Roman fort of Luguvalium. Built to guard the strategic crossing over the River Eden, Luguvalium was superseded in importance by nearby Uxelodunum (Stanwix) and seems to have become mainly concerned with logistics and supplies for the western end of Hadrian's Wall.*

reviewed and it was decided that Uxelodunum would become the garrison fort for the *ala Petriana*, the largest cavalry unit in Britannia, whose commander was the most senior officer on the wall. (Although no physical evidence of the unit's presence has been found here.) This meant 1,000 horses and men had to be accommodated, so the fort needed considerable alteration. The northern and southwestern rampart walls were demolished, as were all the buildings within the fort. The defences were pushed farther northwest and southwest and included three large double gateways (two on the north and one central in the northwestern rampart) beyond the line of the wall, as was the requirement for a cavalry fort. Three ditches were dug in front of the northern rampart. The fort now enclosed something over 3.75ha (9.25 acres).

The forts were built by the *legio VI Victrix* and later by *legio XX Valeria Victrix*. The only altar stone dedicated to a deity is one to the Mother Goddesses of the Household.

The fort now largely lies beneath Saint Michael's Church. The stump of the southeastern rampart is visible in the churchyard and a small section of the northern rampart can be seen in a hotel car park.

LUGUVALIUM (CARLISLE)

Few remains can still be seen of the fort or town. However, many Roman artefacts associated with the wall are now in Tullie House Museum in the city. Luguvalium guarded one of the most important river crossings into Scotland and the timber fort here pre-existed Hadrian's Wall and has been dated to AD72–73. It was probably the original western terminus of the Stanegate.

The second fort was also timber and located just south of the castle to guard the crucial River Eden crossing. It was certainly occupied from AD78–79 until it was demolished in 103. The

Uxelodunum Fort
Location: Stanwix, north bank of Eden
Status: Few remains
Fort: 13th from E; 13km (8 miles) from Camboglanna; 13km (8 miles) from Old Church on the Stanegate
Built: Turf infantry fort – c. 121; stone infantry fort – c. 160s; cavalry fort – c. 200
Dimensions: 177m (580ft) by 213m (700ft) when complete, covering an area of about 3.8ha (9.3 acres)
Gates: N allows road to Castra Exploratum at Netherby; S opens out to Stanegate
Vicus: Causeway across Vallum to S

Milecastle 66 (Stanwix Bank)
Status: No visible remains
Type: Unknown
Builder: Unknown

Eden Bridge

Luguvalium Fort
Location: Carlisle, S of River Eden, on the Stanegate
Status: Few remains *in situ*; bath house
Fort: Separate from wall
Built: AD72; demolished and rebuilt 103–105; stone fort erected c. 165
Dimensions: up to 3.8ha (9.3 acres)
Gates: N allows road to Castra Exploratum at Netherby; S opens out to Stanegate
Vicus: Causeway across Vallum to S

Turret 66A: Unknown

Turret 66B: Unknown

Milecastle 67 (Stainton)
Status: Unknown
Type: Unknown
Builder: Unknown

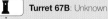
Turret 67A: Unknown

Turret 67B: Unknown

Milecastle 68 (Boomby Gill): Unknown

Temporary camps: Naotler Hill 1 and 2 to W of wall

▲ *Carlisle Castle outer gatehouse and keep. The castle was built into a formidable fortress and Carlisle became a vital border city in the defence of northwestern England. Nearby Tullie House Museum contains a wealth of local and western-wall Roman artefacts.*

next timber fort was built immediately on the same site, to much the same specifications, and was occupied by a garrison well into the Hadrianic period. The garrison stationed there appears to have been reduced over time, until it was withdrawn altogether during the Antonine period. By the time the garrison was returned after the abandonment of the Antonine Wall, the importance of Luguvalium had transferred to the fort at Uxelodunum, only 800m (half a mile) away. The latter became the most important fort on the western side of the country.

A new – and this time stone – fort was built at Luguvalium in c. 200 by men of the *legio XX Valeria Victrix*. They stayed until sometime between 275 and 325, by which time the fort was garrisoned by a legionary cohort that appears to have been mainly concerned with logistic affairs and quartermaster's functions (much as the cohort at Coria did).

Parts of the fort now lie under Carlisle Castle keep, but lengths of the southern and eastern ramparts lie underground between the castle and the A595 road. The eastern ramparts have been extensively studied and have enabled archaeologists to establish that the successive forts were all built on much the same footprint – a platform some 3.2ha (8 acres) in size – and to the same alignments.

Successive forts were built by the *legio II Augusta*, the *legio XX Valeria Victrix* and the *legio IX Hispana*.

The units known to have served at Luguvalium are the *ala Petriana* from Gaul and the *ala Augusta*. But due to Luguvalium's lack of importance not much else is recorded. A number of inscribed votive stones – including one to Mars Ocelus – have been found, as well as 14 altars (including one to Mars Belatucader and another to Victorious Mars) and nine tombstones. Luguvalium established the only known school of British stone carvers and masons working with the local sandstone. It lasted between the Antonine period until well into the 3rd century.

The *vicus* at Luguvalium first developed on the south bank of the Eden and then later spread to the north as an additional smaller settlement. Due to the longevity of Roman settlement in the town and its important location, the *vicus* apparently thrived. The defences of Luguvalium encompassed some 28ha (70 acres) and became an important trading point and leisure area. This flourishing civilian area continued well into the 5th century.

▶ *Although not much remains* in situ *of the Romans in Carlisle, the city is proud of its heritage and guides visitors around its many Roman sites. It is thanks to them that it became established as one of the most important trading and commercial cities in the northwest.*

A great many Roman soldiers retired and remained here and it seems that Luguvalium was awarded a civil charter as a consequence.

CROSSING THE EDEN

The Romans built a bridge – the third and final bridge on the wall – to cross the river Eden and sited Milecastle 66 on the north side across the river from Luguvalium. The river rises on Mallerstang Common, high on the limestone fells, flows north and westwards across the North Pennines to arrive at Carlisle, and then merges with other rivers to run into the Solway Firth. One of the sandstone blocks that comprised the Roman bridge has a carelessly cut inscription that reads 'Century of Vesnius Viator'. This is the authorisation from an inspecting officer that he has checked the stonemason's work and passed it.

The river was dredged in 1951 when almost 100 stones from the original Roman bridge were recovered. Many of them were placed in nearby Bitts Park.

▼ *Carlisle Roman bath house excavation in September 2017. It was discovered during work to move Carlisle Cricket Club's pavilion, which had been damaged during Storm Desmond. Many tiles show the Imperial stamp. An important discovery was an inscription stone with the name of* ala Petriana – *the first such to be found in Carlisle.*

Peter Savin

Temporary camps: Boomby Lane 1 and 2 to W of wall

 Turret 68A: Unknown

 Turret 68B: Unknown

 Milecastle 69 (Sourmilk Bridge): Unknown

 Turret 69A: Unknown

 Turret 69B: Unknown

 Milecastle 70 (Braelee): Unknown

 Turret 70A: Unknown

 Turret 70B: Unknown

 Milecastle 71 (Wormanby): No visible remains

Temporary camp: Burgh-by-Sands to S of wall

 Turret 71A: Unknown

Turret 71B: Unknown

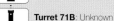 **Aballava Fort**

Location: Burgh-by-Sands
Status: No visible remains; robbed for local buildings
Fort: 7.25km (4.5 miles) W of Uxelodunum
Built: First, 800m (half mile) back from Turf Wall; second, infantry fort, built c. 130s, is aligned on the stone wall
Dimensions: c. 170m (557ft) (N–S) by c. 135m (445ft) (W–E), covering 2.3ha (5.75 acres)
Gates: Originally N, W and E gates N of wall; stone fort aligned with wall with W, S and E entrances to S
Vicus: To SE

 Milecastle 72 (Fauld Farm)
Status: No visible remains
Type: Originally turf replaced with stone
Builder: Unknown
Dimensions: Internal, 19m (62ft 4in) wide (E–W); N–S unknown

 Turret 72A: Unknown

 Turret 72B: No visible remains; Turf Wall turret excavated

FROM LUGUVALIUM TO CONCAVATA

▼ *Aerial view east of Concavata (Drumburgh) The straight line of the wall is visible between the road and the shore as a cleft running from bottom left to the centre of the photo, then slightly altering direction to run to the top right.*

ABALLAVA (BURGH BY SANDS)

Centuries of erosion from both wind and waves around the Solway Firth and Cumbrian coast have obliterated almost all traces of Roman occupation. This was, however, a strategically important area, as hostile marine raiding parties from the north and west constantly harried the coast.

The area around Burgh by Sands is dotted with Roman military encampments, which were all placed at this strategic location to guard two nearby Solway fords, frequently used by raiding parties from the northern tribes, especially the Selgovae to the north and possibly also the Novantae in the northwest. Aside from the Hadrianic fortifications, there are two earlier auxiliary forts and a number of marching camps. Evidence of a small civilian settlement has also been found outside the fort's southeastern defences.

Probably the first Roman building was the watchtower that lies near the southeast gate of the earliest fort. The four-post timber tower was protected by a circular V-shaped ditch 1.8m (6ft) deep and 2.3m (7ft 6in) wide, accessed by a southeast gateway and surrounded by a timber-fronted rampart up to 4.6m (15ft) wide. Pottery shards date the tower to about 120, but it was not in service long before it was demolished to make way for the first fort.

The earliest fort was built on the crest of a high ridge and covered about 2ha (4.9 acres). When it was excavated in 1978–1979 it was revealed to be one of the original forts built specifically for Hadrian's Wall but, for reasons unknown, set 800m (half a mile) back from the original Turf Wall on the site of an earlier watchtower. It was protected by a 4.9m (16ft)-wide ditch and revetted rampart of beaten clay. The ditch was later expanded to 7.3m (24ft).

The second fort was built on the site of Turret 71B and across the line of the Turf Wall to avoid the marshy ground to the south. It was probably built to shelter an infantry garrison and, accordingly, the stone wall was realigned to incorporate the new fort along its northern side. Early 20th-century excavations point to the fort being built at the same time as the wall was being rebuilt in stone. It has been hard to ascertain the size of the fort, but best estimates suggest an area of a little over 2.4ha (6 acres). It was garrisoned until well into the late 4th century.

The third fort was not discovered until it was revealed by aerial photography in 1977, when it was found 1.2km (three-quarters of a mile) west–southwest of the wall fort. The site showed two successive large forts, which were occupied during the first half of the 2nd century. The first fort covered about 2ha (5 acres) and the second almost 3.4ha (8.5 acres). The forts appear to run alongside a Roman road that followed the lumpy ridge of Fingland Rigg, which was a westwards extension of the Stanegate frontier system to an auxiliary fort at Kirkbride.

The first known garrison was the 500-strong *ala I Tungrorum* cavalry troops from Gallia Belgica, here in the 2nd century. It was followed by the *cohors I Nervana Germanorum milliaria equitata*, 1,000-strong part-mounted Germans; then the *cuneus Frisiavonum Aballavensium* and then, in 253 onwards, *numerus Maurorum Aurelianorum* – the latter possibly black Numidian cavalry.

Evidence has been found of a small *vicus* to the southeast of the fort, where a damaged tombstone remembered Julius Pius, a native of Dacia. Over the years, eight altar stones have been found here, plus three damaged tombstones.

▶ *Aballava (Burgh-by-Sands) Fort was built at least three times on three different locations. The footprint of the Hadrianic fort is almost completely obscured by the parish church, which inevitably was built with stone robbed from the wall, as was much of the original town.*

The footprint of the Hadrianic wall fort is now almost completely covered by the churchyard. Stone was raided from the wall to build the Church of St. Michael, which now sits on the southern defence line of the fort. The rest of the fort and its buildings were taken to build the town.

There are four temporary marching camps at nearby Grinsdale and another at Beaumont camp.

▼ *Around 253 the fort was garrisoned by* numerus Maurorum Aurelianorum*, who are thought to have been a 500-strong Numidian cavalry unit mustered from the Roman province of Mauretania, now modern-day Morocco. Researchers hope to discover whether their distant descendants still live around the Borders.*

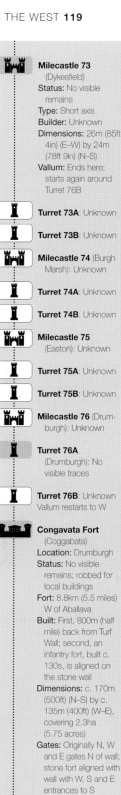

Milecastle 73
(Dykesfield)
Status: No visible remains
Type: Short axis
Builder: Unknown
Dimensions: 26m (85ft 4in) (E–W) by 24m (78ft 9in) (N–S)
Vallum: Ends here; starts again around Turret 76B

Turret 73A: Unknown

Turret 73B: Unknown

Milecastle 74 (Burgh Marsh): Unknown

Turret 74A: Unknown

Turret 74B: Unknown

Milecastle 75 (Easton): Unknown

Turret 75A: Unknown

Turret 75B: Unknown

Milecastle 76 (Drumburgh): Unknown

Turret 76A (Drumburgh): No visible traces

Turret 76B: Unknown Vallum restarts to W

Congavata Fort (Coggabata)
Location: Drumburgh
Status: No visible remains; robbed for local buildings
Fort: 8.8km (5.5 miles) W of Aballava
Built: First, 800m (half mile) back from Turf Wall; second, an infantry fort, built c. 130s, is aligned on the stone wall
Dimensions: c. 170m (500ft) (N–S) by c. 135m (400ft) (W–E), covering 2.3ha (5.75 acres)
Gates: Originally N, W and E gates N of wall; stone fort aligned with wall with W, S and E entrances to S
Vicus: To SE

Milecastle 77 (Raven Bank): Unknown

Turret 77A (Drumburgh): No visible traces

Turret 77B: Unknown

FROM CONCAVATA TO MAIA

▼ *Nothing remains to be seen of Maia (Bowness-on-Solway) Fort, despite it being the second-largest fort along Hadrian's wall (second only to Uxelodunum). It was built parallel to the coast to guard the most westerly fording point of the Solway Firth and is now covered by buildings.*

CONCAVATA (DRUMBURGH)

Situated on a sandy hillock (actually a drumlin) on the edge of Burgh Marsh, Concavata looks over the extensive mudflats of the Esk and Eden estuaries. It is centrally located between Milecastle 76 and Turret 76A but with no visible remains, other than where the Carlisle–Bowness road makes a right-angle turn in the middle of Drumburgh village showing the perimeter of the western corner of the fort. Short stretches of the Vallum are visible to the northeast.

The Roman name for the fort is recorded in the 5th-century *Notitia Dignitatum* as Congauata. The site was excavated in the early 20th century when the wall foundations were found to be 2.9m (9ft 6in) wide. They also discovered that the fort was built after the wall. Three inscribed stones have

been found here, and the dimensions of the fort imply that it housed an auxiliary infantry cohort of 500 men, but there is no record of who the original garrison was. In the 4th century the garrison was the 500-strong infantry unit the *cohors II Lingonum*, recruited from tribes in upper Germany.

MAIA (BOWNESS-ON-SOLWAY)

Built on a clay platform promontory about 15m (50ft) above the southern side of the Solway Firth at its most westerly fording point, Maia was once the second-largest fort on the wall, covering about 3ha (7.5 acres) and was aligned parallel to the coast, lying west–southwest by east–northeast. The fortifications ran down past the low-tide mark. A long stone building near the west gate (which runs parallel to the ramparts) may have been a

▶ *On a sunny day the garrison had a clear view over the firth to Scotland, where the hostile northern tribes lived. The Roman fortifications ran down past the low-tide mark, but would have been constantly washed away by winter tides and weather.*

barracks; it was rebuilt as a larger building around the early 3rd century. The nearby milecastles and watchtowers along the Solway Firth run all the way to the fort at Kirkbride, linked by a rampart flanked on either side by a parallel ditch. The rampart was probably augmented by a palisade of wooden stakes, but these appear to have been constantly eroded by the waters and they stopped being maintained after a while. The fort may have been occupied until the late 4th century

The first structure here was Milecastle 80, built of timber and turf, but when the nearby wall was built up in stone, the milecastle was demolished and was subsequently lost under the fort. Then, a layer of white clay was laid over the subsoil to support the inner buildings of the new timber and turf fort around the end of the 120s. This was rebuilt in stone about 40 years later.

It is possible that the fort was named after the goddess Maia, who is one of the Pleiades (the Seven Sisters), the daughter of Atlas and Pleione and later the mother of Mercury. Alternatively it could be from Maior – larger – as Maia was the second largest fort on the wall after Uxelodunum/ Petrianum (Stanwix). An inscribed altar dedicated by a tribute indicates that the garrison was probably a mixed cohort that numbered around 800, with 10 centuries.

The Vallum suddenly turns south here and was originally intended to continue along the coast.

Outside the fort's south gate lay a small *vicus* that has yielded a few Roman coins and a number of civilian tombstones. The Tullie House Museum in Carlisle displays one that was probably carved at the Romano-British school there and shows a seated woman feeding a small dog while holding a dove in the other hand.

For 65km (40 miles) south down the northwest coast of Cumbria, the Romans built a number of fortlets and signal towers, now called the Western Sea Defences, and stopped just south of Maryport.

 Milecastle 78
(Kirkland)
Status: No visible remains
Type: Long axis
Builder: Unknown
Dimensions: 19.2m (63ft) (E–W) by 20.7m (67ft 11in) (N–S)

 Turret 78A (Kirkland): No visible traces

Turret 78B: Unknown

 Milecastle 79 (Solway House)
Status: No visible remains
Type: Turf wall short axis; stone wall, square
Builder: Unknown
Dimensions: Turf, 14.9m (48ft 11in) (E–W) by 12.5m (41ft) (N–S); Stone, internal, 17.7m (58ft)

Temporary camps: Brackenrigg 1 and 2 to S of wall

 Turret 79A (Kirkland): No visible traces

Turret 79B (Jeffrey Croft): Most westerly turret on the wall, free-standing

Temporary camp: Knockcross N of wall

 Maia (Mais) Fort
Location: Bowness-on-Solway
Status: No visible remains
Fort: 5km (3 miles) west of Congavata
Built: First, for turf wall; second, stone with wall joining at SE and continuing from NW
Dimensions: c. 420m (130ft) (N–S) by c. 220m (710ft) (W–E), covering 2.8ha (7 acres)
Gates: No N (on sea cliff)
Vicus: To S of fort

Milecastle 80
Status: Unknown; probably replaced by fort
Type: Long axis
Builder: Unknown

THE WESTERN SEA DEFENCES

ALAUNA/CARVETIORUM (MARYPORT)

There is little tangible evidence for the Western Sea Defences – the further extension of the frontier fortifications down the Cumbrian coast. Alauna was an important, if not vital, Roman depot and garrison town south of the Solway Firth and it made sense for the Romans to continue the string of fortlets and watchtowers, but nobody knows where the western/southern terminus of the frontier was. Some historians have suggested it may have just petered out. Milefort 25 has been placed with some certainty at the southern end of Maryport, so they seem to have continued beyond the fort. We also know there was a Roman fort at Burrow Wells near Workington (Axelodunum) and another at Moresay (Gabrosentum) near Whitehaven. These probably formed part of the frontier, although no firm archaeological evidence has been able to confirm this. It is possible, albeit unlikely, the frontier stretched even as far south as the fort at Ravenglass (Glannaventa).

On land originally belonging to the Carvetii tribe (which accounts for the title suffix), this site is only mentioned once in ancient literature. The fort overlooked the Solway Firth and was possibly the administrative centre of the Western Sea Defences – this has been deduced from the size of its footprint. However, virtually nothing remains of the fort although many altar stones have been found around the locality, including 23 dedicated to Jupiter Optimus Maximus.

The fort was originally built on Emperor Hadian's orders by legionaries from the *legio II Augusta* and *XX Valeria Victrix*. It was used as the command headquarters and supply base for all the outposts situated south down the coast. Later work was likely done by the succeeding *cohors I Delmatarum* garrison. Further work was done in the mid-3rd century by detachments from the *legio XX Valeria Victrix*.

The dedicated altars found at Alauna indicate the units billeted here. The first unit to occupy the fort was probably the 500-strong *cohors I Hispanorum equitata*, a part-mounted unit recruited from the Roman Spanish provinces who occupied the fort from about 124–140. They were followed by the 500-strong *cohors I Delmatarum* comprised of tribesmen from the Adriatic coast of present-day Croatia; they stayed about 20 years. A later-attested auxiliary regiment that arrived in the late Antonine period was the 500-strong *cohors I Baetasiorum CR* recruited from Germania Inferior (modern western Germany). They were rewarded with Roman citizenship after their campaigning

▼ Milefortlet 21 sits as high up as possible on this stretch of the Cumbrian coast at Swarthy Hill. It was discovered in 1968, thanks to crop marks revealed by aerial photography. It had two gates, one facing the sea, the other the land. Excavated in 1990–1991, it was only built and occupied during the Hadrianic period.

▲ *Aerial view over Maryport. The outline earthworks of Alauna Carvetiorum Fort is visible to the right and shows its commanding views across the end of the Solway Firth and southwards down the coast. Its size suggests that Alauna was the administrative centre for the Western Defences.*

▼ *This fortlet is the only remaining visible evidence of the string of defensive fortlets and turrets along the western end of Hadrian's Wall. It had a 6m (19ft 6in)-thick defensive wall surrounded on three sides by a 7.5m (24ft 6in)-wide ditch, with the seaward aspect open.*

Mileforts situated every Roman mile ran south down the coast. Two towers were located between each fort.

Tower 0A: Unknown

Tower 0B: Unknown

Milefortlet 1 (Biglands House): no visible remains
Three phases; final dimensions 40m (130ft) by 50m (164ft)

Tower 1A: Unknown

Tower 1B: Unknown

Milefort 2: Unknown

Tower 2A: Unknown

Tower 2B: Unknown

Milefort 3 (Pasture House): No visible remains

Tower 3A: Unknown

Tower 3B: Unknown

Milefort 4 (Herd Hill): No visible remains

Tower 4A: Unknown

Tower 4B: Two palisade structures followed by stone tower

Kirkbride Fort
Location: Kirkbride
Status: No visible remains
Fort: 9.5km (6 miles) to Aballava; 5.6km (3.5 miles) S of Maia
Built: AD80 and then rebuilt as part of Stanegate defences
Dimensions: c. 190m (625ft) (N–S) by c.175m (575ft) (W–E), covering 2.8ha (7 acres)
Gates: No N (on sea cliff)
Vicus: To S of fort

Milefort 5 (Cardurnock): No visible remains

Tower 5A: Unknown

Tower 5B: Unknown

▶ *The best sequence of Roman altars found anywhere in the Roman Empire was discovered at Alauna. They are now in Senhouse Museum. Their inscriptions state the names of the military units and their commanders and many of them are dedicated to Jupiter Best and Greatest.*

Paul Beston

work in Scotland 139–142, as indicated by the designation *CR*.

The *principia* building lies in the centre of the fort and has a clearly defined strong room. Excavations dating back to 1880 revealed what was possibly a Mithraeum just east of the fort, as the remains are very similar to the Mithraeum found at Brocolitia.

▼ *The stone from the fort was comprehensively robbed to build the nearby town of Maryport in the 18th century. However, all the inscription stones were rescued and a record was made of the findings, so we know something of its existence.*

With 0.75m (2ft 6in)-thick stone walls, it measures 14m by 7.6m (46ft by 25ft), with a stone shaft with a carving of snakes indicating Mithras. Another building nearby, which has been suggested as a circular temple dedicated to the Mother Goddess, has an outside diameter of 10.4m (34ft).

In 2012, an intact altar was discovered, face down in a large pit at the edge of Alauna. It seems to have been used as a foundation stone for a massive timber edifice that once sat on the highest point of the ridge overlooking the fort and the Solway Firth. Archaeologists surmise that this shows that the altar had lost its significance, as it

▶ *Senhouse Museum's collection was started by the Senhouse family in the 1570s. It contains some of the most important Romano-British remains so far discovered. It is located beside Alauna and has an observation tower overlooking the site.*

was used as a mere building block – but whether we can generalise about other altars from this specific is open for discussion. This altar bore a dedication to the god Jupiter Best and Greatest. It has been dated to the 2nd or 3rd century and was inscribed on behalf of Titus Attius Tutor,

▼ *Almost all of the temples dedicated to Mithras are found in military areas – such as Brocolitia and, possibly, Alauna. The reconstructed mid-3rd century Mithraeum, in the City of London, shows a similar shape and size to those that would have been on the wall.* Richard Baker/In Pictures via Getty Images

commander of the *cohors I Baetasiorum*. It is on display at the Roman museum in town alongside other altars found here.

The fort was largely robbed of its stone in the 18th century to build the town of Maryport, although a man was hired at the time to record and rescue all inscribed stones, so at least some record and substance of the fort exists.

Alauna had a substantial and thriving *vicus* extending out along the road to the north and east of the fort. It is estimated to have been occupied for 280 years. In time, this became the location of Maryport. Among other finds here are two altar

Milefort 6–8: No known mileforts around the estuaries, but they possibly existed, so were given numbers accordingly

Milefort 9 (Skinburness): No visible remains
Dimensions: 65m (213ft) by 61m (200ft)

Tower 9A: Unknown

Tower 9B: Unknown

Milefort 10 (East Cote): Unknown

Tower 10A: Unknown

Tower 10B: Unknown

Milefortlet 11 (East Cote): Unknown

Tower 11A: Unknown

Tower 11B: Unknown

Milefort 12 (Bitterlees): no visible remains

Tower 12A: Excavated 1966
Dimensions: 6m (19ft 8in) by 6m (19ft 8in) (later reduced)

Tower 12B: Excavated 1956

Milefort 13: Unknown

Tower 13A: Excavated 1954
Dimensions: 3.75m (12ft 4in) by 3.75m (12ft 4in)

Tower 13B: Excavated 1880
Dimensions: 6m (19ft 8in) by 6m (19ft 8in)

Milefort 14: Unknown

Tower 14A: Unknown

Tower 14B: Unknown

stones dedicated by a women named Hermionae, one to the goddess Juno, and the other:

'VIRTUTI AUGUSTAE [....]IANA QUINTI FILIA HERMIONAE VSLLM'
('To the Valour of the Emperor [...]iana Hermionae, daughter of Quintus, gladly, willingly, and deservedly fulfilled her vow')

ROMAN ALTARS

The Romans were in thrall to their gods and worshipped them both in public and private. The state religion involved the worship of a pantheon of gods like Jupiter and Mars, and involved rituals and festivities where offerings of food, wine and animal sacrifices were given to the gods. This veneration also included ancestor worship (each household would have had its own *lares*) and, in particular, the worship of previous emperors and the imperial family.

Soldiers – many from distant parts of the empire – had their own favourite gods and were also prone to show interest in local deities. In Britain, suitably martial gods were Belatucadros or Cocidi – both equated with Mars. Bewcastle was called Fanum Cocidii – Temple of Cocidius. Then there was Sol Invictus, a patron of soldiers, and the god Mithras, whose inscriptions also refer to the god Sol Invictus, although there was no link between the two religions. Mithras worship came in at the end of the 1st century AD and faded out by the early 4th century. Sol Invictus became an official cult of the empire in 274 and continued on into the 6th century, appearing on the coins of many emperors.

The temple was an important place in Roman life and the altar was the most important feature associated with it. The altar was most often placed in front of the temple steps and was usually dedicated to the named deity of the temple by an important citizen, often to fulfil a vow or as a plea for a particular favour. Nearby were often placed smaller, temporary alters to other deities who were associated with the main god or the location. Altars could also be placed at significant locations such as important crossroads or the boundary of a forest.

In 2009 a massive 1.5 tonne stone altar was unearthed at Vindolanda and, most unusually, it was discovered inside the fort. The inscription shows it was dedicated to Jupiter of Doliche, whose cult centre was in present-day southern Turkey. He was originally an ancient weather deity, whose cult spread with the soldiers across the empire, especially in frontier provinces. It was dedicated by Sulpicius Pudens, commanding officer of the *cohors IV Gallorum* (from modern France) in the 3rd century. It depicts Jupiter standing on a bull and holding an axe and a thunderbolt on one side and a jar and a shallow dish on the other. Archaeologists interpret this as evidence of animal sacrifice.

Altars are usually a tall block or cylinder of local stone, decorated with elements associated with the god in question. Popular motifs were grapes and leaves, as well as ox heads and skulls. The altar would also be inscribed with the name of the

The altar to Antenociticus, today housed in the Great Northern Museum, Hancock, was originally in Benwell Temple. The inscription reads:

'Deo Antenocitico et Numinib(us) Augustor(um)
Ael(ius) Vibius leg(ionis) XX V(aleriae) V(ictricis)
v(otum) s(olvit) l(ibens) m(erito)'

('To the god Antenociticus and to the Divinities of the Emperors Aelius Vibius, centurion of Legio XX Valeria Victrix, willingly and deservedly fulfilled his vow')

god it was dedicated to and of the person who dedicated it. This is how we know which cohorts were stationed at the various forts – if an altar has been found with a complete, or at least partial, inscription, then we can know for certain who was where. The altar to Antenociticus from Benwell (illustrated opposite) is typical of many found along the wall and is made up from the following components:

Focus: a bowl-shaped depression for offerings
Pulvini: bolsters (here, bunches of incense)
Capital: head of the altar
Die: inscribed surface
Base: lower section of the altar

In their heyday, altars would have been vividly painted. Often, the dedicatee's name was more prominent than that of the deity the altar was dedicated to: it would give his name, his command and place of origin. The Latin inscriptions were densely inscribed, sometimes with no gaps between the words and often with words split over two lines. But by the late 3rd century, the cutting of monumental inscriptions had largely died out and altars, building inscriptions, gravestones and the like were being repurposed for use as hearths and foundation stones and even to patch up the wall.

In 1870, 17 altar stones made from local St Bees sandstone and dedicated to Jupiter were discovered in a field 300m (980ft) northeast of the fort. They were buried at regular distances in an area containing 57 pits, each of about 1.2m (4ft) square, the whole encircled by an outer ditch. The conclusion was that they had been buried for their own protection.

Most had the lettering *IOM* in the top line of inscriptions – meaning Iuppiter Optimus Maximus – Jupiter Best and Greatest. Most of the stones were dedicated by the commanding officers of the various garrisons. A possible explanation for this is that on every 3 January (or the anniversary of the emperor's succession) the troops renewed their oath of allegiance to the emperor and state. Accordingly, a new altar stone was dedicated each year, probably with the sacrificial offering of an ox, maybe by the unit commander, with the last altar stone buried beneath the parade ground so there was only ever one altar stone visible.

However, later excavations revealed that the pits were in fact pot holes, and the altars – far from being reverently hidden – were used simply as supports for the massive timbers that would have held up the surrounding building. The Romans were a pragmatic society and that pragmatism extended to religion.

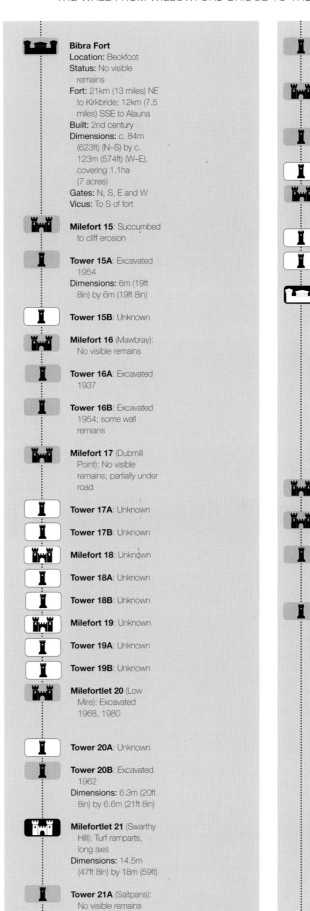

4

THE ROMAN ARMY AND THE WALL

Men of the Ermine Street Guard show off their arms, armour and discipline – as they have for over 50 years of re-enactment. Ermine Street Guard

THE LEGIONS

The legions were the mainstay of the army and of Rome. There were, for the most part, three or four in Britain throughout the Roman period: the *legio VI Victrix*, based in Eboracum, the *legio XX Valeria Victrix*, in Deva, and the *legio II Augusta* based in Caerleon.

A Roman legion was a discrete unit in itself and each was based in a fortress within its own area of a specific province – a complete, self-contained army in miniature with all its weapons, artillery, support staff, transport, stores and ancillary equipment. It was also a microcosm of Roman society, consisting of rank-and-file legionaries who were all Roman citizens, staffed by centurions – the most experienced soldiers who had risen through the ranks – and officered by men of the senatorial and equestrian classes. It was the forerunner of all modern armies in many ways, being endlessly active and constantly practising – a professional standing army – and, undoubtedly, the most evolved in the world at that time in the arts of siege warfare and military engineering.

◀ *The column of Marcus Aurelius in Piazza Colonna, Rome, is similar to that of Trajan. It celebrates the victories of the emperor during the Marcomannic Wars, showing various military scenes. These contribute greatly to our understanding of Roman military equipment of the period.* Jean-Christophe Benoist/WikiCommons (CC BY 2.5)

▼ *Tools were almost as important as weapons most of the time:* batillum *(shovel) and* dolabra *(mattock or entrenching tool).*

THE MEN

Uniquely, and more than any modern army unit, as well as fighting, the legions also built. In wood, turf and stone, they built roads, forts, towers, walls, gates, temples, baths, bridges, granaries, cemeteries and monuments. Wherever they went they created a radical new infrastructure that

▲ *This cast of a panel of Trajan's Column shows legionaries clearing woods for road construction, their shields and helmets on one side.* WikiCommons

certainly must have startled the natives just as much as it increased the speed and spread of Roman civilisation. To be capable of this, a legion contained soldiers who were also craftsmen, including stonemasons, carpenters, plasterers, lead-workers, tool-makers, potters and tilers. Such skilled specialists were called *immunes*, and although they still had to fight when the legion was on active service, they were spared the everyday jobs of guarding, patrolling, firewood collection and latrine cleaning that were the lot of less qualified men, recruits or those on punishment duties. It was these men who built the wall.

Because of these combined capabilities, an entire legion was seldom present at one location. Unless there was a special occasion, such as a parade for an emperor or a change of commander, individuals and units were seconded where and when required. Like a modern-day formation, a legion had its central headquarters, but specialist sub-units would be considerably spread out across its sphere of operations unless the whole legion was specifically involved in a major martial task or relocation. Although Hadrian's Wall had various units of each legion continuously stationed or posted to specific points as required, and their presence would have always been represented and felt by the public at large through flags, shields, symbols and inscriptions, for the most part it was the auxiliaries that permanently or continuously manned the majority of its positions and defences once the wall had been built.

After the reforms to the military by Gaius Marius in 107BC – known as the Marian reforms they started when he became consul for the first time in 107BC – the legions were standardised and put on a professional footing. This included wages paid

LEGIONARY 1st–2nd CENTURIES

The *pilum* had a soft metal shaft that bent once it penetrated a shield to make withdrawal difficult

Roman helmets developed over the years (see p141), with different levels of cheek and neck protection

Lorica segmentata is usually shown on Roman depictions of legionaries, but chain mail was used extensively

The shield was both an offensive and defensive weapon, and carried the legion's insignia

Open sandals were replaced by boots

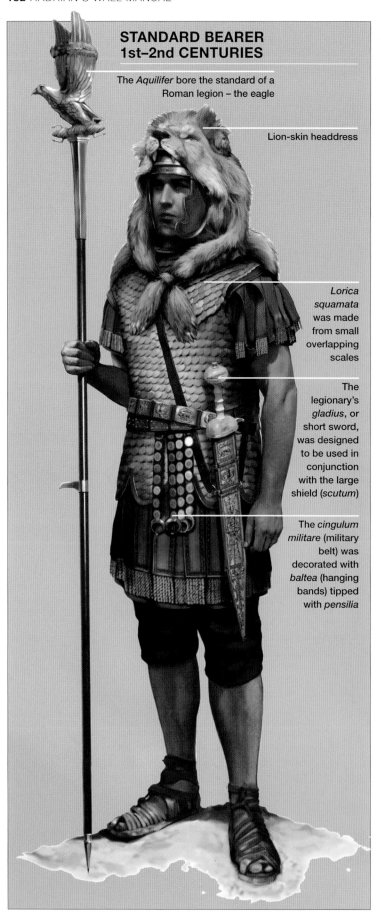

STANDARD BEARER
1st–2nd CENTURIES

The *Aquilifer* bore the standard of a Roman legion – the eagle

Lion-skin headdress

Lorica squamata was made from small overlapping scales

The legionary's *gladius*, or short sword, was designed to be used in conjunction with the large shield (*scutum*)

The *cingulum militare* (military belt) was decorated with *baltea* (hanging bands) tipped with *pensilia*

thrice yearly, a 25-year service contract (20 years with five years as a reservist) and on retirement, the choice of a land grant or a sum of money. By recruiting from the poorer classes and unemployed and later granting all Italian legions Roman citizenship, the army was both considerably democratised and increased in size, thus enabling Rome to field larger forces, maintain its security and continue its successful expansion. While on active service, soldiers were not supposed to get married, but many did unofficially, with the obvious tacit compliance of their superiors, for their families often lived just outside their forts in a local civilian settlement known as a *vicus*. Just as today, if they did not return to their homeland, soldiers tended to retire in the area they had been stationed, where perhaps their wife was from and their children had grown up. The major forts on the wall had significant *vici*, as discussed later.

It is not known precisely how many men were in a legion. Just as with an equivalent modern formation, there was a difference between strength on paper and in reality, with a steady attrition of manpower through war, accident, illness, retirement or postings to other units, while the officers and commander – tribunes and legate – would regularly move off on their own career trajectories. What can be said is that a legion consisted of approximately 5,500 men, primarily heavy armoured infantry, organised into 10 cohorts each of 480 soldiers,

but with the first cohort being double the size of the other nine and containing the best and most experienced fighting men.

THE UNITS

The cohort was the basic tactical unit of the legions – and, unsurprisingly, we see cohorts mentioned in inscriptions all along the wall. A cohort itself was made up of six *centuriae* (centuries) of 80 men, each commanded by a senior centurion with an *optio* serving as his second-in-command. A *centuria* (century) was made up of 10 *contubernia* (tent/mess units) and was commanded by a junior centurion. A *contubernium*, the smallest sub-unit of a legion, was made up of eight men, lead by a *decanus*. These eight men shared a leather tent when on campaign or a pair of rooms when in barracks – one for accommodation and the other for equipment. Additionally, each legion had the *eques legionis* (legionary cavalry) in the form of a 120-man *ala* (wing), who were used as scouts for reconnaissance and as messengers for fast communication. It also had some non-combatants

▼ *The* contubernium *lived in goat-skin leather tents when on campaign. Such tents look too small to accommodate eight men and, sometimes, a servant, but it's likely that other duties and watches would ensure that most of the time there would be fewer than that.* Ermine Street Guard

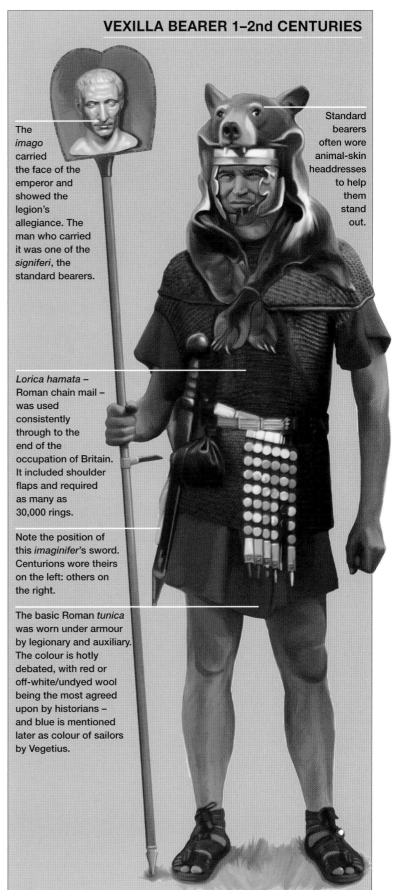

VEXILLA BEARER 1–2nd CENTURIES

The *imago* carried the face of the emperor and showed the legion's allegiance. The man who carried it was one of the *signiferi*, the standard bearers.

Standard bearers often wore animal-skin headdresses to help them stand out.

Lorica hamata – Roman chain mail – was used consistently through to the end of the occupation of Britain. It included shoulder flaps and required as many as 30,000 rings.

Note the position of this *imaginifer*'s sword. Centurions wore theirs on the left: others on the right.

The basic Roman *tunica* was worn under armour by legionary and auxiliary. The colour is hotly debated, with red or off-white/undyed wool being the most agreed upon by historians – and blue is mentioned later as colour of sailors by Vegetius.

▶ *A typical centurion: if he were a primus pilus, he'd be in charge of the first century of his legion's first cohort. Note his laterally crested helmet, his vine stick (*vitis*), which acted as a badge of rank and punishment stick, and his medals, the disc-like* phalerae *and two torques. His sword is on his left side – legionaries carried theirs on their right.* Ermine Street Guard

– as the Romans were sticklers for record-keeping, there was an administrative staff of clerks, along with orderlies for the doctor and the quartermaster and carters to transport equipment and supplies.

When trouble made it necessary a *vexillatio* (plural: *vexillationes*) could be detached from a legion to be sent on a particular mission. Usually consisting of a number of cohorts, a vexillation was a task force assembled and sent off separately or combined with elements from other different legions and units from the *auxilia* into a temporary battle group. The name comes from *vexillatum*,

▶ *There were various types of* optiones *– the equivalent of sergeants in today's armed forces. The* optio centuriae *was a centurion's second-in-command, chosen by the centurion hence the name (*optare *means 'to choose'). Here our re-enactor is wearing an* optio's *ring and holding the* optio's *silver-topped* hastile. Ermine Street Guard

a square flag borne by such a unit, which would feature its parent formation.

OFFICERS AND NCOs

The legion was commanded by a legate (*legatus legionis*). He was a patrician nobleman and member of the Imperial Senate, gaining military experience in order to advance his career. Postings usually lasted three to four years, although an able commander in a time of conflict could see this indefinitely extended. Such military experience was considered essential and by this method the Senate had a good understanding of events on the frontiers. Legates were on an equal footing with each other and subject only to the provincial governor of the province they were stationed in.

The legion's second-in-command was a tribune (*tribunus laticlavius*), who was also a senatorial officer. There were five additional junior tribunes from the equestrian order (*eques;* pl *equites*), making up the primary officers of the command group. The patrician noblemen – the senatorial class – were at the top of Roman society; underneath them were the equestrians (we'd call them knights). Both classes deemed military experience as necessary for political advancement.

On a par, perhaps, with the most senior non-commissioned officers who go on to become officers in modern armies, the third-in-command was a former senior centurion serving as camp prefect (*praefectus castrorum*). Under his control were the other 59 centurions of the legion. Each centurion commanded a century of 80 men and was responsible for day-to-day discipline and order. Again, as with modern NCOs, the centurions were career soldiers who rose from the ranks and formed the backbone of the army with their own heirarchy based on combat record and experience. The very best centurions were promoted to command the centuries of the First Cohort. While the legate and tribunes were political appointees who came and went, assuring that the army was controlled by the men most trusted by the emperor, the centurions were the skilled professionals who would be relied on to run a legion on a day-to-day basis, on campaign and in battle. Centurions could marry, and their wives could live in the barracks with them. They did not march, they rode on horseback and the rank of centurion assured high social status on retirement.

After the key post of camp prefect, the highest post of the centurionate was the *primus pilus*, who was in charge of the First Century of the First Cohort. This was only a one- to three-year appointment and there is evidence that the most experienced centurions changed legions on a

▲ ► *There were a number of flags and symbols carried by the legions. The* aquilifer *carried the eagle of a legion. There's one in this image (above) from Trajan's column. The* signifer *carried the century's* signum *(right) often with a hand atop – dating back to when the maniple (composed of two* centuriae*) was the main Roman fighting formation. A vexillation would have a* vexilifer *to carry a* vexillum *standard (far right).* Conrad Cichorius/WikiCommons, Ermine Street Guard (both in colour)

▼ *The key Non-Commissioned Officers (NCOs) in a century were, left to right:* vexilifer, cornicen, centurion, optio *and* signifier. Ermine Street Guard

regular basis. The seniority then went through the legion's heirachy of cohorts and centuries according to their graded position proven through combat – and their casualty rate was high as they fought alongside the men they commanded in the thick of the action. They stood out. They wore more distinctive armour than the standard legionary – often a hammered bronze muscle cuirass that idealised the human physique, shin greaves and a transverse horsehair crest atop their helmet. They wore their swords on the side at the waist and sometimes on the left, since, instead of a shield,

► Cornicenes *accompanying Trajan on his Dacian expedition as shown on Trajan's Column.* Conrad Cichorius/ WikiCommons

they carried a vine stick (*vitis*) as a symbol of their authority and a non-lethal weapon of reprimand.

Each centurion chose an *optio* from his own century as his second-in-command. The *optio* wore the standard legionary kit with the addition of a more recognisable helmet crest and carried a long staff at least as tall as himself – a *hastile* – used to control and discipline the soldiers.

To enhance unit identity, display allegiance and lead or rally the troops, the legion had a series of standards carried by bearers who were marked out from other soldiers by the animal heads and skins that they wore on parade and in battle (normally a lion, wolf or bear). In order of importance, first, and wearing a lion skin, was the *aquilifer* – the bearer of the legion's silver eagle standard and a position of great prestige, for he was responsible for the safety of the sacred symbol of the legion, whose loss could bring disgrace and even disbandment.

Next came the *imaginifer*, who carried the *imago* – the emperor's image and proof of the legion's loyalty to him. Then came the *signiferi* – trusted men, one for each century, who bore its unique centurial *signum* totems and symbols and also looked after their unit's pay and savings. The standards were revered and used at all important events – battles, parades, rituals and ceremonies.

Besides the standards, sound was used as a signal. In the noise and din of battle, commands had to be clearly understood and three different types of wind instrument were used for specific purposes, with the trumpet the most commonly used on a day-to-day basis. One horn, the *cornu*, was used for anything to do with the legionary colours and the heavier *buccina* horn was used as a mark of the legate commander's authority.

Roman soldiers were deeply superstitious and each legion had an *augur* – a priest who foretold the future through the examination of natural phenomena and the entrails of a sacrificed animal. Other important posts that also paid more were the *medicus* – the physician in charge of the medical facilities; the *armicustos* (quartermaster), a lynchpin in the smooth running of any legion; the *architecti* (engineer), responsible for building, maintenance and repair of all installations and the *ballistarius* (artilleryman), concerned with the heavy weaponry.

EQUIPMENT AND TRAINING

Rome's heavy infantry legions reflect their origins in the armoured hoplite phalanxes of the Greeks,

◄ *The Roman Army used a variety of signalling apparatus, from flags to brass instruments, the latter being sounded by an* aeneator *(aes meaning 'copper alloy'). The main instruments were the* cornu *– sounded by a* cornicen *– and the similar* buccina *or bucina (sounded by a bucinator). There is some debate about the difference between the two, with the main source, Vegetius, suggesting the buccina was curved brass and the cornu horn. Vegetius, however, was writing in the late 4th to early 5th centuries about the legions of the early Principate and is known to lack accuracy.* Graham Sumner

▶ *Practice makes perfect. The Romans trained regularly, as one would expect. Vegetius talks about training with heavy javelins to strengthen the arm, heavier than normal wicker shields and wooden swords – as here.* Graham Sumner

the Etruscans and the Macedonians. Trained to work in an organised unit, such a formation was almost invariably successful against a disorganised barbarian horde often of much greater numbers. For a tribal warrior who prized indviduality and was used to fighting hand to hand, singly or in a melee, such a mode of fighting must have seemed frighteningly strange. The enemy all dressed the same and had the same weapons and they moved and fought as one, as if copies of a single thing. Disconcertingly, they deliberately stayed completely silent until the very last minute as they approached, resisting the natural inclination for war cries except for a roar just before contact. They also had artillery with a range greater than any hand weapons and they never stopped building – complicated siege machinery, enveloping circumvallations and even a fortified camp constructed to a precise plan each night when on the move. They acted as men possessed, without any sense of unique self, half ghosts or automatons controlled by an evil god.

WEAPONS

The primary weapon of the *miles gregarius* – standard legionary – was the *gladius*. The Romans had inherited the metallurgical skills of the Etruscans and knew how to produce a high-carbon steel with which they made a short, 60–85cm (24–33in), sharp sword with a tapered point. Designed for close-quarter combat, it was suitable for slashing and chopping as well as thrusting. Its ridged hilt was made of wood, bronze or even ivory and often personalised and finished in a large spherical knob to provide a snug, sturdy hand grip. When used in a cohesive formation, in conjunction with the long, curved shield (*scutum*), the *gladius* was a very effective and deadly weapon. It was worn on a baldric – a leather and wooden scabbard and belt that looped over the shoulder and hung on the right-hand side. Centurions and officers often wore theirs at the waist.

The distinctive shield itself was large – approximately 1m (3ft) high and 50cm (18in) wide and weighed about 10kg (22lb). It was made of layers of laminated wood glued together at right angles then steamed into shape. The edges were then metalled and completed with a protruding central iron boss that protected the hand and gave the shield an offensive capability. The outer

▼ *The combination of* gladius *and* scutum*, below left, proved as unstoppable in Britannia as it was elsewhere in Europe.* Ermine Street Guard

▼ *One of the panels on the Tropaeum Traiani, below right. The legionary is wearing an armoured sleeve (*manica*), a scale-mail shirt and layers of* pteryges *(strips of leather or linen that seem to have been decorative and worn at either shoulder or hem of mail shirts). The Dacian carries a* falx*, a sword with a curved blade.* CristianChirita/WikiCommons (CC BY-SA 3.0)

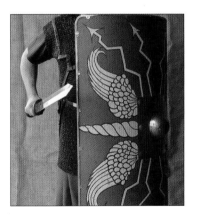 

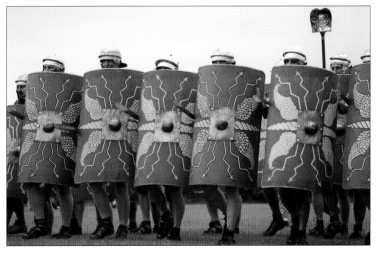

▶ *Legionaries carrying* pila *(in the Tropaeum Traiani). These were important weapons, their heads differing from thrusting spears.* Cristian Chirita/WikiCommons (CC BY-SA 3.0)

◀ *Javelin or spear heads dating to around AD80–100 from the Roman site at Trimontium (Newstead) in Melrose.* National Museum of Scotland/ Bridgeman Images

▼ *The* gladius *(left, drawn, and centre, sheathed) was the sword of the legionary and the longer* spatha *(right) was used by cavalrymen. At the bottom of the photograph a* puglio *(dagger).*

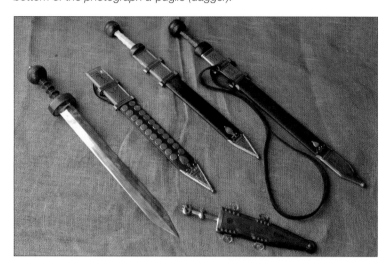

face was covered in leather or canvas and dyed or painted legionary red and then probably emblazoned with Jupiter's crossed thunderbolts combined with individual legion and cohort badges, identifying numbers and colours.

A legionary was also armed with two *pila* – javelins – to thrust at close opponents, pick off individual targets at middle distance or just hurl en masse in a barrage. The *pilum* was designed with a hard iron point and a softer, thin shank that bent on contact and rendered the weapon useless until beaten out straight again. A well-thrown *pilum* could pierce armour or else stick in the shield of an enemy, dragging it down and exposing him to the oncoming crunch of the Roman front rank working in a wall of shields and blades rather like a garden mower. Finally, a legionary also had a dagger (*puglio*) as a side weapon and an all-sorts tool, again often personalised with individual decoration.

▶ *Roman legionaries each with* lorica segmentata, gladius, cingulum militare – *belt with a buckle (*fibula*) and straps (*baltea*) with pendants (*pensilia*) at the end – shield and* pilum. *The helmets are Imperial Gallic and Italic style. These were usually made of iron, with brass decorations.*
Graham Sumner

ARMOUR AND CLOTHING

Except for his arms and his face, the legionary's upper body was completely armoured. On his head he wore a well-made and highly polished bronze helmet (*galea*) with an iron skull-plate, a neck protector extension at the back and a ridged front with hinged side-flaps that could close to protect the cheeks and face. On the top was a plumeholder, enabling the wearing of crests or plumes at ceremonial events and parades. The upper body was protected by an iron-and-steel cuirass of independently moving segmented armour – *lorica segmentata* – made in an intricate arrangement of hoops, strips and plates that were held together with ties or rivetted to a leather jerkin.

We know a lot about this armour because of the pieces discovered as part of the Corbridge Hoard. The pieces on the torso were hinged at the back and hooked at the front to be lace-fastened, with the main chest plates usually fastened by buckle, while the two hooped shoulder guards were attached separately and last of all. When worn with a padded jerkin, this armour was both comfortable and very strong, however, sometimes the rather complicated and high-maintenance *lorica segmentata* was replaced by *lorica hamata* – chain mail that was more flexible and easier to maintain. It was made of small interlocking rings of bronze or iron wired together and sewn on to padded linen or leather. Troops of the *auxilia* tended to be issued with this because they generally fought in a

▲ *The Gallic helmet, with 'eyebrow' decorations, neck guard, cheek guards and brass fittings: the standard helmet of the legions in the 1st century* AD.

▲ *Horse-hair crests and plumes were often seen on 2nd-century helmets. Vegetius suggests that centurions' crests were transverse. It's not clear who wore plumes and crests in battle.*

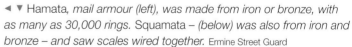

◄ ▼ Hamata, *mail armour (left), was made from iron or bronze, with as many as 30,000 rings.* Squamata – *(below) was also from iron and bronze – and saw scales wired together.* Ermine Street Guard

▶ Lorica segmentata *is much loved by re-enactors and figures strongly on Trajan's Column, although it isn't as widespread elsewhere. It's possible that the column uses it to distinguish between legionary and auxiliary. Nevertheless, sections of armour have been found in many locations – some not known for legionary occupation – including Coria, where the 1964 Corbridge Hoard provided the clues needed to work out how the segments were attached to each other. It was secured by leather ties and hooks, as shown here.* Ermine Street Guard

▶ *An alternative to a baldric – Tiberius Julius Abdes Pantera has two belts, one for his sword and one for his dagger. His tombstone was discovered in Bingerbrück, Germany in 1859. Legionaries often spent many years in the army: Pantera from Sidon died aged 62. He had served for 40 years.*
Pudelek (Marcin Szala)/ WikiCommons (CC BY-SA 3.0)

more open fashion than the close-quarter massed combat in which the legions specialised. There was also a *lorica squamata* made of overlapping small iron or bronze scales wired together and sewn on to a fabric backing. As time went on, both chain- and scale mail came to predominate. Armour was expensive to manufacture but if well looked after could last a lifetime – and more.

Under his armour a legionary wore a linen breechcloth (underpants) and a simple short-sleeved woollen or linen tunic that reached the knees. On his feet were heavily hobnailed sandals (*caligae*) fastened with long leather thongs. In cold weather a legionary wore an additional long-sleeved tunic, three-quarter length leather trousers, closed leather boots with socks and either a hooded *paenula* cloak, like a poncho, or a longer, heavier woollen one known as a *sagum*, made waterproof by its natural lanolin. Around his neck he wore a *focale* – a scarf of wool or linen to prevent his armour chafing. His *balteus* (waist belt) was a *cingulum militare* – a metalled leather belt with a curtain of metal discs on strips at the front, which could be tucked up when working.

▲ *Roman soldiers were extremely superstitious and often wore tokens of gods and other charms.* Ermine Street Guard

▼ *The* cingulum militare *from which hangs a purse (*scrotum*). The sword is attached to a baldric, which is held in position by positioning the straps between the belt and body.* Ermine Street Guard

◄ *From the time of Marius during the Republic, legionaries carried their equipment on a stout stick over their shoulder with their shield over their back. In that period they were known as Marius' mules and little had changed in Hadrian's day.*

Graham Sumner

▲ *By the 3rd century the* lorica segmentata, *large shields, and Gallic helmets had given way to mail, helmets with fuller ear and cheek guards, and a thrusting spear rather than a* gladius. *Shields were often oval (as the cavalry shields) or round.*

Graham Sumner

ON THE MARCH

Besides using strict heirarchical discipline maintained with severe punishments, the Roman Army developed its legions to a high level of fitness and skill with continual training. Stamina and strength were built up using wooden swords

ROMAN HELMETS – 1st–5th CENTURIES

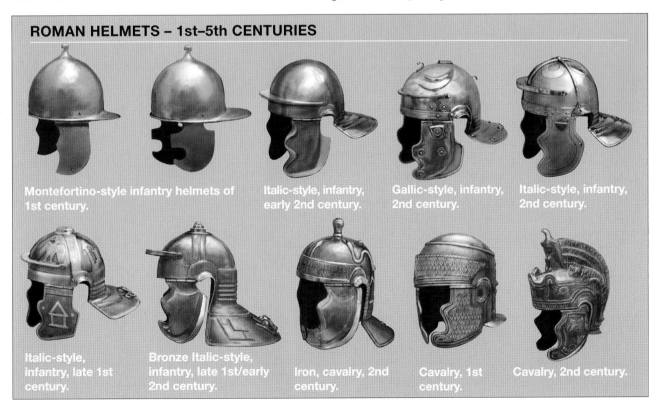

Montefortino-style infantry helmets of 1st century.

Italic-style, infantry, early 2nd century.

Gallic-style, infantry, 2nd century.

Italic-style, infantry, 2nd century.

Italic-style, infantry, late 1st century.

Bronze Italic-style, infantry, late 1st/early 2nd century.

Iron, cavalry, 2nd century.

Cavalry, 1st century.

Cavalry, 2nd century.

LEGION AND CENTURION – 1st CENTURY AD

The centurion wears a transverse crest, his sword on the left and carries his *vitis* (vine stick)

Three standards are illustrated: (L–R) the *signum* identifying the unit's century; the *vexillum* identifying the legion; and the *imago* (representation of the emperor)

On the march, legionaries carried their *pila*, slung their shields on their backs and carrried their personal equipment on a wooden frame

and shields filled with lead, which were heavier than the real versions. This was followed by increasingly skilled real-weapons training, the integration of each man into the unit and then of the units themselves together, for seamless cooperation. Endless parade-ground practice was necessary to be able to carry out manoeuvres swiftly in real time on the battlefield.

The Marian reforms had reduced the lengthy, cumbersome supply train that followed a legion everywhere. There were still transport carts and mules, but to speed up movement and toughen the troops, a legionary carried a lot of his own kit as he marched. He used a forked pole called a *furca*, fastened to which was a satchel (*loculus*) containing a few personal items, money and small tools. Next, he carried a rolled-up cloak with perhaps some spare clothing; a net bag for three days' supply of foodstuffs (including *buccellatum*,

a dried hardtack that lasted indefinitely); and a waterskin, cooking pot and mess tin. He also had to carry a few stakes, a wicker basket, and either a mattock, a mezzoluna-bladed turf cutter or sickle, a pickaxe or a spade. This was to construct primarily turf-and-timber defences but also to overcome obstacles when on the move. All this was in addition to his military equipment. How did he manage it? It seems from recent finds that Roman shields, with their canvas or hide surfaces providing protection from the elements, also had rings fitted on the inside near the rim. This enabled a shield to be hung on the legionary's back, with the *furca* then able to rest on the shield's upper rim and its different elements hanging behind it on the other side cushioned by the softer ones. This would leave one hand free or swappable for relief. Helmets were fastened in front to the chest armour.

▶ *The basic Roman artillery was the* ballista, *which came in various sizes and fired a stone ball. The smaller* catapulta *or* scorpio, *fired arrows, and also came in different sizes as shown in these two photographs: (below right) a metal-framed double-shot as shown on Trajan's Column and a smaller, single-shot, version (right). It is said that the range of the late 4th-century heavy* ballistae *was over 400m (1,200ft).* WikiCommons; Ermine Street Guard

ARTILLERY

Torsion artillery learnt from the Greeks was further refined by Roman metallurgical skill and its increasingly metal construction gave Roman artillery a greater strength, range and accuracy. A legion came equipped with some powerful missile weapon systems – 4th-century writer Vegetius says 55 *carroballista* – no doubt with their own specialist crews who operated and maintained them. The heaviest were the onagers (*onagri*), large, one-armed catapults firing the biggest of mainly stone ammunition and named after the wild ass because of their huge recoil. Requiring a specially built firing base and a crew of eight to operate, 10 such weapons were assigned to each legion, one for each cohort, according to Vegetius. Next came the smaller, two-armed catapults. Crossbow-like in appearance and design, they were operated by winding back a windlass held by a rack and pin or cog. The bigger ones were known as *ballistae* and the smaller as *scorpiones*, but there is some confusion beween the two in the primary Roman sources. The *ballistae* had a crew of two or more, while the *scorpiones* were one-man operated. They had a considerable reputation for accuracy. They all fired iron-headed bolts of different sizes and were sometimes mounted upon carts for mobility.

◀ *The* onager *was similar to the medieval mangonel, using the stored torsion power of rope to fire projectiles. A siege engine, it didn't have a great range.* Ermine Street Guard

THE LEGIONS IN BRITAIN

Of the legions used in the Claudian conquest of Britain, *legio XIV Gemina* left c. AD67 for the Balkans and c. 110 *legio IX Hispana* left for Germania and did not return, although there was an unsubstantiated belief – promoted by Rosemary Sutcliff's brilliant novel *The Eagle of the Ninth* – that it had been wiped out during Agricola's campaign in Caledonia. (Tacitus, writing in the 1st century, says that they were ambushed in camp and almost overwhelmed but rescued by the timely arrival of cavalry sent by Agricola.) The three legions that remained in Britain were *legio II Augusta*, *legio VI Victrix* and *legio XX Valeria Victrix*, supported (and far outnumbered) by various attached units of the *auxilia*. These three legions carried out all the main building of the Hadrianic and Antonine walls, roads, forts, camps, watchtowers, milecastles and other defences in the north of the province and elsewhere.

LEGIO II AUGUSTA

Legionary fortress: Isca Augusta (Caerleon)
Emblem: Capricorn – the star sign of Augustus. The winged horse Pegasus and the war god Mars also featured for a while but by the late 3rd century only Capricorn is attested

▼ The remains of the Caerleon 6,000-seat Roman amphitheatre, where soldiers and citizens of Isca came to relax and enjoy entertainment like animal hunts and gladiators in combat.
Shutterstock

As its name implies, *legio II Augusta* was formed by Octavian Augustus sometime around 25BC. It saw prior service in Spain, Germany and Gaul and was part of the invasion force of Britain in AD43, when it was commanded by the future Emperor Vespasian and campaigned in the southwest of the country against the Durotriges and the Dumnonii, successfully storming various hillforts. Things went really wrong for the legion in AD60–61 when, in the absence of its legate commander during the Boudiccan rebellion, the camp prefect elected to ignore an order to mobilise from Governor Suetonius Paulinus, with the consequence of his later suicide and the legion's fall from favour.

Legio II Augusta was dispersed over a wide area

for a time and was then stationed at Glevum from AD66–74. In AD69 – the Year of the Four Emperors – a vexillation from the legion supported first Otho, then Vitellius, against the claim of Vespasian, but after their defeats the whole legion reaffirmed its allegiance to him.

It was then transferred west for the conquest of Wales in AD74–78 and began to build at Caerleon what would become its main fortress headquarters for more than 200 years. Inscriptions found in both places testify to its part in the construction of Hadrian's and the Antonine Walls in 122 and 139–142 respectively.

In 196 the legion backed the claim of Governor Clodius Albinus for the emperor's purple, but after he was defeated by Septimius Severus the legion fell out of favour again for a time, until it proved its loyalty to the new emperor in his Caledonian campaigns of 208–211, moving temporarily to Carpow. It then moved back to Isca Augusta during the reign of Alexander Severus, and remained there until the late 3rd century.

The final mention of this legion occurs in the *Notitia Dignitatum,* which states that it (or part of it) had moved to Richborough in Kent as part of the Saxon Shore defences.

LEGIO VI VICTRIX

Legionary Fortress: Eboracum (York)
Emblem: Bull

Legio VI Victrix was another legion founded by Octavian Augustus, in AD41. It took part in various Roman civil wars before moving on to take part in the conquest of Spain, where it stayed for nearly a century and won its title of *Victrix*. In AD68 it supported Spanish governor, Servius Sulpicius Galba, in his claim to the purple and marched on Rome against Emperor Nero.

In AD69 the legion was moved to the Rhine area to put down the Civilis rebellion and stayed

there some 50 years. In c. 119 it was relocated by Emperor Hadrian to subdue trouble in northern Britain and was based in the legionary fortress at Eboracum (York), replacing *legio IX Hispana*. The legion built the bridge over the Tyne at Pons Aelius (Newcastle) and in 122 it began work on Hadrian's Wall. Twenty years later it was again involved in the construction of the Antonine Wall from 139–142.

In 197 the British legions supported the claim of Britannia governor Clodius Albinus for the title of emperor, but were defeated by Septimius Severus. When Severus began his Caledonian campaign the Sixth helped build the massive camp at Carpow along with *legio II Augusta* and no doubt shared it with them. There is also a mention of *legio VI Vitrix* during the reign of the usurpers Carausius and Allectus (286–296).

In 306 Constantine was proclaimed emperor at Eboracum, the legion's headquarters fortress, so it must be assumed that it supported his cause. The final reference to the Sixth is at the end of the 4th century in the *Notitia Dignitatum*'s list of Roman Army units, reponsible to the Dux Britanniarum conducting the northern defences from Eboracum. It is not known precisely but the Sixth was probably withdrawn to the continent by Stilcho in 402 or by Constantine III in 407.

LEGIO XX VALERIA VICTRIX

Legionary Fortress: Deva Victrix (Chester)
Emblem: Black Boar

Legio XX Valeria Victrix was also formed by Ocatavian Augustus, c. AD31. It saw action in Spain in the Cantabrian Wars from 29 to 19BC, then moved to Illyria where it won its Valeria title for courage in the Pannonian rebellion. Following the destruction of three legions in the AD9 disaster in the Teutoburg Forest, it was then posted to Germania. In AD43 it was chosen as one of the four legions used by Claudius to invade Britain. After the defeat of Caratacus, its first legionary fortress was built at Camulodunum (Colchester), the erstwhile capital of the British Trinovantes tribe. Around AD55 *legio XX Valeria Victrix* moved to Burrium (Usk) in southeast Wales, where it fought against the Silures, and in AD66 it transferred to Viroconium (Wroxeter). In AD60–61 it was active in the suppression of Boudicca's rebellion and possibly won its title of Victrix for courageous service in this war.

In the civil war of AD69CE, *legio XX Valeria Victrix* favoured the emperor Vitellius and a vexillation took part in his march on Rome, returning only after the victory of Vespasian. In AD71–74 it served under its legate, Agricola, in the north of the province and the conquest of the Brigantes. In AD75, the legion

was transferred back to Viroconium (Wroxeter), from where it launched the conquest of North Wales under the now governor Agricola. In AD78–84 it was with him in the Caledonian Highlands, building a new legionary fortress at Inchtuhill on the River Tay with the intention of permanence.

However, in AD88 the conquest of Caledonia was abandoned and the legion was transferred to the Legionary Fortress at Deva (Chester). Originally built by *legio II Adiutrix*, it was now rebuilt in stone. As with the other legions in the province, *legio XX Valeria Victrix* was involved in the construction of both Hadrian's Wall (122–125) and the Antonine Wall (c. 140). It, too, was drawn into the 196 attempt on the purple by provincial governor Clodius Albinus. The British legions were transferred to the continent, but were defeated by Septimius Severus in the spring of 197. The Caledonians had exploited this reduction in manpower to invade the north of the province and in 208 Severus came to Britain to retaliate with a counterstrike campaign in which *legio XX Valeria Victrix* took part. It returned to Deva Victrix during the reign of Caracalla (211–217) after the final Roman withdrawal from Caledonia.

In the reign of the usurpers Carausius and Allectus (286–296), the legion was inevitably part of the Carausian revolt that established the brief Britannic Empire until it was regained for Rome by Constantius. It seems probable that the legion left Deva Victrix sometime at the end of the 3rd century because the port had silted up and that it probably left the province when the usurper Constantine III took the bulk of the legions for his doomed campaign of 407. Alternatively it could have been disbanded when Constantius I Chlorus reconquered Britain.

▲ *The legionary fortress of Eboracum was first built in wood by* legio IX Hispana *around* AD71–74 *before being rebuilt in stone 107–108. The fortress housed the major military base in the north and increased considerably in size. This photo shows the remains of the so-called 'multangular' tower built on the northwest corner.*
Shutterstock

THE AUXILIA

The *auxilia* (auxiliaries) were a fundamental and vital part of Rome's influence, reflecting its realistic democratic process of inclusion and reward for effort and service to the common cause. The Roman legions themselves fought above all as infantrymen, but they were experienced with horses, and the pre-Marian Roman Army had relied on the equestrian class – the *equites* (we'd call them knights) – for its horsemen. However, the Marian reforms discouraged this practice and severely reduced the number of Roman cavalry. Instead, the Romans began to develop auxiliaries, initially from those countrymen that did not have citizenship, then from foreign tribes of recently conquered territory and later even from outside the empire – in particular, horsemen skilled in the art of mounted warfare who filled a gap in the Roman military and who became steadily more important as the empire grew.

As with the legions, recruitment was voluntary and the reward for 25 years' service was citizenship for the soldier and his family. Julius Caesar put the process on a proper footing with his recruitment of Gallic horsemen, transforming them and the *auxilia* cavalry with a standardised structure similar to that of the legions. Later, after the Augustan reforms, the *auxilia* were developed to become an integral part of the Roman Army, including light and heavy cavalry, light infantry and specialised units, such as archers or slingers, specifically to support and supplement Rome's armoured punch of heavy infantry.

Following various revolts carried out by enlisted *auxilia* in their province of origin – such as the Batavian revolt of AD69–70 – the Roman rule became that of relocation for *auxilia* units, away from their homelands, with the option to return individually on retirement. The *auxilia* recruited in the western provinces took their unit names from their original tribes or regions. Based on a foreign frontier, they maintained their identity with recruitment from the homeland when possible. As time and the empire went on, however, and units became settled, they began to lose their unique identity to their locality, through intermarriage

▼► *There were two basic infantry shields in the 1st and 2nd centuries* AD. *One was the legionaries' rectangular shield, which provided a strong defence, but also had offensive capabilities. Older versions had curved sides. The smaller, round shields would have been carried by* signifer, aquilifer, vexilifer *and* cornicines *whose other equipment made carrying a full shield too difficult. Note the leather shield cover.*

◄◄ Auxiliary infantryman with thrusting spear (hasta)*, mail and an oval shield* (clipeus) *– as also used by auxiliary cavalry and later by legionaries.*

◄ Doubled cingulum militare *showing the* fibula *(buckle) and attached pouch, dagger with wooden scabbard and knife.*

and retirement as well as local replacement. In this way, foreign soldiers became integrated with the local population. Almost all the permanent garrisons that manned Hadrian's Wall were from the *auxilia*. By the 2nd century, large numbers of such troops had been recruited in Spain, Gaul, Thrace, Anatolia and Syria and the *auxilia* reached parity in numbers with the legions in infantry and provided all the army's cavalry and archer support.

In 212 Emperor Caracalla granted Roman citizenship to all free inhabitants of the empire, and the distinction between legions and *auxilia* began to blur, in time becoming irrelevant, with many Roman citizens also joining the *auxilia*.

◄ The auxiliaries were often formed from conquered peoples. This tombstone of an archer of cohors I Hamiorum sagittaria *– Syrians – was found at Housesteads. It dates to the 2nd century AD. Hama was conquered in AD63 and some 60 years later a unit was in Britain at Magnis. Note his composite recurved bow.* Paul Beston

▼ Auxiliary infantry as seen on Trajan's Column. Note that their spears are no longer in place. It is estimated that by Hadrian's reign there were considerably more auxiliaries than legionaries in the Roman Army. This is nowhere more true than in Britain where, by Trajan's time, there were more than twice as many auxiliaries than legionaries: around 36,000 (including more than 10,000 cavalry) compared to three legions – maximum 16,500 men. WikiCommons (CC BY-SA 3.0)

There were six basic types of *alae* and *cohortes*:

- *ala quingenaria* had 16 *turma* and therefore 512 men
- *ala milliaria* had 24 *turma* totalling 768 men
- *cohors quingenaria peditata* had 6 centuries (of 80 men each) with a total of 480 men
- *cohors milliaria peditata* consisted of 10 centuries making 800 men
- *cohors equitata quingenaria*, made up of 6 centuries and 4 *turma*, had 608 men
- *cohort equitata milliaria* the largest formation of all, having 10 centuries and 8 *turma*, making a total of 1,056 men.

There was generally only one *ala milliaria* in any province and there were only seven in total. There were also specialist units of archers and slingers, light and later heavy cavalry and even barge- and boatmen. Living quarters were arranged by *contubernia* on the legionary model – 10 for infantry cohorts and eight for cavalry units – with one barrack block for each century, while two *turmae* occupied a barrack and a stable.

The highest-ranking officer in the *auxilia* was a senatorially appointed tribune who commanded an *ala milliaria*. An *ala* was commanded by a **prefect** who was an equestrian officer or else a native noble with Roman citizenship. A *turma* was commanded by a **decurion** with two **principales** as subalterns and a **signifer** making up the command group. The auxiliary infantry was also commanded by **prefects** and their centuries were commanded by **centurions**.

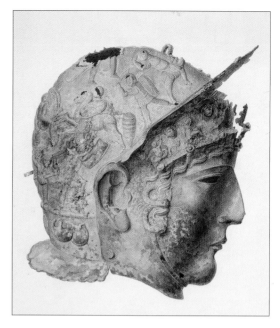

▲ *The Ribchester helmet was discovered in 1796 (apparently by the son of a clog maker). Today on show at the British Museum, it dates to the 1st–2nd centuries AD and is a wonderful example of a cavalry sports helmet – although it is probably missing a sphinx figurine on top.* Graham Sumner; Society of Antiquaries of London, UK/Bridgeman Images

▶ *This re-enactor is wearing a Gallic helmet with a face mask. While these masks are usually identified as being for tournaments, there is a view that they were also used in combat. The restricted view would have made such usage difficult, but not impossible.*

▼ *Oval shields, that on the left modelled after* cohors I Tungrorum, *as used by auxiliaries and cavalrymen.*

THE UNITS

The *auxilia* were not formed into whole legions but rather smaller *cohortes* and *alae* (wings). The cavalry was organised into *alae* of *turma* – the basic sub-unit of 32 men. The infantry cohorts were organised in much the same way as their legionary counterparts. There were also units of mixed infantry and cavalry.

EQUIPMENT

The equipment and attire of the *auxilia* infantry was similar to that of the legions, receiving almost identical weaponry, armour and training. However the cavalry arm of the *auxilia* was different, with its equipment considerably lighter and with quite

▼ *Trajan's Column has many cavalry scenes: here Roman cavalry chase the Sarmatians, who are clad in scale armour. Note the cavalry helmets and oval shields.* WikiCommons

▲ *Between April and October 2017 the Hadrian's Cavalry exhibition 'Turma' toured the museums on the wall. The culmination was a show of massed horsemen – a full* turma *or troop of 30 (some believe the* turma *was of 32 riders), as can be seen in these photographs. Note centre right the* draco *(serpent) standard and noisemaker that was possibly adopted by the Roman cavalry from one of their defeated enemies – possibly the Dacians or Sarmatians.* Graham Sumner

◄ *Metope from the Adamclisi Tropaeum Traiani showing a mail-clad cavalryman. Roman horses are thought to have been around 13 or 14 hands high (1.3–1.4m/4ft 4in–4ft 8in). Experiments have shown that most manoeuvres must have been carried out at a canter (some 40kph/25mph) because, without stirrups, trotting is difficult, as is achieving accuracy with weapons.* CristianChirita/ WikiCommons (CC BY-SA 3.0)

▲ *The Romans didn't have stirrups, which didn't reach Europe until the late 6th century with the Avars. To ensure rider stability, it was important to sit firmly in the saddle, which had four horns as shown here (the rider is sitting behind the saddle so it can be seen). The rider's weight forces the horns to lock around his legs.* Ermine Street Guard

a few specialist variations reflecting their particular country of origin in dress and weapons. The legionary *scutum* was obviously impractical on horseback, as was the *lorica segmentata*, and so the *auxilia* tended to favour round or oval shields and wore simpler helmets and chain mail or scale mail. They also used longer spears, sometimes had a quiver of light javelins or darts attached to the saddle and had a longer sword called a *spatha* adopted from the Celtic cavalry auxiliaries. At this point in time, stirrups had not been invented and although special saddles prevented a man from being unhorsed, it still required much skill to fight on horseback. Certain tribes were renowned for their horsemanship and recruited for just such skills.

▲ *Roman tombstone erected in memory of Rufus Sita, a Thracian cavalryman of the 2nd century AD. It was found in Gloucester.* Getty Images

▼ *This 1st-century AD cavalry helmet was found in Ely, Cambridgeshire. Primarily decorative, the bronze outer would have had an inner iron headguard.* WikiCommons

▶ *Re-enactor's cavalry helmet. Note that it covers the ears – as was usual with cavalry helmets – and is longer at the neck than an infantry helmet.*

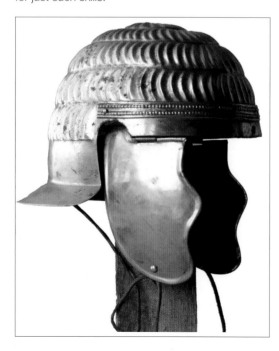

NUMBERS

The sheer size of the auxiliary presence in the province of Britannia cannot be overstated, In c. 130 there were some 56 units, with the cavalry having 11 *alae* of about 1,000 men each, and the infantry having 45 cohorts – a total of over 36,000 men, far outnumbering the three provincial legions. *Auxilia* cavalry were stationed at strategic points, such as the Hadrian's Wall headquarters fort at Uxelodunum (Petrianum). This was the largest fort on the wall and was garrisoned by an elite cavalry regiment some 1,000-men strong – the *ala Petriana* from Gaul, whose name the fort became known by. There were *alae* at Cilurnum, where the wall crosses the River Tyne and at Onnum by Dere Street – the main road north. The terrain in the area of the wall made such mounted units perfect for patrol and response. The local confederation of

tribes known as the Brigantes were famous both as horsemen and breeders, so the *auxilia* would have known some as friends and traders and others as skilful foes.

The 2nd century saw the growth of *numeri* – paid units that were not part of the Roman Army, raised exclusively from non-Roman peoples who kept entirely their own traditional dress and weapons and were attached to legions or battle groups as required.

AUXILIARY CAVALRYMAN 1st–2nd CENTURIES

Cavalry wore chain mail or scale armour

They carried a thrusting spear rather than the javelin or pilum of the infantry

Key to the Roman cavalryman's success was his saddle, made from wood with pronounced horns and a leather cover

Cavalrymen used the *spatha*, a longer sword than that used by men of the infantry

The Romans did not use stirrups

Shields were smaller than those of the infantry, and were oval in shape

Horse harnesses often included tinned or silvered decoration and hangers

THE AUXILIA IN BRITAIN

Many different units of *auxilia* served on the wall over its long duration, but not all of them have left archaeological evidence that has yet been found. Some of those that are attested by primary evidence are listed below.

COHORS I BAETASIORUM QUINGENARIA PEDITATA

The First Cohort of Baetasians was an auxiliary infantry unit of 500 men from the Germanic tribe of Baetasii who came from Lower Germany between the Meuse and the Rhine. The unit was first based near Mamucium (Manchester) before relocating to the Bar Hill and Old Kilpatrick forts on the Antonine Wall c. 139–161. Then, following its abandonment, the cohort transferred to Alauna (Maryport), a command and supply base for the coastal defences on the Cumbrian coast south of Hadrian's Wall. Finally, in the 4th century, there is a mention in the *Notitia Dignitatum* of the Baetasians garrisoning the Saxon Shore fort of Regulbium (Reculver) in Kent.

COHORS I HAMIORUM QUINGENARIA SAGITTARIA

The Hamian Cohort was an auxiliary unit of 500 infantry archers recruited from Hama in the Orontes valley of northern Syria. It was first stationed at Magnis (Carvoran) on the Stanegate as part of the wall garrison. From 142 to 157 it transferred to the Bar Hill fort on the Antonine Wall during its second phase of occupation. Around 163–166 it then transferred back to Magnis, where the unit rebuilt the fort in stone.

There is some tantalising evidence in the form of an archer's tombstone from the 2nd century found at Vercovicium (Housesteads) that the unit perhaps was stationed there or elsewhere along the wall. Its men wore distinctive conical helmets and chain-mail hauberks and used powerful recurve composite bows made of wood, bone and sinew and carried short axes as secondary weapons. With the abundance of wild game in the plentiful woodland close to the wall is thought that the prime function of the Hamians was perhaps in the provision of meat and game for the garrisons.

COHORS I TUNGRORUM MILLIARIA PEDITATA

The First Cohort of Tungrians was an auxiliary infantry unit of about 1,000 men from the Tungri tribe of southeastern Gallia Belgica in the Brabant and Hainault districts of modern Belgium. Around AD85 it built the first wooden fort at Vindolanda on the Stanegate, where a centurion of the unit died and was buried c. 100. The next inscription puts the Tungrian cohort at the Brocolitia (Carrawburgh) fort on Hadrian's Wall sometime between 122

▼ *The site of the Roman Fort on Bar Hill above Twechar, East Dunbartonshire, Scotland.*
Shutterstock

and 138. It was then posted north to man two forts, Cramond and Castlecary, on the Antonine Wall between 139 and 161, before returning to Vercovicium on Hadrian's Wall, where a final inscription dated 205–208 records its presence. The *Notitia Dignitatum* notes that the unit was there until the end of the 4th century.

ALA I TUNGRORUM

The First Tungrian Wing was an auxiliary cavalry unit of 500 men also from Tungrian Gallia Belgica. During the ferocious revolt of the Batavian *auxilia* in AD69, the Batavians had been joined by Tungrians from their neighbouring tribe. It took five Roman legions to subdue them, commanded by the veteran general Qunitus Petilius Cerialis, who brought them with him to his next posting in Britain. Documents from Deva (Chester) and Eboracum record the unit's presence in Britain during the early 2nd century. It operated on the Antonine Wall between 140 and 160, stationed at the largest fort, Mumrills, where an altar to Hercules Magusanus was dedicated by a Tungrian officer, Valerius Nigrinus.

COHORS I VARDULLORUM MILLIARIA

The First Cohort of Vardullians was an auxiliary infantry unit of 1,000 men from the Varduli tribe who lived between the Basques and the Cantabrians in Hispania Terraconensis – modern-

▼ *Auxiliary cavalry played an important role in the garrisons of Hadrian's Wall as was attested by the 2017 cavalry exhibition.* Graham Sumner

▶ *The Antonine Wall – Vallum Antonini – at Rough Castle, Bonnybridge. Like the western end of Hadrian's Wall, it was built of turf, probably with a palisade on the top, with a deep ditch to the north. This small fort was garrisoned by* cohors VI Nerviorum – *as attested by inscriptions found in the area.*
Shutterstock

day northern Spain. The unit is attested at a number of forts across northern Britain, the earliest one being Castlecary Fort on the Antonine Wall. It was next posted to Coria (Corbridge) on the Stanegate, before moving to a number of forts on Hadrian's Wall, including Cilurnum (Chesters) and Onnum. There is also evidence for the Vardullians at the small fort of Cappuck in the Roxburghshire Borders region, at Longovicium (Lanchester) in County Durham and finally, in the late 3rd century, at Bremenium (High Rochester) in Northumberland.

COHORS II THRACUM

The Second Cohort of Thracians was an infantry and cavalry auxiliary unit of about 500 men from modern-day Bulgaria. The unit is known from a tombstone at Mumrills on the Antonine Wall, which commemorates the life and death of Nectovelius, son of Vindex, a Brigantian (from modern-day northern England) who died after nine years of service with the unit. This cohort is also known from multiple inscriptions from the Cumbrian coast fort at Moresby.

COHORS IV GALLORUM QUINGENARIA EQUITATA

The Fourth Cohort of Gauls was a mixed auxiliary unit of about 600 men from Gaul (modern-day France). The unit may have been part of the force that invaded Britain in AD43, and it is known from inscriptions at Comboglanna fort on Hadrian's Wall, Habitancum (Risingham) and Vindolanda, as well as Castlehill fort on the Antonine Wall. At Castlehill, the unit's commander Pisentius Iustus dedicated an altar to the Goddesses of the Parade Ground

and to Britannia. The unit's final attested service was at Vindolanda on Hadrian's Wall.

COHORS VI NERVIORUM

The Sixth Cohort of Nervians was an auxiliary infantry unit of about 500 men from Gallia Belgica (modern-day Belgium). The unit saw service on both Hadrian's Wall and the Antonine Wall, with inscriptions at the Hadrian's Wall fort of Aesica (Great Chesters) and at Rough Castle fort on the Antonine Wall. At Rough Castle, the unit dedicated an altar to Victory and recorded its construction of the fort's headquarters building (*principia*). The altar inscription notes that for part of the time the unit was stationed at Rough Castle, it was commanded by a centurion from *legio XX* named Gaius Flavius Betto.

COHORS I, III, VIII & IX BATAVORUM

The Batavi came from the area of the Dutch Rhine delta and were much appreciated by the Romans as their finest auxiliary troops. Tough, aggressive, yet well disciplined, they were renowned for their horsemanship and their river-crossing capability, which they used to swim the Weser during the campaigns of Germanicus. Writing in the 2nd century, Cassius Dio also tells of their crossing of the Medway in a surprise tactic used by Aulus Plautius against the British in AD43. The Romans initially treated them as equals; they were not required to pay tribute and Batavian units had their own commanders. However, when a high-ranking Batavian nobleman was executed on false charges and another held in Rome without trial it led to a rebellion that spread to northern Gaul and

▶ *Cramond is 16km (10 miles) east of the Antonine Wall. A milestone found at nearby Newbridge marks the presence of* Cohors I Cugernorum. Shutterstock

Germania and became a real threat to the Roman Empire. When the uprising was finally put down, *legio X Gemina* was then stationed in a fortress in the Batavian heartland. Various mixed units of infantry and cavalry are attested in Britain, serving in Agricola's campaigns in Scotland during the late 1st century and at sites along Hadrian's Wall, including the forts at Magnis and Brocolitia and at Vindolanda on the Stanegate.

COHORS I AQUITANI

The First Cohort of Aquitanians was another auxiliary infantry unit of 500 men recruited from the Gallic tribes of the Bassin Aquitain, the Guyenne, and the Gascogne regions of southwestern France. It formed the original garrison of the Brocolitia Fort on Hadrian's Wall, but part of it was withdrawn to the Pennines, to the Brough on Noe garrison fort (Navio), which was not big enough to hold the whole unit. It is finally attested at the Saxon Shore Fort of Branodunum in Norfolk during the late 3rd century.

COHORS I CUGERNORUM

The First Cohort of Cugerni was another 500-man auxiliary infantry recruited from the Cugerni tribe who hailed from Germania Inferior, between the Meuse and the Rhine. Like the neighbouring Batavi and Baetasii tribes it was highly rated by Rome as one of their best auxiliary units. It served on both Hadrian's and the Antonine Walls – a milestone proves its presence near Cramond on the Firth of Forth, before being moved back to man a fort at Pons Aelius close to the bridge itself.

▼ *Replicas of altars from the Brocolitia Mithraeum. The inscriptions identify* cohors I Batavorum – *3rd century AD.*

Shutterstock

MILES GREGARIUS

Just as important as the military imperative was the consideration of the soldiers' personal needs. Such a huge state-funded operation invariably had its shadow civilian counterpart – the *vicus* (plural: *vici*)– a settlement that grew up just outside legionary bases and forts and was often partly built by the soldiers themselves, to cater for their time off and enable them to relax in civilian surroundings. Here they could drink, gamble, eat different foods from the basic army rations and seek female company. Often their unofficial wives and families lived in the local *vicus*, for if life on the wall was not tolerable then the troops would become restive, then rebellious. At the most distant, bleak and inhospitable outposts and forts a rota must have been used to rotate the troops back to the larger forts that had a nearby *vicus* to make life on the frontier much more normal and bearable for the soldiers. Partly determined by geographical location and proximity to major roads and routes, some *vici* and Roman camps grew to become towns that continued after the Roman occupation. Others, less well situated, died out after the soldiers had left.

Cold-weather clothing must have been the norm for a lot of the time in northern Britain. The famously thick full-length British cloak, the *birrus*, was much sought after to keep warm, rather than the usual *paenula* or *sagum*, and there were many other items of cold-weather kit that are rarely worn by today's re-enactors, such as socks (*udones*), as mentioned in a Vindolanda letter, *fascia* leg bindings, scarves (*focale*), or headgear. But as any hillwalker knows, it's what happens when you get back from a long, cold, wet day that's important and a hot bath house and good drying facilities are the key elements to outdoor living. Above all, the cold was kept at bay by staying active, but hot water and hot food were highlights of Roman culture and the Romans went to great lengths to ensure their baths were never too far away.

In fact, more time was spent in the everyday business of living and the maintenance and running of installations than actually fighting.

▶ *The Romans ate more meat than Britons and animals such as pigs and sheep got bigger during the Roman period. There were a number of animal introductions, including pheasants and a number of fruits and foodstuffs, such as spelt, hitherto alien to the British.*
Ermine Street Guard

There were long interludes of peace in between bursts of trouble, where the border became almost a symbolic entity – though one that generated much wealth and activity in its area. Aside from the normal intensive training and patrols, the military would adjust its role to that of customs officers and border police. Their clout was more than physical, it was also financial, since the demands on the local economy by the army for grain, horses, wool, leather, pork and beef and other commodities would bring increasing wealth. Life was also made easier with the importation of luxuries that the troops were used to, such as wine, olive oil, pepper and *garum* – the fermented fish sauce that the Romans used in much of their cooking. Camp midden heaps reveal a good balanced diet featuring much local produce as well. The army supplied chiefly grain, but meat and fish featured regularly in the soldier's diet. Perhaps some even acquired the taste for locally brewed beer over that of wine. Hunting game was a popular recreational pastime.

THE SOLDIER'S LIFE

Camp life for the Roman soldier began with a trumpet call to assemble at daybreak for roll call before breakfast. He would be in his squad's sleeping quarters (eight men to a room, with their equipment stored in another close by). As the roll was taken the officers and centurions would converge on the *praetorium* to receive the day's orders and passwords. Vigorous training then ensued – the Roman Army didn't get where it was by reputation alone: its soldiers trained hard. There are a number of earthworks showing that they honed their skills at siege warfare as well as route marches, manoeuvres and weapons' drills. All soldiers were taught all weapons along with other crafts and skills, changing jobs frequently to ensure that such skills were spread widely among the legion and that no one was irreplaceable, although there were always specialists (such as *optiones* – subordinates of the centurions, the equivalent of sergeants – and *immunes* – specialists, often craftsmen or artisans such as carpenters or blacksmiths) who were given dispensations from basic brute physical tasks to teach their particular skills to others or to carry out their expertise.

Watches and other regular duties – on the wall, this meant manning watchtowers and milcastles – were rotated so that vigilance was always maintained. When one's turn for rest and recuperation came, there were the baths and the *vicus* in which to relax. A Roman soldier's life was well paid, well provisioned and well equipped, with the rewards of citizenship, land and status guaranteed for those who reached retirement. When the wall was built and for at least a century after, there was no shortage of willing recruits.

▼ *A table laid with Roman food: introductions to Britain included cherries and chestnuts. While wheat and oats were cultivated in Britain before the Romans it was they who encouraged its spread.* Ermine Street Guard

5

CIVILIANS AND THE WALL

It may seem a wild frontier today, but the Roman Army's 300-year stay along the wall saw many towns and civilian settlements grow alongside the forts. Shutterstock

THE VICI

Across the Roman Empire, wherever there was a border fort there was almost always an accompanying *vicus* – a nearby civilian settlement that grew alongside but was independent from the fort. However, the *vicus* was on land owned by the military. Although it was administratively independent from the Roman military it was probably tolerated as a necessary adjunct for the benefit of the inhabitants of the fort, providing entertainment and a place to relax with female company away from the eyes of the commanders.

▼ *A model of Condercum (Benwell) Fort as it might have looked in the 3rd century. Note the regular alignment and spacing of the* vicus *buildings flanking the roads leading to and from the fort.* Tyne & Wear Museums/Bridgeman Images

Very little information has come through the centuries about the lives of civilians associated with Hadrian's Wall. They are barely mentioned in the Vindolanda letters that have otherwise provided us with so much invaluable information. As for the native Britons, almost nothing is known from Roman sources; they clearly were of no importance for the occupying authorities. It is thought that in the early years of Hadrian's Wall civilians were strictly kept out and away by the Vallum. Nevertheless, these civilians were under the nominal protection of the army, who doubtless kept a close eye on what was happening there. Despite the enormous number of non-military personnel at Vindolanda– and by extension the other forts along the wall – by AD100 it seems that native Britons

were completely excluded, or perhaps chose to stay away, from the wall.

The only mention of Britons in the Vindolanda letters shows that the Romans viewed them with contempt, perhaps because they had proved useless as recruits or inept as enemies. There was no record or indication of assimilation and acculturation between Britons and Romans and nothing to indicate that the Britons were in any way adopting or even aping the Roman lifestyle. Some Britons are known to have been recruited into the Roman Army, but following Roman form would not have served in their homeland. British units were raised and some soldiers did serve in Britain but they were most likely given Romanised names and therefore disappeared into the records among all the other names.

▲ *An impression by artist Richard Sorrell of the busy street life at Vercovicium (Housesteads) vicus. This grew to become a substantial settlement that was rebuilt at least twice in Roman times.* Historic England/Bridgeman Images

◄ *There is certainly strong evidence for the presence of women at Vindolanda, but how many there were in the fort is more difficult to surmise. There would have been the commander's wife, for example – but it's difficult to quantify.* Ermine Street Guard

Most evidence for the life of the *vicus* has been discovered at Housesteads (Vercovicium) and Vindolanda, but even there, despite all the archaeological excavations, the full extent of the civilian settlements has not become clear. Remnants of timber buildings that comprised the *vicus* have been found beside a number of forts along the wall including at Chesters (Cilurnum), South Shields (Arbeia) and Wallsend (Segedunum), but it is difficult to establish the exact parameters of the latter as this has long since disappeared under modern housing. Conversely, absolutely nothing has been found to suggest that a *vicus* ever existed at Bewcastle: perhaps it was just too remote and likely to be attacked by outlaws to attract civilians.

Every *vicus* grew to accommodate the soldiers and provide them with goods and services not officially offered by the army. The settlement would contain all the camp followers and hangers-on associated with any military establishment, people who were useful for providing a wide range of services for both the military and the individual soldiers. The army is known to have been allowed in exceptional circumstances to requisition goods, services and animals from the *vicus*, but not as a matter of course.

By the period of the Vindolanda letters the Roman occupation of Britain was sufficiently

established for senior officers to have their families and a range of domestic staff with them. The letters make it clear that it was the norm for equestrian officers to keep a full family household with them, including children and slaves, at or nearby the fort – meaning the *vicus*.

In AD21 the Roman historian Tacitus wrote a fictional speech (*Annals*, 3.33), supposedly for the Roman Senate, in which he criticised the growing habit of senators taking their wives with them on

ROMAN TOWNS

It's always dangerous to be too specific, but broadly there were four types of town in Roman Britain.

The highest-ranking were the *coloniae* (singular *colonia*) usually based around land granted to legionaries on retirement. These retiring soldiers received a military diploma, a source of considerable information today, granting citizenship to them and their dependents. There were more Roman citizens in these towns and they were administered in accordance with Roman practices. Examples are Colchester and Lincoln. London and York didn't start as *coloniae* but reached higher rank as they developed.

Next were the *municipia* (singular *municipum*), with a more mixed population and more likelihood of local laws. The population didn't become Roman citizens. Examples are Verulamium and Dorchester.

Third were the *civitates* (singular *civitas*), usually market towns and capitals of tribal areas – although not every tribal area had one. Examples are Carlisle, the capital of the Carvetii, and Exeter of the Dumnoni.

Finally, there were the *vici* that developed around Roman forts and other military sites.

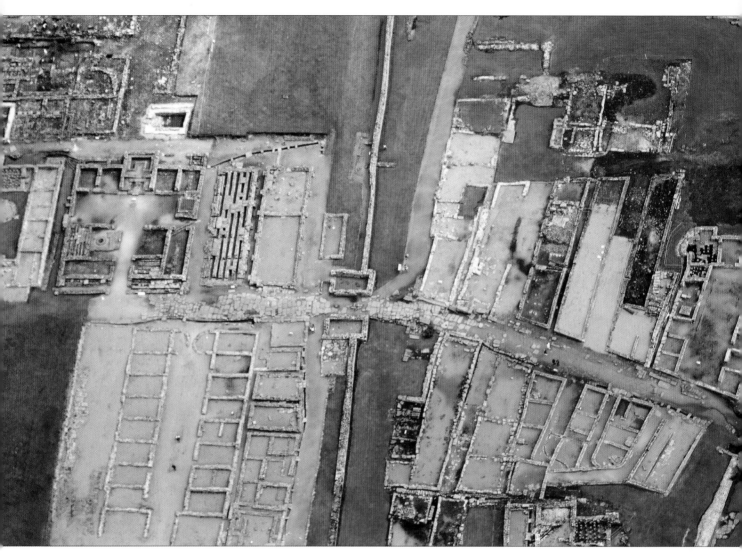

▲ *A closer view of the fort entrance shows just how closely the buildings of the* vicus *encroached on the south gate of Vindolanda. At Vindolanda the earliest* vicus *was started within the remains of the old rampart on the western flank of the fort. It comprised a mansion and several long row buildings with one-room chambers for up to six travellers, plus a fine bath house. These would have been used by Roman officials working and moving along the wall. Indeed, one of the houses is said to have been prepared – and possibly used by – the Emperor Hadrian.*

postings. This no doubt reflects a commonly held view among conservative Romans:

'An entourage of women involves delays through luxury in peacetime and through panic in war. It turns the Roman Army into the likeness of a procession of barbarians. Not only is the female sex weak and unable to bear hardship, but, when it has the freedom, it is spiteful, ambitious and greedy for power. They disport themselves among the soldiers and have the centurions eating out of their hands.'

Little archaeological evidence has been found to fill in the detail of the *vicus*: most of the inhabitants would have been poor, living in mud and timber dwellings with few personal possessions, leaving nothing for archaeologists to get excited about. Some of the bigger and longer-established *vici* evolved enough to have stone-built administrative buildings, but the most evidence comes from the rare coin find, scraps of bone and pottery shards and the occasional altar stone or tombstone. If the lack of Roman artefacts in native settlements is anything to go by, it appears that they did not even trade with each other. It seems that the Romans largely left the Britons to their own affairs, provided they did not make trouble for them and paid their taxes as required. We do not even know any ordinary British names from Roman sources.

There is a note on the back of a wheat account from a man who describes himself as a *homo trasmarinus* (man from overseas), with a grievance about how the army treated him. His complaint suggests that he was a civilian purveyor of goods and therefore one of many non-military merchants working to supply the army and, furthermore, that these people were not local Britons. At this period, the Rhineland, especially the Batavian area, was rapidly urbanising and developing a thriving commercial class. Furthermore, there is a distinct lack of evidence in Britain for the existence of a mercantile class supplying and earning a living off the Roman Army. So the *vicus* did not supply the forts in any official ways.

Native Briton settlements have been found at the Milking Gap roundhouses within a walled enclosure to the west of Housesteads between the Vallum and the wall, contemporary with the occupation of the wall. Other native settlements have been found at Housesteads, Birdoswald and Wallsend, causing archaeologists to revise their theory that the Romans cleared settlements from the frontier areas.

The *vici* themselves were often temporary, as the inhabitants moved with the soldiers, though with a garrisoned fortification like Hadrian's Wall the *vicus* itself would just refresh with new camp followers when the previous incumbents packed up and followed their particular bit of the army. By the late 2nd century the forts along Hadrian's Wall were permanently occupied, as the units were stationed there for the long term. Accordingly, the *vici* became larger and better established and even started to flourish as the inhabitants were no longer moving on with the soldiers.

Among the Vindolanda letters, a number of receipts suggest that people living in the *vicus* paid rent. This certainly implies that the properties were allocated to civilians and that, in turn, may have been tied in with specific work relating to the fort. In fact, the entire *vicus* may have been thoroughly ordered and regulated by the military, with any misdemenours punished by them.

It is thought that most of the buildings in the *vicus* were either single- or double-storey houses, some of them with storage space in the roof. At Housesteads, long slots in some of the stone thresholds are interpreted as the casements for large shutters, which would indicate taverns and shops similar to those found in Rome's Trajan Market. One building at Vindolanda contains cooking facilities that are clearly too large for domestic use, so it must have sold food to passing soldiers and civilians.

Starting from the late 150s, following the Roman withdrawal from the Antonine Wall and the recommissioning of Hadrian's Wall, the *vici* were well-enough established and probably accepted by the Roman military for them to flourish and expand in extent. There's evidence for this thanks to the scientific advances in geophysical technology that have shown that the *vici* at Castlesteads,

▲ *A 2nd-century stone relief of a butcher's shop. Roman shops were typically small and run by the family who lived and worked on the premises. Shutters would open the shop directly on to the street, although some had small enclosed serving rooms like this one.*
Museo della Civiltà Romana/Roger Viollet, Paris/Bridgeman Images

Birdoswald and Halton Chesters extended across the Vallum after this period.

Next to nothing is known for a fact about the people who actually lived and worked in the *vici* because they left barely any traces of their lives. Extrapolating from the uniform building styles, sizes and structures of the stone foundations of the *vici* at Vindolanda and Housesteads, it seems most likely that the *vici* were deliberately established and constructed by the Roman soldiers themselves rather than allowed to grow as an ad hoc collection of buildings randomly assembled by civilians – this goes against previous theories of sporadic and spontaneous construction. If this is the case, then the occupants would have been organised and there would have been rules and regulations, such as that the approaches to the fort must not be

▼ *Stone relief of a blacksmith's shop dating from the 3rd century. All the tools would still be familiar to a blacksmith working today.*
Museo Nazionale d'Abruzzo/Bridgeman Images

◄ *Recreation of how a Roman wheelwright's workshop could have looked at Vindolanda. Many of his woodworking tools would be familiar to modern carpenters. Thousands of wooden objects have been excavated at the site.* Vindolanda Trust

► *Roman stone relief from the 2nd century, of a cutlery shop now in the Museo della Civiltà Romana. Most of the stock appears to be knives and billhooks. Romans mostly ate their food with spoons and used their knives for cutting.*
Museo della Civiltà Romana/Bridgeman Images

obstructed, that buildings shouldn't hinder traffic and must lie well back from the road, and that the dead must be buried in designated cemeteries well away from the fort and watercourses. At Housesteads, the two closest buildings to the fort do encroach over half of the road leading to the south gate but that had already been blocked up before the *vicus* was even built.

The people who lived in the *vicus* were probably a mixture of craftsmen and traders from other Roman provinces, plus a good proportion of Britons. All of these people would have worked primarily to produce goods and services for the garrison. However, nothing has been found to suggest that local Britons settled in the *vici*; more

likely they stayed in their own nearby settlements. Almost certainly the *vici* contained a number of local women, some of them prostitutes, but also some who became wives or mistresses of the garrison soldiers and it follows that there would be children there as well.

It could have been that a *curator* (liaison officer) would have been officially appointed to regulate the *vicus* and act as an intermediary between the civilians and the occupants of the fort. This was known to have happened elsewhere in the Roman Empire but no evidence exists for it in Britain. However the Romans did like order and did apply the same rules and regulations across the empire. It is also possible that the inhabitants of the *vicus* would have been subject to Roman military law and judged accordingly if they transgressed.

Part of the reason for civilians living in the *vicus* would have been for protection from marauders. Brigands would have been very foolhardy to attack a civilian settlement so close to armed and trained soldiers. Occasionally, around some of the more remote northern *vici*, defensive fences have been detected, but this does not appear to be the case with the larger forts where the presence of the garrison was deterrent enough.

Towards the end of the 3rd century many, though not all, of the *vici* were in noticeable decline and a number of them seem to have been abandoned altogether. Those settlements at Vindolanda, Vercovicium, Banna, Onnum, Segedunum and Arbeia in the wall area, and farther off at Alavana (Watercrook), Bremetenacum Veteranorum (Ribchester), Voreda (Old Penrith) and Manucium (Manchester) also declined. The reasons for this probably varied from fort to fort, but the most likely explanation is that the soldiers started to receive their salaries in goods and equipment, meaning that they had less disposable income to spend in a non-military settlement. Furthermore, there may well have been far fewer soldiers garrisoning the forts anyway, as the Romans started to withdraw from Britain.

The *vicus* at Malton bucked the trend as the settlement lasted into the following century. Survival there might have been due to a thriving pottery industry and good trading relations with Cataractonium (Catterick), Coria (Corbridge) and Luguvalium (Carlisle).

It is not known what happened to the residents of a *vicus* when it was abandoned. Most likely the traders simply moved into nearby towns to continue making a living and returned to the forts to trade at weekly markets. The remnants of markets have been discerned at Newcastle, Wallsend and Vindolanda.

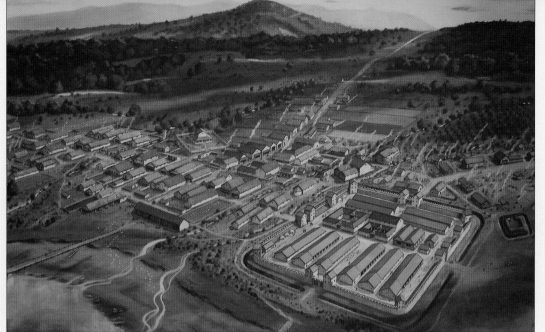

◄ *View looking east over the fort and* vicus *at Ravenglass (Glannaventa). The consensus of opinion is that the* vicus *developed along the roads and by the streams running through the area, particularly Swine Gill and Town Gill. Note the baths (red building just outside the fort).*
Graham Sumner

GLANNAVENTA (RAVENGLASS) VICUS

A geophysical survey over 35ha (86.5 acres) was undertaken in 2013 and 2014 by the local archaeology project (supervised by various professional experts) and has demonstrated that the Ravenglass *vicus* had buildings to the east and northeast of the fort. In places the survey was hindered by the vegetation and marshy ground, and complicated by detritus left by the construction of the railway. However, exploratory excavations confirmed the presence of large timber buildings and evidence for industrial activity, particularly iron-working but possibly also glass-making. Nothing was found to indicate any pre-Roman settlement in the area. The Glannaventa *vicus* itself would have grown around the Roman fort in about 130 and was mainly developed along the sides of the main roads. Only in the 2nd century did it start to extend any farther away, and even then, only to a maximum of about 200m (655ft).

During the latter half of the 2nd century, the area outside the north and east of the fort became more occupied and streets developed until the *vicus* extended to cover about 5ha (12 acres). It is possible that a market place was established – this would explain the 20m (65ft)-wide section of road. The *vicus* also started to extend westwards towards the coast, and might support the theory of the construction of a port here.

A number of domestic artefacts have been discovered that lead experts to conclude that the residents of the *vicus* were not high status, but that they appeared to aspire to the Roman lifestyle, when their use of Roman pottery is assessed. Local pottery shards have been found that came from southern England and the Midlands. Also, the remains of traded amphorae from Europe show the inhabitants had contact with the Mediterranean world through the Roman garrison.

Thanks to centuries of agriculture, particularly ploughing, Roman remains have been dispersed and spread, making analysis of the site difficult. Magnetic data shows that there are traces of a couple of roads running northeast of the fort and of settlements along the roads, as well as possible industrial activity; beyond 130m (425ft) eastwards, evidence has been found for ploughing and drains, but nothing of any real note. However, it appears that the settlement did not extend any distance towards the coast.

The beach was also carefully explored for Roman evidence – particularly material eroding out of the cliff – but the few pieces found cannot conclusively be ascribed to the fort itself.

The *vicus* here appears to have declined in the latter half of the 3rd century and may even have disappeared by the 4th century. This concurs with *vici* activity at other sites along the wall, as the Roman military presence drastically declined in numbers and the consequent demand for the services of the inhabitants also disappeared.

▼ *The bath house at Ravenglass. Maryport was probably the end of the western defence wall although there is much debate about how far south it came. Ravenglass, much farther down the Cumbrian coast, was an important port and supply centre that linked in with the overall defences.*
WikiCommons/August Schwerdfeger (CC BY 4.0)

VINDOLANDA

Vindolanda is the jewel in the crown for research on Hadrian's Wall country thanks to the indefatigable work of the Birley family, after archaeologist Eric Birley bought the Clayton estate of Chesterholm in 1929. His family continue his work to this day every summer, as he was followed first by his sons Robin and Anthony, and now his grandson Andrew. What is today the Vindolanda Trust continues to excavate and preserve at Vindolanda, and rarely a year goes by without remarkable finds. The trust's discoveries have transformed understanding of how life was lived on and around Hadrian's Wall, particularly through the finding and description of the Vindolanda 'letters', rare caches of ancient Roman letters written on thin slices of wood and preserved in the anaerobic conditions of the site.

▶ *Aerial view of Vindolanda clearly shows the stone-built buildings of the* vicus *outside the confines of the fort. In fact the* vicus *would have spread much farther, but many of the buildings would have been made of timber and mud and all trace of them has long since disappeared. As the fort grew, so did the* vicus, *particularly in the 3rd century when it was greatly enlarged and rebuilt in stone – these are the foundations we see today. The village was largely abandoned, for unknown reasons, in about 285.*

▲ Reconstruction of a Nymphaeum at Chesterholm House. Dedicated to Holy Nymphs (water spirits), it sits beside Bradley Burn, just east of the fort itself.

▲ In the 2011 excavations around 300 round huts were uncovered under the north wall. They were used up to c. 208, when the fort was abandoned.

▲ The first bath house on the site was built to the south of the fort by the Batavian garrison. The size reflects the fact that it was 1,000-men strong. Shutterstock

▶ The Romans were masters of water management: how to get it into and around the fort, how to control rainwater and how to dispose of it. Here at Vindolanda even the humble drains are beautifully constructed.

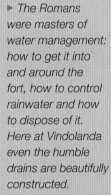

▼ The 3rd-century bath house is situated outside the walls to the northwest and would have been in use until the fort was abandoned in the 4th century. Shutterstock

▲ *Dr Andrew Birley shows off a complete iron sword still contained within its wooden scabbard. It was probably abandoned because of its bent tip, which would have rendered it useless as a weapon.* Vindolanda Trust

▶ *This piece of harness was found looking almost like new. It is made of copper alloy and was found among many other cavalry items in the barrack buildings.*
Vindolanda Trust

▼ *Unmistakable, a wooden Roman lavatory seat was discovered deep down in the pre-Hadrianic trenches and is thought to be the only surviving Roman wooden loo seat. Its remarkable preservation is due to the anaerobic, oxygen-free conditions of the mud.* Vindolanda Trust

RECENT FINDS

There have been numerous finds at Vindolanda in recent years, including:

1992   Largest discovery in the world of a cache of letters or ink tablets.
2006   A bronze and silver fibula, with the name Quintus Sollonius impressed into the surface and featuring the figure of Mars.
2010   The body of a child aged 8–10 years old in a shallow pit in the barracks. Disturbingly, it appears the arms may have been bound.
2014   A very rare Roman wooden toilet seat.
2014   The only gold coin ever found at Vindolanda. It bears the image of the Emperor Nero thus dating it to AD64 (or 65).
2016   Discovery of 421 Roman shoes for men, women and children.
2017   Spring: 25 ink tablets dating to the 1st century AD.
       Summer: Uncovered the cavalry barracks that contained numerous items of military paraphernalia including textiles, arrowheads, swords and ink tablets all dating to around 105.

▲ *In summer 2016, a collection of 421 Roman shoes was found in a ditch alongside general debris, including dog and cat skeletons. The shoes were for men, women and children and ranged from baby shoes to adult boots and bath clogs.*
Vindolanda Trust

▼ *The first gold coin found at Vindolanda appeared in June 2014. It is an aureus showing the head of Emperor Nero and dating from AD64–65. It represents half a year's salary for a Roman soldier.*
Vindolanda Trust

LIFE IN AND AROUND THE FORT

Vindolanda was originally a fort guarding the Stangate, but it was so well established that it remained in use after the building of Hadrian's Wall – as did Coria. It lies almost exactly halfway along the length of the wall but about a mile south.

The fort was continuously occupied from about AD85 to around 370, then after the Romans left Britain it fell into disrepair and ruin. Like other forts along the wall, Vindolanda was thoroughly robbed over the centuries for its stone, reaching a peak, apparently, in the 18th century. It disappeared from the historical record for centuries until it was mentioned by topographer and historian William Camden in *Britannia,* his chorographical survey of Great Britain and Ireland published in 1586.

Confirmation that the Romans called the fort Vindolanda was discovered when an inscribed altar was found on the site in 1914. The fort was classed as a *castrum* or auxiliary fort, meaning that it started as a fortified military camp that provided secure shelter and home to Roman soldiers and all their equipment, baggage and supplies when they were not fighting. It is one of the most excavated and studied sites along the entire length of the wall.

There is no evidence that Vindolanda was ever attacked by Picts raiding from the north or by hostile British natives from the south. It existed at the very edge of the Roman Empire for almost 40 years as a frontier garrison, before the building of Hadrian's Wall to the north provided a protective barrier from hostiles of all persuasions.

The first fort (known as Period I) at Vindolanda was built c. AD80 at the virtual centre of the

THE ERAS OF VINDOLANDA

Thanks to the Roman habit of demolishing their fort each time they were posted elsewhere, a number of eras have been ascribed to classify and understand Vindolanda.

Period I	AD80–85
Period II	AD85–c. 92
Period III	97–105
Period IV	105–122
Period V	122–140
Period VI	140–160
Period VIA	160–c. 208
Period VIB	208–c. 213
Period VII	213–280/300
Period VIII	300–c. 367
Period IX	367–410
Period X	410–c. 550

Stanegate – the frontier road that ran east to west across the Pennines. It was built at a time of high tension between the natives and the Romans in the usual playing-card profile. The first indication of activity at this site is a small wood-and-turf fort, whose remnants were discovered 4m (13ft) deep in waterlogged soil. It was protected by a large earth rampart surmounted by a wooden palisade, and covered an area of about 1.5ha (4 acres). All of this building now lies deep under successive forts and its only remains are the outlying defensive ditches. The age of the fort is tentatively dated thanks to the remains of samian pottery found in the lowest level of the fort ditch. Even more excitingly, writing

▼ *Reconstruction of a* chamfron *– horse-head armour – based on finds discovered around Vindolanda. Designed to protect the horse's head in battle it was also a decorative piece made to reflect the status of the rider. It is thought that such harnesses were made at Vindolanda fort.*

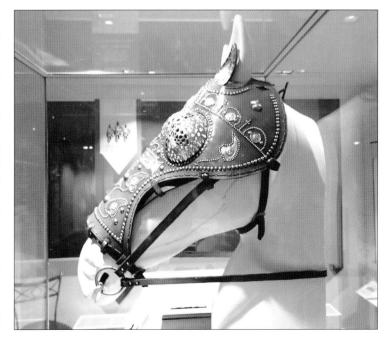

tablets discovered in the western fort ditch reveal that the part-mounted, 500–1,000 strong *cohors I Tungrorum* was the first garrison in about AD85.

The second fort was much bigger, covering an area of about 2.4ha (6 acres) and built in a square profile overlapping almost completely the earlier fort's footprint. Constructed of turf and timber, it had a large earthern palisade-topped rampart protected by a defensive ditch. This new fort was probably built by the 500–1,000-strong, part-mounted *cohors IX Batavorum equitata millaria*, although the Tungrians may still have been garrisoned at the fort. But archaeologists have been puzzled by the fort's poor construction from green, unseasoned woods, wattle-and-daub walls, and floors made only of beaten clay or earth. Their best guess is that the troops needed to throw the fort up quickly and then rebuild it properly when the political climate was calmer. The fort probably contained barrack blocks, but archaeologists can't be sure, as wrecking crews from each cohort completely demolished their predecessors' accommodation. It was in one of the rooms of this iteration that many of the Vindolanda letters were found.

However, it was during Period II that Vindolanda transitioned into an established settlement, with the first bath house (discovered outside the southern gate), a Romano-British temple, paved roads and sewers – in short, all the trappings of an established settlement.

In Period III the *cohors IX Batavorum* was still probably the garrison and it set about rebuilding the existing fort with better-quality materials. Although the fort was still predominantly turf and timber, proper building materials were also used, such as seasoned oak, stone flooring, lead pipework, flagstone or plank floors and so on. By now the fort certainly had four gates, although only the southern gateway has been found: it had been repositioned slightly, probably to avoid a gully that would have caused subsidence problems. Barrack accommodation has been found, as well as a bath

GARUM

Essentially fermented fish sauce, garum was made in a variety of ways for different purposes. It could be used as a flavouring or, among the poor, as an accompaniment. The best, an expensive luxury made from mackerel, was mostly eaten by the Roman elite. Their fish sauces were made from whole fish and fish brines, making a more refined sauce. The poor man's version was traditionally made from the blood and guts of tuna, but varied according to the available fish and various components.

Geoponica (XX.46), a 20-volume, 10th-century text of agricultural lore, provides the most detailed description of the recipe:

'Into a jar or bowl add 1 quantity of salt to 8 quantities of small fish entrails (e.g. mullet, anchovies, sprats). Leave to ferment in the sun for several months then siphon off the liquid (*liquamen*) and strain.

Use as a seasoning directly into cooking to flavour soups and stews or use as an accompanying sauce or condiment. The remaining paste is made into *allec*.

Wine, herbs and spices can also be added.'

A quicker version is just to boil the fish in strong brine, then add oregano (*origanum*) and strain until clear.

There were different types of garum:

Liquamen	Thick, whole fish sauce, sometimes made with added viscera to produce a strongly flavoured, fishy, salty and oily liquid.
Allec	The solid paste left after the liquid is siphoned off.
Muria	Made from gutted and beheaded fish. The result is milder and paler in colour.
Haimation	A black liquid made from just fish blood and viscera.

▼ *The Romans introduced over 50 new kinds of food to Britain, many of these were successfully grown in the south, but would rarely make their way as far north as the wall. Garum and wine would have been imported.* Ermine Street Guard

house in the southeast just outside the fort. Thanks to the continual fires used to heat the water, bath houses were a real fire threat and, like ovens, were built outside the confines of the fort proper.

The remains of Fort III lie at varying depths across the site. This is explained by the fact that the site was hugely uneven, but each time the fort or the buildings within were demolished, the rubble was used as fill-in, and over the decades the ground was levelled. Wrecking crews were rigorous about demolishing ground-level buildings, but just filled in the dips without demolishing the contents: hence the survival of the *praetorium* (commander's building) but not the barracks.

The *praetorium* was built for Flavius Ceralis. This is the best and most thoroughly examined building at Vindolanda, which has been excavated over a 30-year period between 1970 and 1990. The western wing of the building is 50m (165ft) long and contains kitchens, animal pens, storehouses, workshops for iron-working and leather-cutting,

walkways and living spaces in over a dozen rooms. Remarkably, some walls around 50cm (18in) high have survived, as have the flagged or planked floors. But most extraordinary of all, in the southern section, hundreds of fragments and pieces of writing tablets were found – the largest collection ever discovered. Their existence is due to complete chance: when the Cerialis family was leaving the fort their personal letters and old fort documents were gathered up and taken to burn by the demolition crew. The crew lit the bonfires and left, but a heavy rainstorm (still typical of the area) put out the flames before they could consume the wooden letters, leaving an absolute goldmine of information about daily life in and around the fort. The actual living quarters of the Cerialis family are presumed to lie under the unexcavated east side of the fort, which lies hidden under later remains.

The fort was suddenly abandoned around 105. It seems that Emperor Trajan needed the *cohors IX Batavorum* to fight for him against the Dacians

▶ *'The great Apicus was pleased to go out to dine: even gourmets grow depressed at home.'* Martial's quip reminds us how similar the Romans were to us, and it's unsurprising that even legionaries should want to ensure they had decent grub. The auxiliaries brought a truly cosmopolitan range of nationalities to Britain, and with them an equally diverse range of Roman foods and flavours. The list is no doubt incomplete but includes cabbages, broad beans, parsnips, peas, radishes, turnips, celery, carrots and mustard. Fruits and flowers include cherries, medlars, plums, damsons, apples, roses, lilies, violets and pansies.' Ermine Street Guard

HOUSEHOLD OF FLAVIUS CERIALIS, THE PREFECT OF THE *COHORS IX BATAVORUM*

c. AD92–103

Length of tenure probably three or four years

Inventory (fragmentary list of household contents):

Scutulae	plates/dishes
Paropsides	side plates
Acetabula	vinegar bowls
Ovaria	egg cups
Lanx	platter
Compendiarium	strong box
Lucerne	lamp
Panaria	bread baskets
Calices	cups
Trullae	bowls

Personnel
  Flavius Cerialis
  Wife
  Slaves   minimum of two (one called Privatus)

(modern Romania) and the cohort had to abandon Vindolanda quickly. The men serviced their weapons, saddlery, tents, etc., and left in a hurry sometime in the late summer of 105, without their usual clearing up of quarters, so leaving piles of leather scraps, general litter and tools. The site was abandoned and the elements started to erode the buildings. After lying vacant over the autumn, the buildings were razed to the ground in mid-winter and then covered with a layer of turf and clay in preparation for the next fort.

Period IV Fort was built by the 1,000-strong *cohors I Tungrorum* in late 105 or early 106. Although still predominantly made of turf and timber, the fort's profile changed to become an elongated card-shape, enclosing a 3.6ha (9 acre) compound. It also had a new high earth rampart topped by a wooden palisade and protected by ditches. This new fort was altogether grander and included the biggest and most extravagantly appointed wooden building on site. Built near the west gate this huge two-storey (or more?) courtyard building was possibly built in anticipation of the emperor making a visit to inspect his prospective wall. The two barrack blocks that were built in the south have revealed many exciting archaeological finds, including more writing tablets.

In 2006–2007, a 65m (210ft) hall was discovered on the western edge of the fort.

The sheer scale of the building implies the occupation of a legionary force but no other evidence for its presence has as yet been found.

Period V Fort was built by the 500-strong infantry *cohors I Tungrorum* (probably) at the same time as Hadrian's Wall was being constructed just a couple of kilometres to the north. Remarkably little has been discovered about this iteration of Vindolanda: it was likely built on much the same profile as the previous fort, still of turf and timber and guarded by a huge earth rampart and most likely with an encircling ditch. Only the north gate has been found, although there may have been up to five more. The remains of a number of buildings have been found, but archaeologists have been unable to identify their purpose.

This was a very busy period for the fort, as it was at the heart of the construction for Hadrian's Wall, sheltering people and supplies intended for the frontier curtain. Supporting evidence for this pivotal role is the discovery in 2002 of a number of huge bread ovens, including one almost 10m (30ft) square. By 130 Hadrian's Wall was completed and the huge numbers of people and supplies moving through Vindolanda disappeared and the fort returned to normal. It was now no longer a frontier fort and its 1,000-stron garrison was cut in half. The empty barracks were demolished and most of the workshops abandoned.

Emperor Hadrian died in 136 and his successor Antoninus ordered his army in Britain to move 160km (100 miles) north and establish a new walled frontier. While most of the forts on the wall were abandoned or mothballed, Vindolanda remained active. The previous fort(s) were demolished and covered by clay and turf. A new turf-and-timber fort was erected, but it is not known which cohort was responsible; not much at all is known about this period. Buildings of this era are (probably) the earliest currently visible. A 4m (13ft)-high earth rampart was built and three large defensive ditches were dug to guard the western flank. Very little is known about the internal layout and, as yet, no stone-built structures dating from Period VI have been found. In the middle of Period VI more work was done to make stronger facilities, which may indicate a new garrison moved in. This era fort is still being excavated and it is hoped that it will reveal even more startling finds than has its predecessors.

The fort dating from Period VIA (also known as Stone Fort I) lies largely under later forts and is accordingly little understood. It dates to the period of the return to Hadrian's Wall after the Antonine Wall proved unsustainable. At this time the outer fort was rebuilt in sandstone with walls over 5m (16ft 6in) high. It contained the usual commander's house, barracks, granaries, stables and workshops, but when the *principia* was excavated in the 1930s it was found to be the most impressive building, constructed to the highest visual quality, built anywhere along the wall, in any era. Its architecture included an upper storey of adobe, Ionic and composite columns, decorative statuary and a painting of the sun god Apollo in his chariot. Furthermore, the building faced south instead of north. Archaeologists believe, on this evidence, that the unknown garrison were of Spanish or North African origin and maybe even legionaries. However, despite its impressive appearance and beautiful stone-cutting and facings, the fort, intentionally or not, was not built to last: the foundations were inadequate and were prone to subsidence within a few years, the facing stones were not cut to withstand movement, and the core of the walls were filled with rubble bonded by clay rather than mortar. Within 50 years entire sections of wall collapsed as their foundations gave way.

To the west of the fort extensive civilian settlements appeared. This included an industrial area and a temple built to the same extremely high standards as the *principia*. Unfortunately, centuries of agricultural ploughing around the landscape have obliterated all but fragments of the structure. What remains is of much higher quality than is found in any other *vicus* and includes a large bath house. The favourite explanation for this is that this area was occupied by the local cohort while legionaries lived in the fort itself.

Emperor Septimius Severus arrived in north Britain in 208 (bringing his warring sons Caracalla and Geta with him) to campaign against the rebellious northern tribes. At the start of period VIB – the Severan period – the remaining standing walls were systematically dismantled and the entire fort was razed to the ground, with only part of the western wall retained. The new fort was surrounded by a massive ditch and rampart earthwork, probably topped with a wooden palisade. The main street ran east–west through the fort and was surrounded on both sides by barrack blocks and workshops carefully built with small cut stonework. Access roads wide enough for commercial carts separated the buildings. It was clearly a busy and important fort.

Outside the fort to the east and southeast a series of mysterious circular huts have been found – nothing similar has been discovered anywhere in the Roman Empire. Five or 10 to a row, each cluster is built differently but they are all served by good roads and drains. No explanation has

been found for them. In 211 Emperor Severus died in Eboracum, his son Geta immediately had his brother Caracalla murdered and the northern campaign was abandoned; consequently, Hadrian's Wall again became the fighting frontier.

Period VII Fort (also known as Stone Fort II) became the definitive Vindolanda and the one most excavated and seen today. It existed through a period of peace and prosperity and accordingly

◄ There's an aqueduct leading to the bath house. It starts at a water tank fed by a spring. Today, most of it has been reconstructed, although there are some original sections. CM Dixon/ Getty Images

▼ Located in the vicus*, the bath house was an important recreation area for the soldiers and their families, as well as providing more prosaic but vital washing and toilet facilities.* Shutterstock

appears to have thrived. It was built by the new garrison, the *cohors IV Gallorum*, who had been there since at least 213. The fort resumed the typical Roman playing-card shape and returned to facing north. It was built of squared sandstone blocks on some of the earlier foundations of Fort VI-A (a fatal error as subsidence proved a perennial problem), with extensive inner buildings. The military bath house was built just outside the western gates where it would have been accessible to the entire Vindolanda community. A little farther away lay the *vicus* either side of the road leading out of the fort's western gate. Almost certainly laid out by military planners, it had residential, religious and industrial zones, surfaced roads, drainage channels and aqueducts. Some of the buildings boasted substantial stone foundations. Over the decades of ever-increasing population, the *vicus* became crowded and filled with ad hoc buildings, and evolved into a crowded maze of alleys and dead ends. It became so crowded that much of the western ditch was back-filled to provide more space for shops and houses for the wide diversity of inhabitants. Another *vicus* has been discovered recently to the north of the Stangate, but this has yet to be explored.

At the end of the 3rd century, Vindolanda fort and *vicus* were completely abandoned – why and for how long is unknown, but probably tens of years. No coins or pottery from the 4th century have been found there. But around 300, life at the fort resumed, and the long-abandoned *vicus* was pillaged for stone for the new fort – particularly for the nearby western wall, which seems to have collapsed outwards in the interim. The new garrison – about 300 mixed auxiliary, *cohors IV Gallorum* – patched and resurfaced the wall. Many of the old buildings were rebuilt, including the granaries, and new buildings constructed. As with other forts along the wall, the barracks were redesigned to become small, single, free-standing rows of buildings, divided from each other by narrow alleys, each just about big enough for a soldier and his family.

The *vicus* did not revive. Instead, experts believe that the civilians now lived within the confines of the fort itself, as by then there was plenty of room. Also, just by the west gate, a building that was used for decades as a domestic residence was built directly into the clay ramparts. Similar structures have been found on the southern section as well. This all points to a relaxing of relations between Romans and civilians.

At the start of the 4th century, the Roman

▼ *Today, Vindolanda is both a research centre and a powerful, evocative reminder of Britain's historic past.* Shutterstock

Empire was undergoing turmoil: provinces were being broken up, the army was reorganised and bureaucracy expanded. It seems that many of the soldiers in Britain were posted away to deal with problems elsewhere in the Roman Empire and Britain was increasingly left to fend for itself.

Vindolanda remained an important and busy fort. The Period VIII iteration appears very similar to its predecessor physically and was built by the mixed auxiliary infantry and cavalry *cohors IV Gallorum*. The fort seems to have been thoroughly revived and rebuilt, new buildings sited, and civilians well established within the confines. In Britain in 367 the natives banded together and launched a coordinated attack on Roman-occupied Britain. It took a year to defeat them. Some of the wall garrisons were disbanded when a number of soldiers were branded traitors. Archaeologists don't know how this affected Vindolanda, but there were changes.

The Period IX Fort was built by an unknown garrison to much the same configuration as before, but this time the walls were just patched up and supported by buttresses where necessary. The southern and western gates were blocked up, either because the garrison was too small to guard four entrances or perhaps because there was no need for them. But, as the surfaces of the buildings of Period IX are close to the ground surface, much of the detail has been lost to ploughing and general disruption. The Roman Empire was crumbling and the garrison had less muscle to enforce its rule over the land.

In 410 the Romans abandoned Britain, no doubt leaving behind many of their soldiers who had gone native. Vindolanda probably remained occupied to some extent for an unspecified length of time into the 6th century. The traces from this era are faint, but it remained a fortified, inhabited settlement. Parts of the western wall were repurposed for new buildings within the confines of the fort, but these were skilfully made to last, not just casually thrown together. The *principia* became the residence of the head man and the old Roman mustering room turned into a community hall, while other buildings seem to have changed purpose. The granaries were turned into storehouses or perhaps dwellings and a Christian church was built on the south side. Various artefacts have been found across the site indicating a vibrant community full of life, industry and commerce. A Christian tombstone to a Celtic high chief called Brigomaglos was found dating to the late 5th century, so he, too, had made Vindolanda his home a century after the Romans officially departed.

SLAVES

The Vindolanda letters show that slaves lived in the officers' households and on occasion corresponded with each other. Only a handful of letters obviously involved slaves but a number of them were probably written by slaves as they were the people most intimately involved with household matters such as food supplies. One man called Severus wrote to another slave called Candidus (a slave belonging to Genialis) about the upcoming December festival of Saturnalia and some money that was owed for it.

It is unclear whether all the slaves in the *praetorium* also had duties across the unit as a whole, but the tablets suggest that slaves were responsible for at least partially organising the commander's household. It is also impossible to tell whether all the slaves attached to military personnel were personal property (of the officers) or belonged to the unit. They probably worked as personal attendants, batmen and grooms for the soldiers, but no evidence actually supports this.

Typical slave names mentioned in the texts include Primigenius and Privatus, (both common slave names), Rhenus (meaning from the Rhineland), Gracilis, Similis and Audax (all frequent servile names). Many other names are mentioned but the status of those people are unclear, these include the Greek names Hermes, Trophimus, Paris, Corinthus and Elpis.

▼ *Roman mosaic from Pompeii, of a boy slave in a kitchen with fruit and fish.* Getty Images

THE VINDOLANDA LETTERS

Size:	About 20cm by 8cm (8in by 3in)
Material:	Thin strips of birch, alder or oak
Medium:	Ink made from gum arabic, carbon and water
Thickness:	0.25–3mm (3/32in)
Number:	Happily, increasing year on year; cache of 25 more found in summer 2017 bring total over 500
Dates:	c. AD92–103

The first Vindolanda tablets were found in March 1973 by Robin Birley (co-founder of the Vindolanda Trust) and in time proved to be a cache of nearly 500 wooden tablets – but broken into numerous fragments. Now archaeologists know what to look for, numerous tablets have turned up in the digs at Vindolanda.

The first trove of tablets were found in a waterlogged rubbish heap near the commander's house and pre-date the wall. Since then, tablets have been found scattered across the site, including an important cache of around 25 found in June 2017. They were found about 2m (6ft 6in) down in damp, anaerobic soil in a newly excavated part of the site and were in a particularly good state of preservation. These remarkable survivors of early Roman Britain provide a unique insight into the everyday life of the fort and associated *vici* in a way no other source can remotely match. Before their discovery, next to nothing was known about the history of Britain between the end of

Agricola's governorship and the construction of Hadrian's Wall. If nothing else, the letters prove that this northerly border region was safe enough for Roman families.

The first cache of tablets was found in the *praetorium* and date from c. AD92–103 when the fort was under the command of Flavius Cerialis, the prefect of the *cohors IX Batavorum*. They are the daily correspondence of the governor and his wife and various officials and friends in and around the fort. They provide an insight into the daily life of the more important personnel of Vindolanda. Later tablets have been found around the barrack-block and workshop and illuminate the life and work of the common soldier and garrison as a whole.

Such wooden tablets were used for correspondence and record-keeping in parts of the Roman Empire where papyrus was scarce or non-existent. The tablets found at Vindolanda mostly date from between AD97–103 during the period when the fort was occupied by *IX Batavorum* and its sister unit *III Batavorum*, supplemented by a detachment of cavalry from the Spanish *ala Vardullorum*. They are not official records – those would have been kept in the *principia* – but were informal notes and correspondence and were discarded as rubbish and frequently burnt. Their survival is completely unintentional.

The tablets, or letters, comprise smooth-surfaced sheets of locally grown birch, alder or oak, folded in half to make a postcard-size message with the writing contained on the inside leaves and an address on the outside. Most letters

▼ *A very rare and almost complete example of one of the Vindolanda letters. These wooden messages from the ancient past needed careful cleaning and conserving before revealing their contents.* CM
Dixon/Print Collector/
Getty Images

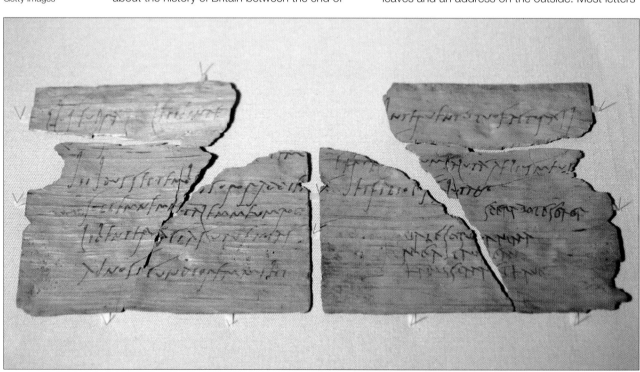

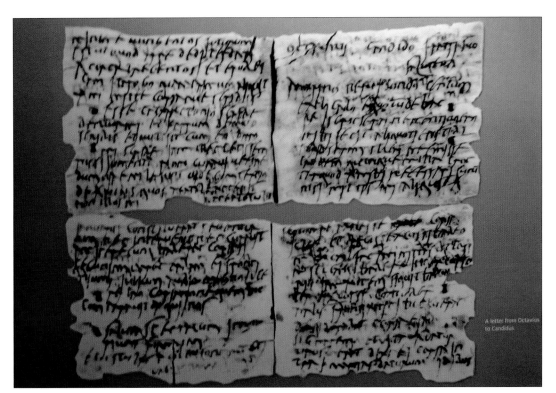

◄ *One of the more complete Vindolanda Letters. It starts 'Octavius to his brother Candidus' and goes on to discuss the supply of goods and an urgent request for money to secure the purchase of cereals and hides. It was found in the room at the end of the barracks building.*

A letter from Octavius to Candidus

followed the same format: they were written by a scribe in two columns, starting on the left side of the sheet and then continuing down the right in the direction of the grain of the wood. The top-left column begins with a couple of lines giving the opening address and naming both sender and recipient, with closing farewell remarks – often added by the sender – at bottom right. When a longer message was sent, holes were punched in the upper corners so the missives could be tied together. When the letter was finished it was scored vertically down the centre and folded. Occasionally, the ink hadn't dried completely and the writing blots on the folding leaf. The address is written on the back of the right-hand leaf in large, spikey lettering and underneath, in smaller cursive lettering, the name of the sender, but this time sloping upwards from left to right. Until later finds in

◄ *Tablets, recently unearthed from a deep trench, as they looked before preservation. They were in such remarkable condition that a few words were immediately legible.* Vindolanda Trust

London, these were the earliest discovered hand-written documents in Britain.

The tablets were not immediately recognised as letters and are so extremely fragile that they may well have been overlooked by earlier archaeologists as mere fragments of wood. Once the pieces are unfolded, the ancient wood rapidly oxygenates and the wood becomes black and unreadable. Transcription is not always possible, because the ink has faded so much, but infrared imaging can sometimes reveal the lost pen strokes. Additionally, however, there are other marks, lines and dots that may or may not also be conveying information. Precise dating of most of the correspondence is near impossible, although a few tablets can be corroborated with known facts. Many of the tablets seem to be locally written and received, but some also arrived from other forts and Roman settlements and also perhaps from Gaul.

The writing is predominantly Roman cursive script, probably written with a reed pen, which was initially very difficult to decipher. The ink is a mixture of gum arabic, carbon and water and it required sophisticated computer technology and expert epigraphists to expose and understand the writing. When scientifically analysed, it became clear that the letters were written in the 1st and 2nd centuries AD and were inscribed while Vindolanda was just a northerly Roman fort, before the great wall was constructed. Most of the tablets now reside in the British Museum in London, although a number are on display back in Vindolanda at the fort museum. Of course, it is hoped that more will be discovered as the site is excavated.

Many fascinating things have emerged thanks to the tablets, not least that there was clearly a high degree of literacy among the Roman garrison. Many of the tablets have now been transcribed

▼ *The conservation process is meticulous and takes time before the inscriptions are made legible. Such finds dating from the Roman world are exceptional and provide fascinating detail and insight into ancient lives.*
Vindolanda Trust

and translated and provide a unique insight into daily life in this far-flung Roman frontier and they prove just how organised and well run the Roman Army was. Many of the messages relay military instructions, work rosters, interim reports and accounts – they show just how bureaucratic and regulated the army was. But they also contain requests for leave (*commeatus*), while other tablets concern the social side of life and trivial matters that passed between ordinary Romans and civilians. For example, one letter mentions a gift of oysters.

The letters include fragmented lists of foodstuffs. One short account lists food items paid for with cash, probably for the prefects (*praetorio*) rather than the barracks. One lists pork (*porcellum*), ham (*perna*), roe deer (*caprea*), venison (*cervina*), salt (*sal*), spices (*condimenta*), a malting cereal (*bracis*) and wheat (*frumentum*). Romans clearly ate a healthy diet of a wide range of foodstuffs.

The largest collection of correspondence (some 60 texts) comes from the household of Flavius Cerialis, the prefect of the *cohors IX Batavorum*, and his wife Sulpicia Lepidina, who lived at Vindolanda c. 97–102/3 and wrote to her friends and to the tradesmen and suppliers of goods she needed. Sulpicia received an invitation to a birthday party (the earliest recorded), and now known as Tablet 291, from her friend Claudia Severa, the wife of Aelius Brocchus, the commander of a nearby fort. The main invitation is probably written by a household scribe, but Claudia herself penned personal greetings at the end in which she called Lepidina her sister.

Possibly the most important tablet, not just for Vindolanda but about the Roman military in Britain as a whole, is Tablet I.154, which gives the strength report of the *cohors I Tungrorum* (c. 92–7) – the only known strength report from Britain. It shows that two-thirds of the unit were away on duty elsewhere. This military unit was based at various times along the wall in Vindolanda, Brocolitia, Castlecary (on the Antonine Wall) and Vercovicium. It is dated 18 May (but frustratingly no year date) and lists 752 men under the command of Julius Verecundus. These included six centurions, 46 *singulares legati* (guard detachment for the provincial governor, maybe of the *legio IX Hispania* [from Eboracum]), seven detachments numbering 456 *absentes* at different (unfortunately unreadable) places, but probably including a centurion in London. Those remaining (*reliqui praesentes*) number 296, and include five centurions, but of these 15 are sick (*aegri*), six are wounded (*volnerati*) and 10 have inflamed eyes (*lippientes*), which left 265 men fit for active service in northern Britain. However, this may not have been the only military strength at Vindolanda at that time. Archaeologists suspect that other units or part units, probably of Batavians, would have been there as well.

They also throw light on the logistics of garrisoning a frontier post. For example, Tablet I.154 describes the double-strength of military *cohors I Tungrorum* that shows it could function with a number of men absent from base at any one time (either assigned elsewhere, on leave or ill). Another letter from Masculus to his superior Cerialis requests orders for the next day's deployment, as well as a plea for more beer for his men.

Analysis of the tablets show that the Roman frontier guard units communicated extensively and clearly to each other and units moved up and down the lines as required. Their speed and flexibility would mean that the native Britons would have been unable to assess accurately the strength of any given fort and that they would have been unaware of the exact numbers of Roman soldiers. Indeed, some forts were probably seriously undermanned at times, but the Britons were unlikely to have known about it.

One of the tablets (II.155) reveals how the men were worked: out of 343 men present, 12 were set to shoe-making, a number were assigned to collecting lead, clay and rubble, while 18 men were building the bath house and others were plastering. The rest of the men were sent to look after the wagons, the kilns and the hospital.

Thanks to the tablets we know that the bath-house keeper (*balniator*) was called Vitalis. That there was a shield-maker (*scutarius*) called Lucius, two vets (*veterinarii*) called Virilis and Alio looking after the horses, a brewer (*cervesarius*) called Artectus (who owed money to the pork butcher for iron and pork fat), and a doctor (*medicus*) called Marcus. The fact that they are mentioned in the letters and worked in the fort makes it distinctly likely that all of these men were also soldiers who specialised in their professions alongside their military role.

It also shows that soldiers hoped for goods and luxuries from their friends and loved ones: from tablet II.346 we learn that an anonymous soldier received some pairs of socks, two pairs of sandals and two pairs of underpants (this confirms a much contested fact that Romans wore underpants [*subligaria*], which were no doubt very welcome in the far north) Another long-held question confirmed that the Romans called the Britons by the unflattering term *Brittunculi* (which translates as something like 'nasty little Britons') – although it is

of course difficult to generalise about this from one mention.

One fascinating tablet indicates that soldiers were issued with goods whose payment came straight out of their salary. From the centuries of Ucenius and Tullio men were issued with an overcoat, a cloak (costing 5 denarii, 3 asses), thongs, towels (2 denarii each), a flask and tallow. Pepper was 2 denarii. Some of these items were checked off, probably indicating that the debt had been paid.

Little is known about the common soldiers themselves, as they were largely unimportant individually. Just some of their first names are mentioned and these are of Celtic, Germanic, Spanish and Balkan origin, which concurs with the units garrisoning the wall – none are British names. The soldiers of the wall were a distinctly foreign occupying force.

Only one text refers directly to the Britons themselves and then only briefly. It may be a note from a departing commander to his successor. It says Britons do not use swords or armour, have no cavalry and do not throw javelins from horseback.

▲ *A 3rd-century tombstone showing an unnamed but wealthy woman. The stone itself was used to repair the walls of the fort in the 4th century. Other tombstones dedicated to women have been found around the site, but only in fragments.*

BIBLIOGRAPHY

BOOKS

An Archaeological Map of Hadrian's Wall (English Heritage, 2014).

Bédoyère, Guy de la. *Pottery in Roman Britain* (Shire, 2004).

Bédoyère, Guy de la. *Roman Towns in Britain* (Batsford/English Heritage, 1994).

Birley, Andrew. *The Vindolanda Guide* (The Vindolanda Trust, 2015).

Birley, Anthony. *Garrison Life at Vindolanda: A Band of Brothers* (Tempus, 2002).

Birley, Robin. *Civilians on the Roman Frontier* (Frank Graham, 1973).

Birley, Robin. *Vindolanda* (Amberley, 2009).

Bishop, M.C. and Coulston, J.C. *Roman Military Equipment* (Shire, 1989).

Bishop, M.C. *Per Lineam Valli 1: An Introduction to Hadrian's Wall* (The Armatura Press, 2012).

Breeze, David J. and Dobson, Brian. *Hadrian's Wall* (Pelican, 1987).

Bowman, Alan K. *Life and Letters on the Roman Frontier* (British Museum Press, 1994).

Crow, James. *Housesteads* (Batsford/English Heritage, 1995).

Edwards, John. *The Roman Cookery of Apicus* (Random House, 1993).

Elliott, Paul. *Everyday Life of a Soldier on Hadrian's Wall* (Fonthill Media Ltd, 2015).

Embleton, R. *The Outpost Forts of Hadrian's Wall in the days of the Romans* (Frank Graham, 1983).

Fields, N. and Spedaliere, D. *Fortress 2 Hadrian's Wall AD 122–410* (Osprey, 2003).

Goldsworthy, Adrian. *The Complete Roman Army* (Thames & Hudson, 2003).

Graham, Frank and Embleton, R. *Hadrian's Wall in the Days of the Romans* (Frank Graham, 1990).

Hill, P.R. *The Construction of Hadrian's Wall* (Doctoral thesis, Durham University, 2003. Available at Durham E-Theses Online: http://etheses.dur.ac.uk/1071/)

Hodgson, Nick. *Hadrian's Wall on Tyneside: An Introduction and Guide to the Latest Discoveries* (Tyne & Wear Archives & Museums, 2017).

Keppie, Lawrence. *Understanding Roman Inscriptions* (Batsford, 1991).

Lindsay, J. *The Romans Were Here* (Frederick Muller Ltd, 1956).

Macdowell, Simon and Embleton, Gerry. *Warrior 9 Late Roman Infantryman 236–565 AD* (Osprey, 1994).

Matyszak, Philip. *Legionary: The Roman Soldier's Manual* (Thames & Hudson, 2011).

Morris, Jason C. *The Groma and the Gladius: Roman Surveyors in the Later Republic* (Victoria University of Wellington, 2010 from https://core.ac.uk/download/pdf/41336648.pdf).

Rohl, Darrell J. *More than a Roman Monument: A Place-centred Approach to the Long-term History and Archaeology of the Antonine Wall* (Doctorral thesis, Durham University, 2014. Available at Durham E-Theses Online: http://etheses.dur.ac.uk/9458/)

Russell Robinson, H. *What Soldiers Wore on Hadrian's Wall* (Frank Graham, 1976).

Scullard, H.H. *Scullard: From the Gracchi to Nero* (Routledge, 1991).

Shotter, David. *Romans and Britons in North-West England* (Centre for North-West Regional Studies, 1997).

Shotter, David. *The Roman Frontier in Britain* (Carnegie Publishing, 1996).

Southern, Patricia. *Hadrian's Wall: Everyday Life on a Roman Frontier* (Amberley, 2016).

Spring, Peter. *Great Walls and Linear Barriers* (Pen & Sword, 2014).

Suetonius. *The Twelve Caesars* (Penguin, 1989).

Wacher, John. *Roman Britain* (Dent, 1986).

Wooliscroft, David. *Roman Military Signalling* (Tempus, 2001).

ARTICLES

Applebaum, Simon. 'Agriculture in Roman Britain', *The Agricultural History Review,* Vol. 6, No. 2 (1958).

Belfiglio, Valentine John. 'Sanitation in Roman Military Hospitals', *International Journal of Community Medicine and Public Health*, 2015.

Fitzpatrick-Matthews, Keith J. *Britannia in the Ravenna Cosmography: A Reassessment*, 2013.

Gallo, Isaac Moreno. 'Roman Surveying' from http://www.traianvs.net/

Habelt, Dr Rudolf. 'Imperial Visits as Occasion for the Erection of Portrait Statues?', *Zeitschrift fu r Papyrologie und Epigraphik* 133, 2000.

Hanson, W.S. 'Roman campaigns north of the Forth–Clyde isthmus: the evidence of temporary camps', *Proceedings of the Society of Antiquaries of Scotland*.

Hodgson, Nick, Bidwell, Paul and Schachtmann, Judith. *Roman Frontier Studies 2009 Proceedings of the XXI International Congress of Roman Frontier Studies Limes Studies*. Archaeopress Publishing Ltd, 2017.

Articles included:

Breeze, David J. 'Hadrian's Wall and the Mommsen thesis'.

Brickstock, R.J. 'Continuing the search for an "Antonine Gap" on Hadrian's Wall'.

Collins, Rob and McIntosh, Frances. 'Life in the Limes; Studies of the People and Objects of the Roman Frontiers'.

Graafstal, Erik. 'River Frontiers or fortified corridors?'.

Symonds, Matthew F.A. 'Smaller Structures on Hadrian's Coastal Frontier'.

Poulter, John. 'The Planning of Roman Dere Street, Hadrian's Wall, and the Antonine Wall in Scotland'.

Welfare, Humphrey. 'The function of temporary camps along Hadrian's Wall'.

Wooliscroft, David. 'Roman Towers'.

Holder, Paul A. 'Auxiliary Deployment in the Reign of Trajan', from *Dacia* (Editura Academiei Romāne, 2006).

Long, George. 'Portorium'. In Smith, William: *A Dictionary of Greek and Roman Antiquities* (John Murray, 1875).

Rickard, J. 'Vegetius 27 April 1296', retrieved from http://www.historyofwar.org/articles/battles_vegetius.html

Schuckelt, Sebastian. 'Evidence for horse armour in the Roman Army and the use of chamfrons by the Roman cavalry' from https://www.scribd.com/document/296437969/Evidence-for-Horse-Armour-in-the-Roman-A

Stephenson, J.W. 'The Column of Trajan in the light of ancient cartography and geography', *Journal of Historical Geography*, 2012 (accessed from http://www.academia.edu)

Symonds, Dr Matthew. 'The Milecastles' from http://www.northofthetyne.co.uk/Images/cameraHome/Milecastles-Hadrians%20Wall.pdf

Zehetner, Stefan. 'The Equites Legionis and the Roman Cavalry', *Journal of Ancient History and Archaeology* No. 2.3, 2015.

WEBSITES

There are loads of good websites on the course of the Hadrian's Wall trail, on the history of Roman Britain and the construction and history of the wall. These are some that were used in the preparation of this book.

https://www.futurelearn.com/courses/hadrians-wall/0/steps/5132
Info on Roman altars.

http://www.roman-britain.org
All-encompassing site: a fount of knowledge on every aspect of Roman studies.

http://www.pastscape.org.uk/
Records held in the National Record of the Historic Environment (NRHE).

http://www.u3ahadrianswall.co.uk/wordpress/contents/
A website whose stated aim is 'to provide all you need to know about Hadrian's Wall except where to eat, drink and sleep'.

https://romaninscriptionsofbritain.org
Online version of Collingwood and Wright's work.

http://structuralarchaeology.blogspot.co.uk
Geoff Carter's iconoclastic site, which undoubtedly ruffles establishment feathers, definitely provides alternatives to some of the theories currently in vogue.

http://www.vindolanda.com
Website of the Vindolanda Trust. Worth keeping an eye on for breaking archaeological news.

http://vindolanda.csad.ox.ac.uk
The Vindolanda Tablets online: a brilliant site that covers the tablets published in *Tabulae Vindolandenses* vols. I and II.

http://vto2.classics.ox.ac.uk
A sister website covers tablets 118–573 from vols. I and II and 574–853 from vol III.

http://s9.zetaboards.com/We_Dig_Vindolanda/index/
Records of discussions and information on Vindolanda including the excellent http://s9.zetaboards.com/We_Dig_Vindolanda/pages/diggers_guide/#periods history of Vindolanda.

http://www.castlesfortsbattles.co.uk/index.html
Excellent photographic coverage of the wall.

http://www.english-heritage.org.uk/
https://www.nationaltrust.org.uk
Much of the course of the path falls under these two organisations. Any visitors to the locations should start here.

https://twmuseums.org.uk/walking-hadrian-s-wall-on-tyneside
Download the excellent Tyne & Wear Museums guide to the wall in Newcastle and on Tyneside.

GLOSSARY

Aelius Hadrian's house name. It was added to many names to show it was created by or honoured Hadrian. There are a number of examples along the wall from locations (Pons Aelius) to units (cohors I Aelia Dacorum)

ala/alae Wing i.e. cavalry unit subdivided into turma

auxilia Auxiliaries. Under the principate the auxilia was a professional force, mostly divided into cohorts, with more men in total than the legions

centuria/centuriae Century i.e. unit of 80 men

cohors/cohortes Cohort, an infantry unit subdivided into centuria and turma

cohors equitata Mixed infantry and cavalry unit

Coria As with many locations in the Roman world, today's Corbridge has a number of names, such as Corstopitum and Corie Lopocarium. It's referred to as Coria in the Vindolanda letters so that's what is used in this book.

Delmatarum From Dalmatia; also seen as Dalmatarum

IOM (Iovi Optimo Maximo). 'To Jupiter Best and Greatest'. The Romans' favourite god: King of Heaven, Protector of Rome

legio Legion, the largest unit of the Roman Army, commanded by a legate in Hadrian's period it was composed of nine cohorts plus a double-strength first cohort and a wing of cavalry

milliaria Strength of 1,000 men (could be used with cohors or ala)

praetorium The commander's house in a fort

Principate The first 300 years of Imperial Rome, from the accession of Augustus (27BC) to 284 when it became the Dominate

principia Headquarters building in a fort

quingenaria Strength of 500 men (could be used with cohors or ala). Actual number of men debated; usually from 480–520

turma/turmae Squadron/company; unit of 32 cavalrymen

vallum. A ditch flanked by mounds dug to the south of the wall after it was completed, probably to create a military zone. The vallum was crossed south of each fort

vicus/vici An unplanned civilian settlement that grew up around forts and other military locations

VSLM (votum solvit libens merito) 'X (person/military unit) willingly and deservedly fulfilled his/its vow.' Found at the end of many inscription stones

ACKNOWLEDGEMENTS

Thanks to all those people who contributed to this book, particularly: Jonathan Forty for the military sections and much of the modern still photography; Sandra Forty for the coverage of Vindolanda and the vicus; Leo Marriott for the aerial photography; Elly for the fort plans; Chris Haines, James Lynn, Rod Sayers and Michael Knowles from the Ermine Street Guard for the information and photos; Graham Sumner for the splendid Roman cavalry photos and artwork; Alan Larsen; Peter Savin; and Jo, Richard Wood and Ian Kelly for company on the walk. All other photo suppliers are credited with the captions. Thanks, too, to Joanne Rippin at Haynes and Lindsay Porter for her editorial skills. The fort plans are based on information that comes from a number of sources including the excellent Roman Britain website.

Much of the material in the sections on surveying and construction was informed by two theses. The first, Peter Hill's The Construction of Hadrian's Wall, was subsequently published in book form. His experience in stonework (he was an apprentice stonemason at York Minster, Clerk of the Works of Lincoln Cathedral and is co-author of Practical Stone Masonry) means that he is undoubtedly an expert. The other is that of Jason C. Morris, The Groma and the Gladius: Roman Surveyors in the Later Republic, which is a little early in subject matter but helps provide information on the position and role of surveyors in the Roman Army. Thanks to Chris Haynes of the Ermine Street Guard who has been re-enacting Roman legionary activities for over 50 years.

INDEX